10/31/96

Fred,

I thought you might enjoy
having your own personal copy.
It is interesting to note that
the majority of the wealth built
in Simpson has been from making
good investments in timberland,
and timberland is simply another
form of real estate.

Best regards,

Al Aymington

P.S. I am looking forward to seeing
a copy of the Weiss family book
"Family Properties"!

Family Trees

Simpson's
Centennial
Story

Robert Spector

Documentary Book Publishers Corporation
Bellevue, Washington

Library of Congress Catalog Card Number: 90-080574
Library of Congress Cataloging Information:
Publication date: October 31, 1990
Spector, Robert, 1947 -
Family Trees, Simpson's Centennial Story

Bibliography
Includes Index
ISBN 0-935503-07-2

FIRST EDITION

Book and cover design: Cross Associates, Los Angeles

PAPERS USED:
Dust jacket; Simpson Shasta Gloss, Book 100 lb.
End papers; Simpson Gainsborough Charcoal, Text 80 lb.
Divider pages; Simpson EverGreen Spruce, Text 70 lb.
Text pages; Simpson Teton Tiara, Text 80 lb..
Photo pages; Simpson Shasta Gloss, Book 100 lb.

Table of Contents

Acknowledgments

The creation of this book would not have been possible without the help of hundreds of men and women throughout the Simpson family whom publisher Barry Provorse and I met during the almost three years that it took to bring this project to completion.

Thanks go to the more than one hundred people – from Pomona, California, to Hudson Bay, Saskatchewan – who openly shared their thoughts and experiences with us. The author particularly appreciated the forthrightness of Gary Reed, Furman Moseley, Susan Reed Moseley and Eleanor Henry Reed.

Thanks also to the Simpson Centennial Committee, which ably and assiduously represented current and retired employees in planning the celebration of the Company's birthday.

The Committee was chaired by Joe Leitzinger, who shepherded this project since its inception. We valued his patience, humor, thoroughness and good judgment, particularly in having Lin Smith as his secretary. Thanks, Lin, for all your help.

Every member of the Committee made a significant contribution: Ben Dysart gave us insights and encouragement, while stressing the accomplishments of rank-and-file Simpson employees.

Cindy Sonstelie helped to make the manuscript "gender-friendly." As the father of a three-year-old daughter, I appreciated her comments.

Gary Snider concentrated on the look of the book and was stalwart in insisting on the highest quality, which according to Gary "begins with the highest quality paper."

Jim Hartley carefully read this manuscript many times in its various manifestations. His writing and photography for the various Simpson in-house publications represented a major source of information.

Bob Seidl was invaluable in explaining the scientific and technical aspects of timber, plywood, overlays, energy, pulp and paper, and his observations on Simpson's corporate and family personality were precise.

Dave James, who represents a bit of the soul of Simpson, served as a gentle but exacting editor. Without Dave and the Simpson publications he edited for many years, this book would lack heart, not to mention several good stories.

Thanks also go to Dr. Robert Ficken, forest industry historian, for the use of his research notes for his biography of Mark E. Reed, *Lumber & Politics,* and for his original research for this book into the papers of the Company and William G. Reed. And thanks to Judy Gouldthorpe for her careful editing of this manuscript.

We are all indebted to Bill Reed for the published interview *Four Generations of Management: The Simpson-Reed Story* and his personal memoirs, *Family Trees,* which he felt "provided invaluable information not only on the business, but also on the people, activities and properties with which the Simpson and Reed families have been associated. Thus, the title *Family Trees* struck me as an interesting pun that referred to the genealogy of the most likely readers of the book as well as the timberlands which have been the basis of our business." (We felt that his title would also be appropriate for the Company's centennial book.)

With the help of these memoirs, the author has tried to tell a good portion of the Simpson story in Bill Reed's own words. In fact, all quotes in this book attributed to him originally appeared in *Four Generations* or *Family Trees,* unless otherwise specified. The book's same use of quotes from memoirs also applies to former Simpson Timber Company President Chris Kreienbaum and Chief Forester George Drake.

Thanks also go to Barry Provorse, who, as always, filled many roles: publisher, co-interviewer, sounding board, editor and friend.

Finally, thanks to Marybeth and Fae Spector, the sturdy branches of my own family tree.

Robert Spector
Seattle, Washington

Foreword

Three years ago, in anticipation of Simpson's 100th anniversary, we made a commitment to rediscover and record our Company's history. The result of this effort is *Family Trees, Simpson's Centennial Story*.

Back in 1946, Simpson Logging Company President Chris Kreienbaum established guidelines for the Company's first publication, *The Lookout:* "We have a good story to tell and we should tell it. Present the facts in a regular, readable way. Tell the truth, be accurate, tell the bitter and the sweet and tell Simpson employees first." In essence, that is what we told Robert Spector we wanted for Simpson's 100-year history. This book was written from our open files, countless documents, and from interviews and information gathered from hundreds of retired and current Simpson employees.

We are proud of the accomplishments and the values of those people who preceded us. Founder Sol G. Simpson, my great grandfather, established the Company policy of retaining the logged-off lands for the generations to come – at a time when most others chose to cut and run. He worked in the woods as a teamster and respected loggers and their work. He made sure that Simpson's logging camps were well kept, and he became one of the first operators on Puget Sound to provide a company health plan.

Later, Mark E. Reed, my grandfather, carried on these traditions and expanded upon them. He carried the interest of loggers to Olympia, where he became Speaker of the House. There, he fought for the state's first medical insurance act, an accident-prevention program, and in 1911 he proposed improvements in the workers' compensation act, which compensated injured workers for both lost wages and medical expenses. He also worked to establish a tax base for timberland that encouraged holding on to land for future timber crops once the last tree had been cut.

He made the town of Shelton a better place to live and work because he knew that a stable work force depended upon the well-being of its community. When the Company's interest expanded from logs to lumber, it built its first mill in Shelton and encouraged other operators to do the same. For the rest of his life, he instructed Simpson managers that the future of Shelton must be considered in every business decision, and that the town must survive.

My father, William G. Reed, picked up the mantle from Sol Simpson and Mark Reed. He built the Company far beyond the dreams of his predecessors, while maintaining their principles. He looked after the welfare of the Company's employees by investing in timberland for future generations. He always felt that he was a part of Shelton, which was his voting address until his death in 1989.

He made the Company's first investment in the paper business in 1951, when he acquired the Everett Pulp & Paper Company, and in the years that followed he was steadfast in his support of Simpson's paper interests.

Family Trees was the title my father coined for his memoirs, which he wrote in the late 1970s after his retirement. We felt that it was an appropriate name for Simpson's centennial history because this Company, since its creation in 1890, has been a family company.

Although Simpson has always been a closely held company, its success has been the product of the balance between its few stockholders and Simpson managers, beginning with Sol G. Simpson, who hired Arthur B. Govey and Mark E. Reed, who later became Sol's son-in-law. When Mark took charge of the Company, he complemented his talents with those of people such as Chris Kreienbaum and George Drake. Following a string of family tragedies, William Reed relied on Kreienbaum and Drake, as well as a new generation of management, including Tom Gleed, Hank Bacon, Gil Oswald and many others.

Family Trees also describes current Company interests, but it will be for future generations to evaluate our contributions. Simpson is the company it is today through the efforts of William Reed and thousands of Simpson employees, and this book is dedicated to this man, and to these men and women.

We are pleased with the talent brought to this project by its author, Robert Spector, and Documentary Book Publishers Corporation. We feel that this book would meet Chris Kreienbaum's wish for an accurate and truthful story told in a "regular, readable way."

Wm. G. Reed, Jr.
Chairman

*This book is dedicated to Simpson's past
employees for their accomplishments, and to the
Company's present employees for their commitment
to the promise of the future.*

And, to the memory of William G. Reed.

Preface

The story begins with trees, majestic trees that pierce the skies and stretch out as far as the eye can see, an arboreal army standing across the verdant wilderness, from the Cascade Mountains, up through Canada and down through the northern part of California. There, ideal soil conditions and abundant rainfall yielded forests of spruce, hemlock, cedar, redwood and another species the white man ultimately named Douglas fir, after the Scottish botanist David Douglas, who called the fir tree "one of the most striking and truly graceful objects in nature." Douglas fir became the foundation of Pacific Northwest and Simpson lumber manufacturing.

In 1778, Captain James Cook, the first English explorer to the Pacific Northwest, sailed into Nootka Sound, on the western coast of today's Vancouver Island, to repair his storm-damaged ships, *Resolution* and *Discovery*. Cook's crew discovered that the strong, straight, even-tapered fir that grew along the water's edge was ideal for masts and spars.

Fifty years later, the first sawmill was built by the Hudson's Bay Trading Company in 1828 at Fort Vancouver, on the Columbia River. Two decades thereafter, Hudson's Bay moved its operations to Puget Sound, where the harbors were more navigable and the timber more abundant than in the Columbia River region. In 1848, the company bankrolled the Puget Sound Milling Company, on the Deschutes River, near what is today Tumwater, Washington.

The California Gold Rush

Gold, discovered in California in 1849, produced a bonanza for the Pacific Northwest lumber industry and forged an interdependence between sparsely populated Western Washington and Northern California, which developed an appetite for Douglas fir lumber, timbers, ties and pilings, used to shore up mining tunnels, support railroad tracks, and frame and finish buildings in California mining towns and cities. Western Washington trees were profitable to harvest and process into lumber, which found ready buyers in the burgeoning California market. San Francisco entrepreneurs – many of them transplants from the Great Lakes timber region – invested in Puget Sound sawmills and employed their own fleets of sailing ships to ensure timely and steady deliveries.

"Skid roads" were built and greased to ease the hauling of logs from deep within Washington forests to railheads, rivers, lakes or tidewaters.

In the rough-and-tumble openness of the Pacific Northwest in the mid 19th century, timber was freely available and aggressively logged. Washington, which became a territory in 1853, essentially was unencumbered by federal laws regulating logging on public lands. The statutes in effect at that time were mostly ignored.

Mill owners, who were more interested in manufacturing, chose to contract out the task of logging to independent operators. In exchange for purchasing logs in advance at an agreed-upon rate, sawmills provided equipment and oxen, and granted these loggers credit at the company store

Congress tried to make some order out of the timber-purchasing chaos with the Timber & Stone Act of 1878, which allowed "any citizen or person who has made a declaration of his intention of becoming a citizen" to acquire a timber claim of 160 acres at a price of $2.50 per acre. As a result, hundreds of thousands of acres were purchased in Washington Territory. As the 1880s progressed, and the United States population grew, so too did the demand for lumber. Timber prices spiraled and lumber companies began to purchase Timber & Stone claims from their owners. Spurred by sawmill improvements, lumber production jumped from 160 million board feet in 1879 to more than 1 billion board feet in 1889.[1]

Railroad Connections

Because no transcontinental railroads serviced the region, the Pacific Northwest had been isolated from large commercial markets. Trade was by sea to California, Hawaii, the east coast of North America, the west coast of South America, Australia and China. Travel to the region was by one of two routes – by boat from San Francisco, or overland to Portland, Oregon, which was then the financial center of the Pacific Northwest.

In the 1860s, the federal government encouraged railroad builders to construct a transcontinental connection to the Pacific Northwest by offering immense grants of land and resource holdings. For example, when the Northern Pacific Railroad completed its line to Tacoma in 1888, it was granted by the federal government 1,866,363 acres in Washington Territory for a mere 1 1/4 cents an acre.

Desperate for cash and new sources of business, the NP encouraged the development of the Pacific Northwest lumber industry so that forest products could be hauled to eastern markets. As the first harvest of the nation's largest source of accessible timber – in Wisconsin, Minnesota and Michigan – approached its end, the NP enticed midwestern lumber manufacturers to the Pacific Northwest with large tracts of cheap timberland and mill sites. The first sawmill to be established on this basis was the St. Paul & Tacoma Lumber Company in Tacoma, in 1888. The NP sold to the newly formed company 80,000 timber-dense acres at the base of Mt. Rainier, within 30 miles of Tacoma, for $3 an acre – the largest purchase of timberland in the 19th century. The mill, in turn, contracted to ship an annual minimum of 75 million board feet of lumber east by rail.[2]

By 1890, Pacific Northwest mills supplied one third of the nation's shingles, thousands of eastbound carloads each year. When the Great Northern Railroad was completed in 1893, Seattle and Everett were joined with the markets in the Midwest and East. With the Great Northern came reduced tariffs, which enabled Pacific Northwest forest products to compete on a national basis.

Logging Practices

In the early logging days, manpower alone moved the logs out of the forest. Not surprisingly, the first trees felled were those closest to the lakes, rivers or tidewaters. As timber demand increased, and the most easily accessible timber had been cut, loggers devised faster and more efficient methods for felling (e.g., replacing the axe with the saw) and transporting logs. Teams of oxen, usually 10 or 12 yoked in pairs, were used to haul larger logs over longer distances to rivers or tidewaters, where they were boomed and floated to the mills.

The logs reached the water via the "skid roads." These roads were built of logs, called skids – some as long as 24 feet – set about eight feet apart at right angles to the line of the haul. In order to reduce friction, "skid greasers" tramped ahead of the oxen, smearing thick grease on the debarked skids. A six-yoke team of oxen, on a one-mile level road, could haul four turns a day, 10,000 to 12,000 board feet a turn. A veteran teamster recalled, "One mile from water, or other landing, was the longest haul you could handle with bulls and still make money."[3]

As loggers plunged deeper into the woods, they needed more efficient and cost-effective hauling methods. The prime movers, oxen, some weighing 1,800 pounds, were slow, needed considerable fodder and could not pull logs uphill, and they were eventually replaced by teams of horses or mules.

Dragging (yarding) and loading logs was made easier by the "Dolbeer donkey engine," a steam-powered machine invented by John Dolbeer, a lumberman and shipbuilder from Eureka, California. This machine, described by author Stewart Holbrook in *Green Commonwealth,* "had a vertical boiler, a single-cylinder vertical engine that powered an upright capstan called a spool. Around this spool went the hemp, and later the wire rope, used to yard the logs" from as far away as a quarter of a mile.[4] The Dolbeer was advertised as being able to do the work of 70 horses or 80 bulls. Although that was an exaggeration, it was still faster and cheaper to operate than bull teams, and it did not require food or shoes and was able to remove logs from terrain too steep for animals. By 1900, steam donkeys were a familiar sight in the Pacific Northwest forests.

Logging Railroads

In order to get deeper into their timber holdings, larger Puget Sound lumber companies began building their own logging railroads. The most ambitious of these lines was planned by Captain William Renton's Port Blakely Mill Company. Located on the south end of Bainbridge Island, across Puget Sound from Seattle, Port Blakely had the largest mill in the world under one roof, and was one of three Puget Sound sawmills with an annual production capacity of 100 million board feet. The Port Blakely logging railroad was planned to begin at Old Kamilche on Little Skookum, a branch of Totten Inlet, the southernmost tidewater on Puget Sound. Kamilche was seven miles south of the embryonic logging town in Mason County called Shelton. Little Skookum (Chinook Indian word for "strong") was a few miles south of Hammersley Inlet, also known as Big Skookum, the waterway to Shelton. The railroad line would haul logs from Port Blakely's timberlands in Mason and Grays Harbor counties to Little Skookum. From there, the logs would be towed northward about 65 miles to the Port Blakely sawmill on Bainbridge Island.

In 1887, to grade the routes for what was to be called the Grays Harbor and Puget Sound Railroad, the Port Blakely Mill Company hired a newcomer to the woods, one Sol G. Simpson.

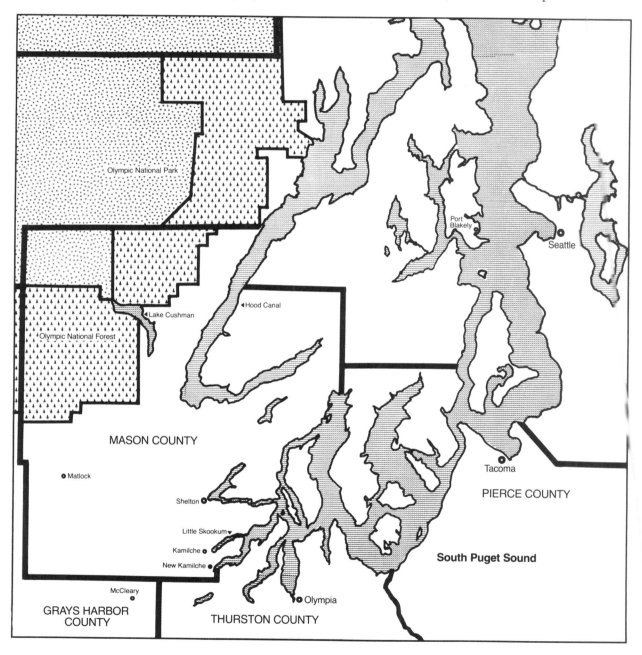

Sol G. Simpson

Sol G. Simpson, a wiry five-foot nine-inch Canadian with a big bushy mustache, was unlike many of the thousands of other ambitious men who trekked to the Pacific Northwest, because he had already crammed a few personal booms and busts into his 44 years. Born Solomon Grout Simpson in 1843, he was the son of Joseph Simpson and Caroline Grout Simpson, who in the early 19th century migrated from Yorkshire, England, to Cote St. Charles, Quebec, a suburb of Montreal, an up-and-coming timber port on the St. Lawrence River. There, the teenaged Sol worked as a timber raftsman, floating spruce and fir logs along the Ottawa and St. Lawrence rivers.

In 1865, at the age of 22, Sol headed to Carson City, Nevada, to find his fortune in the silver and gold mines. His immediate luck was poor and, as his funds dwindled, he turned to what he knew best, logging, as well as a new enterprise, road-grading. Sol was luckier in love than in mining, and in 1876 he married one of Carson City's most eligible young women, Mary James Macon Garrard – "Tollie" to her friends – the daughter of William Mountjoy Garrard, administrative assistant to the governor of Nevada. The Garrards were descendants of Huguenot Protestants who fled from France to London in the late 17th century. They later emigrated to the United States, where William Garrard's grandfather was the first elected governor of Kentucky, which later named a county after him.

In 1878, soon after the birth of Sol and Tollie's first child, Irene Marie, the Simpsons decided to seek a new life in the boomtown of Seattle, Washington Territory. They had lost their house in Carson City but, somehow, had enough money to make it to Seattle, where a second daughter, Caroline, was born. They bought a house and set up a business. Sol worked as a teamster, contracting his horse-drawn scrapers with drag scoops to grade streets for the city of Seattle and railroad beds for the Seattle & Eastern Railroad that stretched to the coal mines around Black Diamond and Renton, on the outskirts of the city.

Working on "The Blakely"

Sol Simpson's work on the Seattle & Eastern brought him to the attention of Captain William Renton, founder of the Port Blakely Mill Company. Renton hired Sol to grade the right-of-way in Mason County for the Port Blakely Mill's Puget Sound and Grays Harbor Railroad, nicknamed "The Blakely." Sol, Tollie, Irene and Anna moved from the planked streets and bustling stores of Seattle about 65 miles southwest to the little valley village of Kamilche, in Mason County.

The steam donkey was invented by California lumberman and shipbuilder John Dolbeer in the 1880s, and by 1900 was a common sight in the Pacific Northwest.

1

Nature battled Simpson and his construction crew at every turn as they slowly worked their way west from Kamilche, through the mud of the rain-soaked Mason County lowlands. "We have hauled rock and ripped, raked the fills where the water had washed them away," Sol wrote in a report to the Port Blakely Mill Company. Thick, brushy undergrowth made every mile a challenge to clear. Sol once kidded a Port Blakely manager, "You fellows move more dirt with a pencil in one minute than I can in a week with all my carts." Eventually the track was extended eastward to the point of the peninsula, where the Port Blakely Mill constructed new docks and, in the process, created the upstart village of New Kamilche. Logging camps popped up all along the railroad line.

Oxen were the prime movers in the Pacific Northwest woods, but Sol, who had used horses to grade city streets and railroad beds, began to explore their potential to move logs. Although horses couldn't begin a wide turn with a heavy load of logs as speedily as bulls, once the horses built up momentum, they were much quicker in pulling even giant logs to the railhead.

Sol was convinced he was onto something, so he peddled his teams of bulls and purchased 60 heavy draft horses, weighing between 1,700 and 1,900 pounds, some costing as much as $500. To ensure ready, available feed for his new four-legged investments, he cleared a piece of farmland near the railroad for raising hay, turnips and carrots. Substituting horses for bulls was, wrote Holbrook, "not only revolutionary, so far as the West Coast woods was concerned, but downright heretical, practically indecent." A logger of that era later told Holbrook: "Everybody thought Sol was just a greenhorn and couldn't last another year." Sol just chuckled at the skeptics, stroked his bushy mustache, hauled logs and kept buying horses. [1]

S. G. Simpson & Company

The owners of the Port Blakely Mill and "The Blakely" railroad held Sol in high regard. "Mr. Simpson," wrote a Port Blakely manager, "is a pleasant man, easy to get along with…a man who is conscientiously honest." They were sufficiently impressed with the quality of his work to hire him to build the railroad that they needed to lug out nearly 200,000 board feet of logs a day. In 1888, he was named superintendent of all Port Blakely operations. [2]

Sol G. Simpson

Located down the tracks from Matlock, Washington, Beeville was the home of Simpson Logging Company and the hub of Simpson employees' social life. Shown (from left) are Sol Simpson, John Campbell, Joseph Simpson (Sol's brother), James Campbell. The women were not identified, but included was Mrs. Arthur Govey. The Campbells were Simpson partners and relatives of Captain William Renton, head of Port Blakely Mill Company, Simpson's major customer.

Most loggers believed in oxen power and shunned the use of horses. Sol Simpson was a teamster who knew the value of a good team, and shortly after he entered the woods as a logger he proved the efficiency of 10-horse teams.

In 1889, Sol's destiny was changed forever when the Port Blakely Mill Company awarded him a contract to harvest and deliver its logs and hand-hewn ties to the tidal booming grounds at New Kamilche. Sol was not one to sit back and watch others build fortunes without giving it a try himself, so as his income grew, he invested in timberlands. (Some have speculated that Simpson was bankrolled by Captain William Renton of the Port Blakely Mill Company.)

In 1890 Sol Simpson formed S. G. Simpson & Company, a sole proprietorship construction firm, which had as its chief assets road graders and horses. He headquartered the Company deep in the timber of eastern Mason County in Beeville, 15 miles west of Shelton, near the village of Matlock. Sol was still closely involved with the Port Blakely Mill Company; two of the partners in S. G. Simpson & Company were brothers John A. and James Campbell, who ran the Port Blakely after the death of their uncle, William Renton, in 1891. (The other two partners were another set of brothers, Ed and C. E. Holmes of San Francisco, who were also associated with the mill.)

Simpson & Company, Holbrook wrote, "appears to have taken over everything on The Blakely line" (including horses, donkey engines, railroads and logging crews).[3] Most of the records of S. G. Simpson & Company have been lost, but an entry from July 1893 showed that all of the 7 million board feet of logs cut by Simpson were purchased by the Port Blakely Mill Company.[4]

Simpson Logging Company

In spite of the depressed economy of 1895, Sol incorporated the Simpson Logging Company that year with the backing of a group of investors that included the brothers Campbell and Holmes. His primary customer was the Port Blakely Mill Company, which needed a large, steady supply of logs to support expanded sawmill operations. (The financing of loggers was a common practice among sawmills.) Another investor was financier Alfred H. Anderson. Each of the founders officially owned one sixth of the Company, which was capitalized at $50,000. Rather than pay cash, the partners subscribed for capital stock, which enabled the Company to borrow money from banks. The new Company's only tangible asset was Sol's construction equipment.

Alfred Horace Anderson

The major turning point in Sol's career came when he crossed paths with Anderson. The six-foot five-inch Anderson was a stylish bear of a man, known for the natty suits that he had custom-made by a tailor on London's Bond Street. Dubbed "The Tall Fir of Mason County," Anderson filled every room he entered with his considerable presence. A man who got things done, he rarely missed a business opportunity. For example, in June 1889, when he learned of the fire that was raging on – and eventually destroyed – the Seattle waterfront, he immediately ordered his logging crew to haul out only pilings. Then he caught the next boat up Puget Sound to Seattle, where he sold those pilings to rebuild the city's burnt-out waterfront. Although an unabashed opportunist, Anderson was not without compassion. In 1890, he personally saved the financially strapped Bank of Shelton – which had been closed for a week – by advancing the bank the funds to pay all depositors who requested their money.

An avid outdoorsman, Anderson once organized and led an expedition to cross the mountainous Olympic Peninsula, which had been only partially explored at the time. (Mt. Anderson in the Olympic range is named after him.) He established a large farm and hunting preserve in Clallam County, where he experimented with soils and procedures for clearing stumps to encourage farming on cutover lands. He was a big man who liked to do things on a big scale – an oversized bed and bathtub were installed in his room at the Shelton Hotel. Even his appetite was Bunyanesque. "For breakfast," recalled Ed Hillier, who used to work for him, "Anderson liked a fairly thick beefsteak about one foot long, a quart of coffee and, if he wasn't really hungry, 10 eggs."[5]

Anderson had been in the region about as long as Sol Simpson, but had arrived with considerably more capital and connections. His father made his fortune manufacturing loggers' clothes in La Crosse, Wisconsin, in the middle of one of the major Great Lakes lumber regions. In 1883, Anderson married a La Crosse girl named Agnes Healy, daughter of lumberman Benjamin G. Healy, who, in addition to lumber, made his fortune in Colorado gold mining and Texas real estate. In the late 1880s, Healy bought several thousand acres of timber in Mason and Thurston counties from the Northern Pacific Railroad. He also invested in the Satsop Railroad, a failing, cash-strapped logging line, created at about the same time as "The Blakely."

Benjamin G. Healy began investing in Washington timber and railroads in the 1880s. He assigned his son-in-law Alfred Anderson to oversee his interests and seek out new opportunities, such as the Satsop Railroad.

Alfred Horace Anderson

(Next page) The Puget Sound and Grays Harbor Railroad, "The Blakely," eastbound to New Kamilche.

New Kamilche was typical of the logging villages that sprang up around Puget Sound during the 1880s. Living quarters were primitive, but its waterfront location afforded its residents transportation to Olympia, the main settlement on the South Sound and the state's capital.

The New Kamilche log dump and tidal booming grounds were the end of the Blakely line for logs that were rafted and towed by steam-powered tugs to the Port Blakely Mill Company, up sound on Bainbridge Island.

Unaccustomed to running a long-distance logging operation, Healy dispatched Anderson and another of his executives, C. F. White, to Washington Territory to take care of his business interests. White (one of the namesakes of Seattle's White-Henry-Stuart Building) handled Healy's timber holdings and his Pacific Mill property, and Anderson oversaw the reorganization of the Satsop Railroad – renamed the Washington Southern Railroad – and the timber along its tributary in Mason County.

Anderson joined Healy in acquiring timberland in Mason, Thurston and Grays Harbor counties. In one of their first moves, they exchanged some of Healy's timber and cash for a half-ownership in the Mason County Logging Company, which was owned by Quebec-born brothers Tom and Joe Bordeaux. To facilitate the harvesting of their timber and delivery to the log markets on Puget Sound, the new partners encouraged construction of the Peninsular Railroad, a common carrier that ran westward from Shelton.

About that time, Sol Simpson was building the Blakely Railroad at Kamilche, a few miles south of the Anderson interests, which is where he and Anderson first became acquainted. After Sol completed the Blakely line, Anderson asked him to help on the Peninsular in Shelton.

Simpson and Anderson got along well and joined forces. The two men and their backers consolidated the holdings of the former Satsop Railroad, the Blakely Railroad and the Simpson and Anderson logging camps into what became the Simpson Logging Company and the Peninsular Railroad Company, both incorporated in 1895. On June 27, 1895, in Olympia, Simpson and Anderson filed the articles of incorporation of the Logging Company, which was equipped to log 100 million board feet a year, a huge output for that time. The Company established its Seattle headquarters in the Sullivan Building and Shelton was listed as a "subordinate" office.

Well aware of the commercial opportunities in the developing Northwest, the founders of the Simpson Logging Company provided in their articles of incorporation blanket coverage for other businesses, including land development, operation of canals and railroads, stage lines, wagon roads, logging roads, plank roads, tramways, operation of logging camps, telegraph and telephone lines, dealing in assorted merchandise, and carrying on a general mercantile business.[6]

The Simpson Logging Company and the Peninsular Railroad Company soon became the business pillars of Mason and eastern Grays Harbor counties. By 1905, the Peninsular had 50 miles of track, including spurs, and its rolling stock consisted of four steam locomotives, 41 flatcars and 173 railroad log trucks, nicknamed "rattlers" because of the way they clattered when being hauled to camp for loading.[7]

Building a Company

The Simpson Logging Company was an unqualified financial success, operating at a profit virtually from its beginning, and soon declaring dividends, which were credited to the stockholders' subscription accounts.

By 1898, the Company was operating eight logging camps and 80 miles of winding tracks on two railroads, one that ran from Kamilche to Summit and a second from Shelton west into the woods operations. By then, Simpson had a collective daily production capacity of a half million board feet of logs (a large amount by the standards of the day). One eight-horse team working out of Camp Two hauled out 204,050 board feet of logs in a single day in 1898 – proof that loggers no longer questioned the economics of horsepower.[8]

Employing the latest machinery was one of Sol's passions. He commissioned Seattle's Washington Iron Works to build a half dozen models of a log-hauling machine called a "Walking Dudley" – a donkey engine and a large wheel on a movable car, with cables mounted on both ends. The $1,500 machine got its name from a noted logging camp character who walked wherever he went. Although the Walking Dudley was more colorful than effective, it illustrated Simpson's philosophy of continually mechanizing production. (Thirty years later, the Company operated the first fleet of gasoline-powered Caterpillar tractors ever used in Douglas fir logging.)[9]

Like most operators, Sol faced a constant turnover of workers, who were liable to quit at any time to head for the saloon or other camps or the coal mines, which paid better. So, in the Company's best long-term interests, he built decent, livable logging camps along the railroad that lured stable, dependable loggers. A good company retail store was almost as important to loggers as a good cook house, so Sol built in Shelton the Lumbermen's Mercantile, which was also a boon to the isolated community of Kamilche. The store provided easy credit as an inducement for loggers to take root and keep working in the community.

Simpson camps attracted a great number of Scandinavian and Finnish emigrants, who came to the Northwest to start a new life. When the would-be loggers arrived at Simpson headquarters, Al Hanlon, a Simpson brakeman, would take a piece of blue chalk and mark on the back of each man's shirt the number of the camp to which he was assigned. The newcomers then piled on a flatcar, their feet dangling over the side, for the 25-mile ride to camp.

When camps moved to new
sites, everything was loaded
onto rail cars. First the gear
was loaded, "then men, wives
and babies," wrote Dave
James. Moves generally were
made over a weekend to avoid
weakening worker
productivity."

Simpson Logging Company Camp Five was located above Matlock, now known as the Palmer Place. (Pictured from the left as identified by Bill Grisdale) first row — Al Leroy, unknown, George Grisdale, "Jack the Ripper,"

unknown, unknown, Eric Odegard, Clarence Brainard and Jim Forrest; second row — unknown, Bill Doty, unknown, unknown, Carl Weiks, unknown, "Boomstick," Frank Fieser, Ed Grout, Bill Grisdale,

Dave Kelly, Jack Clark, George Cline; third row — Fred Anderson, Pete Rambo, Jack Ireland, Joe Stertz, "Old Ninety," unknown, Levi Cline, Plummer Cox, Ed Cook; back row — Cleve Anderson, Krise, Joe Zink,

unknown, unknown, Ted Callow. Bill Grisdale, "Scotty" Forrest and Ed Grout lived in the cabin to the left.

Simpson encouraged a family feeling among owners, managers and workers; Sol, in fact, hired three of his brothers – George, Joseph, who eventually became general logging superintendent, and J.R. (also known as "Bob"), who was a camp foreman. As Sol achieved greater success, more relatives came west. His nephew George Grisdale first worked on The Blakely in 1893, and was Simpson's logging superintendent from 1906 to 1929. Another nephew, Will Grisdale, worked his way up from common laborer in 1898 to camp superintendent. When he retired in 1948, Will quipped, "I never received a check from another company – and they were all good."

Sol was concerned about the health of his loggers, who were involved in a dangerous – sometimes deadly – occupation. At a time when most loggers were uninsured, Sol was one of the first operators on Puget Sound to provide a company health plan, through the Sisters of Providence, who operated St. Peter's Hospital in Olympia. Each month, the Company deducted 75 cents from the wages of each worker and matched that amount to pay for the plan.

The success of the Simpson Logging Company opened up other opportunities for Sol. In the middle of 1898, he and Anderson built a cedar shingle mill on Buck's Prairie, 10 miles out of Shelton, and installed machinery acquired from the Sylvia Mill Company, at Montesano. In January 1899, Sol, Thomas Bordeaux and M. A. Healy organized the Black Hills Logging Company, which acquired timber holdings in Thurston County, and in 1900, Sol, Alfred Anderson and a young Simpson lieutenant, Mark E. Reed, started the Phoenix Logging Company, which was located in Potlatch, on Hood Canal in Mason County. Sol was also a partner with the Bordeaux brothers and other loggers in the Shelton Hotel Company, and eventually became financially involved in the Capital National Bank of Olympia.

Stewardship of the Land

Logging operators viewed timberland acquisition as something of a chess game, where they jockeyed for control of strategically situated tracts. After they removed the timber, "Most lumbermen peddled what they could to stump ranchers or town builders and gave the rest back to the county in lieu of taxes," wrote historian Murray Morgan. "Lumbermen considered holding cutover land in the same light as retaining old mistresses – sentimental and damned uneconomical."[10]

Sol Simpson, on the other hand, took a long-term view of timberland ownership, preferring in most cases to hold on to cutover acres of stumps and brush. (This was a lesson he learned in 1888, when he was superintendent of the Port Blakely operations. That year, Sol had the assessor in Shelton put Port Blakely's logged-off land in Mason County on the tax rolls at $1 per acre. Port Blakely, in turn, agreed to maintain its ownership and pay taxes on its land.) Other operators would eventually follow suit, thanks to the changing relative value of the land and the timber. William G. Reed, Sol's grandson, once noted, "When timberland was purchased in the 1890s for $10 per acre, Simpson accounts recorded the value as $5 an acre for the land and $5 for the timber. Fifty years later, purchases were recorded at $1 per acre for the land and from $1 to $5 per thousand ($25 to $250 per acre) for the timber."[11]

Sol Simpson knew early on that the end of the trees was inevitable. Grant C. Angle, editor of the *Mason County Journal,* wrote that Sol, "...strained his resources in buying timber lands far beyond current needs, and also set the policy of retaining the logged lands for the generation ahead."[12]

Bill Reed speculated that his grandfather bought land in order "to secure rights-of-way and to acquire timber when homesteaders or others did not want to keep responsibility for managing the land. He looked at timber as a one-time crop and the land as a potential for some other use, usually farming. A lot of stump ranches were started and many were cleared, but most did not work out." In the early 20th century, the family holding company, Simpson Investment Company, repurchased several sections of cutover timberland within the Logging Company's Shelton operating area for tree farming.

Independence

Although Sol's name was on the door, the Simpson Logging Company was essentially a "captive" of the huge Port Blakely Mill Company. The Simpson Logging Company in 1899 purchased its first logging locomotive – a 42-tonner – from Port Blakely; Port Blakely held first option on all logs harvested by the Simpson Company and could buy them at below market value. Under the terms of the agreement, Simpson was able to sell on the open market only logs not desired by Port Blakely.

Sol became fed up with this arrangement. In 1902, he declared independence from the Port Blakely Mill Company and demanded to be paid according to what the market would bear. In a polite but firmly written letter, he informed the Port Blakely Mill that he had "taken the liberty to advance the price of logs to the Blakely Mill to the same [price] as other mill companies are paying," which was "but a fair proposition for us." He assured the Blakely people that they would have the first call on anything the Simpson Logging Company had, at prices equivalent to what Port Blakely would pay other loggers.[13]

Sol was now a strictly commercial logger, free to sell to the highest bidder. Although Simpson and Port Blakely remained closely aligned, Simpson had taken an important stride toward becoming an autonomous company.

Mark E. Reed

2

Mark E. Reed

Luck, goes the old saw, results when preparation meets opportunity — an apt description of the encounter, in 1897, between Sol Simpson and Mark E. Reed, a quiet, lanky 31-year-old native of Olympia whose diversified resume represented a brief lifetime of honest effort that had produced more failure than success.

Mark Edward Reed had weathered tragedy literally from his birth on December 23, 1866. Four days later, complications from the delivery took the life of his mother, Elizabeth Finley Reed, a frail woman who had lost three other children to disease. Mark and his older brother, Tom, were the only offspring of Elizabeth Reed's to live beyond infancy. (Their father later remarried and had other children, including Emma, who married Dr. George W. Ingham of Olympia, and Thomas Avery Reed, who worked as a clerk in the Lumbermen's Mercantile in Shelton.)

Mark's father, Thomas Milburne Reed, was born in 1825 in Kentucky of Irish-Scots parentage. An ambitious young man, Tom Reed set out on his own path at the age of 18, finding work as a country schoolteacher and, later, as a clerk in a general store, all of which was too mundane for a man with dreams. In 1849, the 24-year-old Reed answered the siren song of the California Gold Rush and joined the migration to the West to try his hand at gold mining in the booming counties of Sacramento and El Dorado. But his luck wasn't much better than Sol Simpson's in Nevada and, in 1857, he accepted an offer from the Wells Fargo Company to serve as its agent in Olympia, Washington Territory.

Tom was more adept at mining votes than gold. He represented Lewiston, Idaho, in the territorial legislature at Olympia in 1862 and 1863, and was elected Speaker of the House. In 1864, he became a representative to the newly formed Idaho legislature and prosecuting attorney of Nez Perce County. He then entered the bureaucracy as a clerk in the U.S. Surveyor's office in Olympia, rising to the top position in 1872. Five years later, he became territorial auditor. When Washington achieved statehood in 1889, Tom was a delegate to the state's first constitutional convention, and became Washington's first auditor. A canny politician who valued social contacts, he organized the first Grand Masonic Lodge in Washington and filled the post of secretary until he died in 1905.

Tom's political success did not extend to his private business ventures. His financial troubles in 1884 forced Mark to drop out of the University of Washington after only a few months and return to Olympia to manage the family grocery store.

Felled by axe, saw and man power, large trees took many hours to cut and buck, and once loaded on cars they served as favored seating for camp-hopping photographers such as Darius and Clark Kinsey, and Edward and Asahel Curtis.

Shortly thereafter, Tom's fortunes changed and Mark was able to attend the California Military Academy in Oakland, where he graduated in 1887. The academy, a watershed experience in Mark's life, instilled in him a lifelong appreciation for discipline and regimentation, which he later passed on to his sons. An officer in Washington's first National Guard unit, Mark felt that military training tended to "impress upon the youth the necessity of obeying their superiors and brings to their attention their obligation to promptly act when a definite purpose is set before them for consummation."[1]

After graduation, Mark worked for retailers in Los Angeles and San Francisco, before returning to Olympia in 1889 to serve as a deputy to his father, the state auditor, and to become active in the local Masonic lodge. Mark also studied law with Olympia attorney James A. Haight and, although he didn't complete his legal training, he recalled for a newspaper interviewer, it "helped me out of many a spot. Every young business man should have some knowledge of the law."[2]

Mark was at a crossroads in his life. Olympia provided obvious political and business advantages, but his hometown exacted a high personal and emotional price. Mark was filled with a restless urge to blaze his own trail away from his father and his older brother, Thomas M. Reed, Jr. Unlike Mark, young Tom Reed seemed to sail through life, graduating from the University of California, then attending Princeton Law School. He became an eminent attorney, was named to the Thurston County bench in 1893 and later was appointed as a federal judge in Alaska.

Family pressures were compounded by a lack of opportunity in Olympia, an idyllic setting, but an economic backwater, which had been bypassed by the transcontinental railroads and had lost the race for supremacy to both Seattle and Tacoma. Fortunately, opportunity lay just a few miles from Olympia in the woods of Mason County.

In 1893, armed with dreams, ambition and a small amount of cash savings, Reed and an experienced logger named Ike Ellis formed a logging company, Reed & Ellis. The partners purchased a tract of timberland on Cranberry Creek, near Shelton, and built a primitive railroad with tracks made from wooden poles. Teams of oxen hauled logs a mile down to tidewater, where the logs were dumped and floated to Oakland Bay, in southern Puget Sound.

Reed & Ellis became, in Holbrook's words, "one of the quickest logging failures in Puget Sound history" – a casualty of the economic depression of 1893, which was precipitated, in part, by overproduction and falling prices. Reed and other disgruntled loggers placed the brunt of the blame on sawmill operators, who had the freedom to unilaterally establish the amount of board feet in a shipment of logs and, consequently, how much the loggers would be paid. The system bred obvious abuses, and Reed vowed that one day he would reform such unfair – and often corrupt – business practices.[3]

This logging camp was typical of Mason County accommodation in the early 1890s.

Seated between the commanding officers of his senior class at the California Military Academy was Mark E. Reed.

19

A turn-of-the-century logger, wrote Edwin Van Syckle in They Tried to Cut It All, slept "...in a bunk on straw called 'California Feathers,' and warmed himself by a big iron stove in the middle of the bunkhouse." He hung his wet underwear and socks {which were washed in used bath-water boiled in five-gallon kerosene cans on the bunkhouse stove} on rope around and above the stove where they would steam and reek of sweaty wool. The water on the stove was always kept warm to provide a little moisture in the room.

Dressed for the elements, which usually included rain in excess of 100 inches each year, men wore suspenders and paraffin-coated canvas pants, commonly called "tin pants." Van Syckle observed, "The pants, stiff when wet and with their permanent knee bend, would be stood in the corner near the bunk, like a half-man ready to jump."

Bunkhouse bathing – washing a 200-pound logger's body in a 20-gallon lard bucket – was an art form. In winter, the make-shift bathtubs were moved as close to the bunkhouse stove as one could get without getting singed.

Dave James wrote, "Within the bunkhouse, beds ran at two levels and the inter-mingling snores sounded like bees buzzing in a jug."

20

Broke and disappointed, Reed returned to Olympia, where his political connections landed him the job of secretary to the state land commissioner. Working in an office that regulated a half million acres of state land, he became familiar with land titles and ownership, and sales of timber from the lands granted to the state by the federal government. Although Reed scored high marks for his work, he lost the job – a political patronage position – when the Republicans were voted out of office in 1896.

A few months later, he was hired by C. J. Lord, president of Capital National Bank of Olympia and an old family friend, to oversee the bank's interests in a bankrupt logging company in Mason County. Reed was hardly an experienced logger, and except for his bushy walrus mustache didn't look like one. Although he wasn't afraid to get his hands dirty, he was unprepared for the harsh reality that he found at the logging camp. Years later, he recalled the experience:

When I arrived at camp carrying my blankets, I reported to the foreman and asked him where I should go. He pointed to the bunkhouse and told me I could leave my blankets there, but I would have to build my own bunk. I asked for lumber and he told me to find some down at the hog lot….I built something like a bunk, and then went down to the barn to rustle straw to fill it. Over this I spread my blankets. That night the hard boards and the odor of hogs kept me awake for a long time; and I vowed then that if I ever had charge of a real camp I would provide decent furnishings for the men who worked in the woods.[4]

Logging Camps

The idea of "decent furnishings" in logging camps was almost revolutionary. Set deep in the woods beside the logging railroad tracks, the typical early camp was a ramshackle collection of small temporary cedar shake bunkhouses, a cook house, a blacksmith shop, a few family dwellings, and sometimes a company store.

In the bunkhouses, 20 or 30 work-toughened men were crowded together in sometimes filthy conditions that were pleasing only to lice and bedbugs. The kind of man who chose the logging life was, wrote Edwin Van Syckle in *They Tried to Cut It All*, "defiant, intractable, recalcitrant, insubordinate, pugnacious, refractory and often quarrelsome. He was unattached and footloose, and mostly unencumbered by matrimony…. His was an outdoors job with nature and peril, in places where misery was rain six or more months of the year…however, he did not complain of the work itself, for there was savor to it."[5]

Loggers rose hours before sunup and quietly ate generous helpings of eggs, flapjacks, biscuits and potatoes and drank plenty of coffee. (Not surprisingly, the quality of the food was an important consideration for any logger. An inferior cook would get the food thrown back in his face – or worse.) At the end of the day, loggers had little else to do but stick around the bunkhouse to either sleep or – more likely – play stud poker. (Drinking in camp was usually taboo.)

Camps were remote. Most logging companies felt that roads would make it too tempting for men to leave during the week. Before the roads were put in to Simpson camps by volunteer loggers using equipment provided by the Company, the Company railroad was the only way in or out.

Dave James described transportation by "crummy" or caboose in his book, *Grisdale: Last of the Logging Camps:*

> *Riders sitting on hard benches remember their bones felt as if they had carved their initials in the wood during a long ride. Camp Three women rode a caboose into Shelton. The train schedule allowed them two hours for shopping before the train returned to cross that heart-pounding steel bridge 350 feet above Vance Creek. It was a swaying 17-mile journey filled with clicketty-clacketty racket. Camp Five people would ride speeders (small motorized carriers) along railroad tracks to Frisken Wye near the Mason County line. There they caught logging trains going into Shelton. This meant a 70-mile round trip, often done in skin-soaking weather.* [6]

The loggers with families at Simpson camps built their own houses. Max Schmidt, Jr., retired Northwest timberlands manager, who grew up in Simpson camps, recalled camp housing: "The architecture varied. Some expanded on what had been rail bunkhouses. Others went heavily to shakes, which they split on their own time. Extending water lines to these huts and shanties among the stumps took months. Families made do with showering privileges at designated hours in a bath house built for single workers." Schmidt's father, Max, Sr., or "Dutch," was the first to install indoor plumbing in his house. [7]

The Simpson/Reed Union

Soon after he began working in the woods, Reed got the break he was hoping for when he crossed paths with Sol Simpson. Despite their dissimilar backgrounds, they established an instant rapport. Simpson, a customer and stockholder of Capital National Bank, hired Reed away from C. J. Lord and made him foreman at Camp One, near Lake Nahwatzel in Mason County. Sol recognized – and called upon – all the talents that Mark had developed during his personal odyssey. As a general troubleshooter, Reed fulfilled a variety of roles. His retail background made him a natural to manage Simpson's Lumbermen's Mercantile Company, a two-story red-frame building on Railroad Avenue in Shelton. The "LM," as it was called, was

Nome, Alaska in the late 1890s, following the discovery of gold.

Simpson & Co. Miners Supplies Provisions – Building Material, Etc., Nome, Alaska in 1902. The Simpson store and other interests were sold or just closed up a short time later when Sol Simpson withdrew from Alaska following a near tragedy at sea.

The Simpson Logging
Company office was built at
Beeville, on the Blakely
Railroad near Matlock. It
was known as the "Little Red
Camp." Mark Reed is
pictured sitting on the lawn,
Mary "Tollie" Simpson
sitting to the left on the porch,
Sol Simpson standing to the
right of the office entrance,
and Arthur Govey standing
at the far right.

Sol Simpson's office, complete with telephone, a light bulb and pinups.

(from left) J. R. "Bob," Joseph and George Simpson assisted their brother Sol in managing his railroad construction and logging business enterprises.

There were no roads, only trails and tracks. Loggers sometimes celebrated town visits with beer at the Bear Tavern in Shelton.

Simpson Logging Company Camp Four was built in the 1890s.

the commercial center of the little town, with $50,000 worth of goods in stock: "Everything from a Needle to a Locomotive" was its slogan. Later, Reed reorganized and streamlined Simpson and Anderson's railroad holdings and helped the two partners set up the Phoenix Logging Company, which remained an important Simpson affiliate company for many years. In early 1900, Reed was sent to temporarily manage the affairs of the Capital National Bank of Olympia.

Reed was finally on the fast track that had always eluded him. Robert Ficken, author of the biography *Lumber and Politics, The Career of Mark E. Reed,* observed that the meeting of Reed and Simpson "brought to an end Reed's search for meaningful endeavor and opened the way to business success and political power."[8]

Politics was in Mark Reed's blood. He became mayor of Shelton, population 800, in 1906, which was the beginning of a long, fruitful and often frustrating political career. At the same time, he was becoming one of the driving political forces of the logging industry, helping form the Puget Sound Timbermen's Association, an affiliation of independent loggers who fought to reform the procedures of scaling (measuring the logs). The timbermen's group lobbied successfully for the passage of a bill that set up a system of impartial state and county log scalers who would (at least in theory) establish fair values for logs.

Alaska Lure

When the steamer *Portland*'s fabled "ton of gold" cargo from the Klondike of Alaska arrived in Seattle in 1897, the Gold Rush was on. Many loggers tossed aside their axes and, with only meager grubstakes, booked passage on the next ship north.

Sol could not resist the allure of the Alaska gold strike, which had already made a wealthy man of his brother-in-law C. D. Lane, the husband of Tollie's sister Anna. Too old and too busy to pan for gold himself, Sol invested in retail and banking enterprises in Alaska, and he invested in the transportation business between the Klondike and Seattle, which, with the help of banner newspaper headlines, had become "The Gateway to Alaska." In 1900, Simpson started the White Star Steamship Company in partnership with Lane, who was the owner of the richest strike in Nome, the Wild Goose Mine. Simpson and Lane, who had already established his own steamship line in southeastern Alaska, bought three steamers for the Seattle-Nome run and Mark Reed was sent to Alaska to be the line's agent and to oversee Sol's other financial interests.

Reed had gained Simpson's personal and professional trust. The alliance of the two men – and the future of the Simpson Logging Company – was sealed in 1901 when Mark returned to Seattle to marry Sol's high-spirited older daughter, Irene. Mark had to return immediately to Alaska, so he and his new bride spent their honeymoon on the Company ship heading north to Nome.

Soon, internal and external events dramatically altered the lives of the newlyweds. As the number of new discoveries dwindled, Alaska gold fever subsided. Irene was in the early stages of pregnancy and sailed on one of the White Star steamers back to Seattle to have her baby. She almost didn't make it. The ship lost a rudder at sea and was missing for several days. Terrified that Irene and the rest of the passengers had perished, a shaken Sol Simpson wired Reed to "close up everything in Nome to the best of your ability and come home as soon as possible.... I don't care what becomes of Alaska. Not all the gold of Nome would induce me to take another chance on another steamship." The ship that carried Irene was found safe and was towed into Puget Sound.[9]

The end of the steamship line was not the end of Sol's troubles. A bevy of lawsuits filed by the ship's passengers almost ruined him. Settling with the plaintiffs and his creditors, Sol lost not only the ships, but also his holdings of Seattle tidelands, and most of his other assets. Ironically, just about the only thing Sol was able to salvage was his minority interest in the Simpson Logging Company, which the creditors didn't think was worth much. Years later, Tollie Simpson jokingly referred to her "$50,000 corkscrew," which was all that was left of the Simpson venture in Nome.

Changing of the Guard

The Alaska steamship misadventure took much of the life out of Sol Simpson, who eventually contracted a form of leukemia. For the last years of his life, he lived in Seattle, far from the smells and sounds of the woods. He died on May 5, 1906, during a visit to Mark and Irene Reed's home in Shelton. In his obituary, the *Mason County Journal* wrote: "He was almost the only one of the old-time loggers who had weathered the storms which beset the industry under old methods, and had reached a prosperous and influential position."[10]

Although Anderson, who was occupied with his diversified interests, officially became president of Simpson Logging Company, it was managed by Reed, who was also general manager of the Peninsular Railroad, the leading logging line in the state, which transported the logs of the dominant companies in the region – the Simpson Logging Company, the Mason County Logging Company and the Western Washington Logging Company. Simpson Logging Company had grown to 300 employees and five camps, and was cutting up to 300,000 board feet of timber daily. Reed moved its headquarters to Shelton, the Mason County seat, which enjoyed such amenities as direct steamboat service to Seattle, Tacoma and Olympia, and was the home of the Company-owned Lumbermen's Mercantile.[11]

Sol and Tollie Simpson, with two of their grandchildren, Sol Simpson Reed and Frank Campbell Reed, in Beeville.

Shelton School classroom of the 1890s.

Turn-of-the-century Shelton, Washington.

With Anderson's backing, Reed moved quickly to protect Simpson family interests in logging and railroad operations. At the time of his death, Sol personally owed $260,000 to The National Bank of Commerce, and the bank's president, Manson Backus, called the loan. Unable to work out terms with Backus, Reed was directed by Anderson to arrange a new loan for the Sol Simpson estate with Anderson's friend N. H. Latimer, manager of Dexter Horton & Company of Seattle.

Anderson then dispatched Reed to California – with $360,000 borrowed from Dexter Horton & Company – to buy Simpson Logging Company stock held by descendants of the original Port Blakely Mill Company investors. Following consummation of the deal, Anderson rewarded Reed with a four-percent interest in the Company. Awarding managers a small stock ownership was a common practice among lumber companies, and the cachet of ownership made Reed, the only one qualified to run Simpson, an equal among his peers in the industry.

The remaining 96 percent of the stock was divided evenly between the Anderson family and Simpson Investment Company, which represented the Simpson family. (The Investment Company was an unusual arrangement in the forest products industry. Many years later, the Reed family revived the Investment Company name, though its purpose was different.)

Reed's next move was to recapitalize the Simpson Logging Company. The original 500 shares increased to 15,000 shares and the cash value from $50,000 to $1.5 million. Rather than the addition of new capital, this growth primarily reflected the increase in timber values during the first few years of the 20th century that was caused by the massive influx of outside investors from the Midwest, including midwestern lumberman Frederick Weyerhaeuser. (In 1900, the Great Northern Railway Company sold 900,000 acres of timberland to Weyerhaeuser at $6 an acre – one of the largest single land transfers in U.S. history.) Also, the supply of available timber was decreasing because of the creation of national forests, where large stands of Western Washington timber were reserved for the public domain. [12]

The San Francisco earthquake and fire of 1906 created a surge in demand for Puget Sound lumber, which enabled Anderson to quickly retire the debt he and the Simpson Investment Company had incurred when they bought out the Logging Company's Port Blakely stockholders. Although the Logging Company endured some very flat years until World War I – except for business generated by the building of the Panama Canal – Reed maintained Simpson on a modestly profitable course.

The Death of a Founder

While Reed ran the various Simpson/Anderson holdings, Anderson dabbled in his myriad business and political activities. (Anderson was involved with several corporations but never wanted to be bothered with details, preferring to draw the big picture two or three years ahead of time and assign somebody else to follow through.) After winning a seat in the Washington State Legislature, Anderson proved himself to be a politician who could get things done, particularly in helping Washington state acquire federal lands. Anderson also served on the committee that chose a new site for the University of Washington and is credited with helping secure large timber holdings as future income for the university. Holbrook wrote that Anderson was "highly able on the floor [of the legislature], and he displayed a wit and a power that amazed the professional politicos."[13]

Anderson fell ill in late 1913, but stubbornly insisted on taking a long-planned trip to Europe. He left Seattle in February 1914, and got as far as London, where he began to feel worse. Too weak to travel, Anderson remained in London for two months, until he was able to sail to New York City. He died in April at the Waldorf Astoria, an appropriate setting for a man of sumptuous tastes.

With Anderson's death, Reed assumed the helm of the Simpson Logging Company as well as the Phoenix Logging Company, the Peninsular Railroad, the State Bank of Shelton, the Lumbermen's Mercantile Company and the Shelton Navigation Company (Mason County's only public transportation), which operated steamships on lower Puget Sound. Reed also was appointed executor of the Anderson estate (he already held the same position for the Simpson estate). The $5 million-plus Anderson estate was, according to Robert Ficken, "the largest aggregate of private capital in the Northwest, making Reed one of the region's major financial figures."[14]

Ensuring Shelton's Future

3

Ensuring Shelton's Future

Some say the dawn of the modern community of Shelton began when Mark E. Reed established his home there. Shelton was an isolated forest village, barely connected to Olympia by a rough, hilly road. Before the modern highway was built in 1922, supplies were brought in from Olympia on barges or on company-owned sternwheelers, such as the *City of Shelton* and the *S. G. Simpson.*

In an era when the stereotype of the lumberman was a "cut-and-run" exploiter of the forests, Mark Reed chose to build (but not own) a community. He had found "in his business, in his family, and in Shelton the security and stability he had lacked for so many years," wrote Robert Ficken.[1] Reed's son Bill recalled, "Everybody in the community looked up to him almost as a father figure. If a guy was having trouble with his wife, he'd come in and say, 'Gee, Mark, would it be all right if I got divorced?'"

The Kneeland House. The Kneelands were logging pioneers in Mason County, like the Simpsons, Bordeaux, Drahams and Fredsons. A Shelton landmark and a welcome sight for loggers fresh from the camps, Kneeland House meant indoor plumbing, hot showers and a mattress filled with something other than straw.

Mark made it clear to everyone in the Logging Company that the future of Shelton must be considered in every business decision – and that the town must survive. In August 1914, when a fire destroyed most of Shelton's buildings and businesses, he ordered the immediate construction of a new fireproof business block. He directed many Simpson, Anderson and Reed funds to the construction of important Shelton public structures, including the Sol Simpson Memorial Town Hall and Public Library. (At the building's dedication, Reed noted that "Sol Simpson's…dream was the industrial upbuilding of Mason County and the beautification of Shelton as the county seat." The same could be said of Reed himself.)[2]

In 1915, as a member of the Washington State Legislature, Reed arranged for $140,000 of a $200,000 appropriation for the Olympic Highway to go to Mason County. In 1923, he got the state to help Mason County pave Shelton's main street as part of the highway north to Port Angeles. Two years later, he negotiated for the state to reroute the Olympic Highway through Shelton.[3]

Arthur B. Govey

After Anderson's death, Reed was one of only two directors on the board. The other director was Vice President Arthur B. Govey, who was born in London, England, and came to Mason County in 1889, when he was 18. His first job in the woods was greasing skids to ease the way for log-pulling bulls. In 1891, Sol Simpson hired Govey as a camp clerk, to handle the payrolls, maintain supplies, buy food for the animals and see to the welfare of injured workers. Govey was known as a kindly and generous man. Having seen more than his share of maimed loggers, he worked tirelessly for the development of Shelton General Hospital and often anonymously paid the doctor bills of needy injured loggers, according to Emma Richert, who served as secretary for both Govey and Reed.

Govey was a loyal, earnest employee who developed a reputation for tight-fisted money management. "He sits on the lid," was how Mark's son Sol Reed once laughingly described Govey, who saved and reused rubber bands, paper clips, string and the backs of envelopes, which he used as scratch pads. At the time, Simpson paid its workers in gold coins, and Govey enjoyed clinking the $20 gold pieces on the counter as he dispensed wages to each logger coming in from camp. (On paydays, the town marshal watched the Simpson offices from a warehouse window across Railroad Avenue, a .30-30 rifle across his lap, ready to fend off robbers.)

Lumber and Politics

In 1914, following his second two-year term as mayor of Shelton, 47-year-old Mark Reed was elected to the Washington State Legislature. He was motivated by a desire to find a solution to the logging industry's growing labor problems (particularly the radical influence of the Industrial Workers of the World – the I.W.W.) and to reform the system of taxing owners of logged land. A canny politician and organizer who was respected and well connected in the Olympia area, Reed rapidly ascended the political power structure, eventually becoming the first native-born Washingtonian to be Speaker of the House.

Although Reed became the legislature's designated spokesman for the views of big business, he was reform-minded when it came to the health and job safety of workers. During his career, he sponsored legislation that established the state's first medical insurance act, an accident-prevention program, and a state medical board to administer employer-employee contributions and pay doctors' bills. These Reed proposals were a giant step beyond Washington state's innovative 1911 Workers' Compensation Act, which compensated injured workers only for lost wages, not for medical expenses.

In the summer of 1917, the I.W.W. sponsored a series of bitter and angry strikes, protesting working conditions – bedbugs, unclean housing and bad food – in the mills and camps of Western Washington. Mysterious forest fires occurred and there was talk in the mills that someone had hammered spikes into the sawlogs. Some workers who stayed on the job during strikes were beaten. Logging camps and then sawmills began to shut down. Reed abhorred the tactics of the "Wobblies," as the members of the I.W.W. were called, but supported their demand to reduce the workday from 10 hours to eight. (Before the strike, Reed had urged the industry to adopt on its own a similar plan.)

The growing mood of danger in mill towns such as Centralia, Aberdeen, Everett and Tacoma prompted Reed to move his family, first to Seattle for a year and then to California for about 18 months. Reed remained in Shelton (which had no strikes during that period) to run the business and consult with fellow lumber operators in other towns who were under the siege of the Wobblies.

Mark Reed (on right) with a fellow Solo (a card game) player, "Father" Pritchard, the town banker.

The S. G. Simpson, *the second and fastest steamer in Shelton Navigation Company's fleet, offered direct transportation between Shelton, Olympia and other ports on lower Puget Sound. It hauled passengers and freight, and occasionally served as a water ambulance, transporting injured loggers from Shelton to St. Peter's Hospital in Olympia.*

Offering "Everything from a Needle to a Locomotive," Lumbermen's Mercantile (on right) was located in a two-story red-frame building on Railroad Avenue and was the largest store in the county.

The strikes threatened to affect national security because the United States, which was then mobilizing for war, needed to maintain uninterrupted production of spruce lumber for airplane fuselages and fir lumber for ships. Reed went to Washington, D.C., on behalf of the Northwest lumber industry, which agreed to supply lumber, virtually at cost, for construction of sixty 3,000-ton merchant ships. He also became one of the trustees of the United States Spruce Production Corporation, which was formed to ensure the flow of spruce for the war effort.

A professional soldier with a persuasive personality, Colonel Brice P. Disque, was assigned the task of restoring order in the production of spruce lumber. The lumber industry, led by Reed and George Long of Weyerhaeuser, decided to cooperate with the forceful Disque, who used as his weapons soldiers and logic. By February 1918, loggers got their eight-hour day. Disque supplemented that action with a series of reforms, including upgrading camp living conditions. Production improved as the influence of the I.W.W. was diminished.[4]

After World War I, Reed led the way in the state legislature for labor reform by backing an increase in workers' compensation benefits and pushing through legislation that recognized the rights of trade unions and restricted the granting of injunctions against union activity. Citing such efforts, the Washington State Federation of Labor in 1923 called Reed "honest, honorable, fearless and upright...a great mountain of righteousness." Simpson had no organized unions when Reed died in 1933, but both the Lumber and Sawmill Workers of the AFL and the International Woodworkers of America of the CIO won contracts in the early 1940s.[5]

At the peak of his political career, Reed was often thought of as a logical candidate for governor. In 1923, he told the *Seattle Post-Intelligencer:*

> *I think now, just as I have thought all along, that the party should find some man who has not such large and dominating interests as I have. I do not know whether I can get loose from them or not, and I will say that I am making right now a careful survey of them (including plans for new mills in Shelton) to see what might happen if I did put them aside, as I would have to do if I became a candidate for governor.* [6]

After weighing those responsibilities, he chose not to run for the office, which he almost certainly would have won. He said that he owed the Anderson and Simpson families, particularly the widows of Sol Simpson and A. H. Anderson (who owned most of the stock in the Simpson Logging Company), "a very lasting obligation.... I feel that theirs is the first call upon me."[7]

Reed's decision disappointed his supporters. A typical reaction was this commentary in the Seattle political newspaper, *Argus:* "Were a vote to be taken today to find the most influential man in the Republican party in this state, Mark Reed would, I believe, win by a handsome majority. It is quite generally believed that he could have any office within the gift of the people."[8]

Improving the Loggers' Lot

When it came to camp conditions, Reed put his money where his mouth was. Always mindful of his humiliating experience in a logging camp in 1896, he hired good cooks and made sure that Simpson camps were sanitary. In 1917, the Company built a $25,000 portable camp on wheels – 12 railroad cars, with steam heat, electric lights, drying rooms, a dining room and separate sleeping quarters. Two years later, Simpson built new fixed-site camps to replace those that had been damaged in a series of dry-season forest fires in 1918. After touring Simpson's rebuilt Camp One, a reporter for the newspaper of the Loyal Legion of Loggers and Lumbermen (4L) called it the best he had ever seen, with "showers running water hot and cold, electric lights, excellent bunkhouses, a good school and 4L hall."[9]

Despite these amenities and strict safety precautions, the woods remained a dangerous place, where injury was a way of life. In 1920, Reed helped finance Shelton General Hospital, the first such medical facility in Mason County, which until then was without ambulances and emergency wards. Previously, an injured logger had to be taken into Shelton on a crew rail car. With some camps as far as 20 miles from town, the ride was almost as traumatic as the injury. After a layover at the Shelton Hotel (where he was often looked after by Mrs. Sol Simpson), the injured logger would be hauled by boat to St. Peter's Hospital in Olympia. The easier access to the new Shelton hospital helped relieve much suffering for injured loggers.

A Move to Manufacturing

Simpson's immediate postwar surge in earnings owed more to the appreciation of timber than to operating profits. But in the severe recession of 1921, the price of lumber plummeted and so did log purchases. To keep Simpson's crews busy, Mark Reed reduced the price of logs almost by half, which allowed Simpson to harvest at normal production rates at a time when virtually all of its competitors were shut down. Consequently, Simpson emerged from the postwar period stronger than ever, and clearly established itself as the dominant independent logger on Puget Sound.

Still, loggers and manufacturers were confronted with skyrocketing taxation of their land. Washington state property tax levies, accounting for 70 percent of state revenue, had tripled between 1910 and 1920. In order to ease the tax burden, landowners cut their timber, causing immediate overproduction. Many owners walked away after timber was harvested and let the land be taken by the counties for nonpayment of taxes. Reed saw that overcutting would eventually result in shortages. High taxation, he observed, "intensified a desire on the part of the owner to liquidate and get out from under the tax burden" without gaining an acceptable return.[10]

Simpson, which by the early 1920s was a large landowner, was an exception in the industry because it had chosen to retain its land and pay the taxes. Bill Reed speculated that his father acted on two primary premises: "First, the land would probably eventually have value for farming or some other purpose.... Second, if we let the land go for taxes, not only would the public image of the Company suffer, but more importantly the Company would simply have to pay higher taxes on the rest of its property."

According to Bill, Mark Reed never bought logged-off land, as such, and usually didn't even want the land under the logged trees. Like most loggers in those days, Mark preferred to buy timber, not land, leaving it to the private landowner to hold the land or let it go for taxes. Consequently, much of the timberland in Simpson's operating area ended up in county ownership. Years later, when Bill became president of Simpson, the Company purchased most of this land from the counties.

Logging companies also were faced with dwindling lowland supplies of timber and mounting costs because logging operations were being moved onto rougher, higher ground. In the mid 1920s, Simpson had to build the Skokomish River Bridge, then the fifth-highest logging span in the world, in order to reach timber in the foothills of the south Olympic Mountains.

As logging areas moved to higher ground, Simpson loggers faced larger stands of hemlock. Although hemlock was used in the manufacture of pulp, there was practically no demand in the United States for hemlock lumber. Only the choice grades found markets, and then at a poor price. Box factories were the only buyers of lesser-grade hemlock and usually offered only a "take-it-or-leave-it" price. [11]

The overabundance of hemlock posed a severe problem for Mark Reed: how to meet the challenge of converting the "useless weed tree," as he called it, into a good economic resource?

Reed decided to get into the hemlock lumber production business and to reorganize the Company's operation on a more efficient basis. His decision was influenced, in part, by the experience of a colleague, pioneer Grays Harbor lumberman Alex Polson, who had gambled on cutting and stockpiling millions of board feet of hemlock when the lumber market was soft after World War I. When the East Coast found itself in a lumber shortage, Polson made a killing. [12]

Aside from a few small sawmills, Shelton had never been a manufacturing community. The timber logged by Shelton companies had been transported up Puget Sound for cutting into lumber at Port Gamble, Port Ludlow, Port Blakely, Tacoma and Seattle. The *Mason County Journal* aptly described Shelton's predicament:

While Shelton never slumps to the extent of other communities in dull times, it never gets very high when things are flourishing elsewhere because it only gets one crack at the logs which shoot through to the extent of millions of feet every year. With a good-sized mill and some incidental factories, the local payroll would be increased several times, and the town and the people reach high C occasionally, instead of being just normal when the logs come down. [13]

Reed devised a multistage strategy to integrate Simpson's operations.

The first part of his plan involved a longtime friend, colleague and customer Henry McCleary. McCleary had worked in and around sawmills since 1890, and at the turn of the century, he had built a small mill on the banks of Wildcat Creek in eastern Grays Harbor County. By 1910, his Henry McCleary Timber Company had become the largest door factory in the world, producing 138,000 units a month. To ensure a work force for his operations, McCleary established the company town that bore his name and was dominated by his personality. [14]

Reed and McCleary had participated in many large business dealings together and built up a shared and long-standing trust. As early as 1912, the Simpson Logging Company had supplied a portion of the logs used by McCleary's mill. McCleary, who in January 1924, had purchased 100 million board feet of what was reputed to be "the finest timber stand in southwest Washington," supported Reed's plan for a major industrial building program on the south side of Oakland Bay at Shelton.

Starting in 1924, the harbor (Oakland Bay) was dredged and about 30 acres of tide flats were converted into an industrial site by driving 2,000 pilings across the flats to dam up what the mud dredgers would extract from the bay's bottom. The development would include a $1 million fir mill for the Henry McCleary Timber Company, which would produce lumber and veneer. The McCleary Mill started sawing in the latter half of 1925 and had a daily capacity of 300,000 board feet.

Simpson's hemlock sawmill, called Reed Mill, opened in July 1925, with a daily capacity of 150,000 board feet and a crew of 50. Reed Mill was designed and built for speed. According to the *Mason County Journal,* "No time is lost in sawing the logs and passing the cutting through the plant and over the yards and docks." By September, 2 million board feet of squared logs had been barged to Olympia on their way to Japan. S. E. "Ed" Gange was the Mill's first general manager, and he was later succeeded by its sales manager, Chrysogonus H. "Chris" Kreienbaum, who would become one of the most important men in Simpson's history. [16]

In 1924, to help ensure Shelton's future, Simpson entered the hemlock lumber manufacturing business with the opening of Reed Mill. The Company dredged Oakland Bay, filled the tide flats, and built a pier and a power plant that supplied electricity and steam to Reed Mill and the McCleary Mill. The new mills used logs that had previously been towed or shipped by rail to mills outside Shelton.

Family quarters could usually be determined by the nature of the laundry drying on the line. Of camp housing, retired Simpson Timberlands Manager Max Schmidt, Jr., recalled, "The architecture varied. Some expanded on what had been rail bunk-houses. Others went heavily to shakes which they split on their own time."

In 1917, Simpson Logging Company designed a portable camp mounted on railroad cars that could easily be moved to new remote logging operations. The 12-car camp was equipped with steam heat, electric lights, drying rooms, a dining room, kitchen and sleeping quarters.

A centrally located steel and concrete power plant supplied both mills. Reed and McCleary, according to W. H. Abel, McCleary's attorney, agreed to what was officially called the Joint Power Operation with a handshake, "without a scratch of a pen between them to determine their rights and liabilities...."[17] Carl Macke, who had worked for more than 20 years for the Henry McCleary Timber Company, most recently as chief electrical and mechanical engineer and purchasing agent, was appointed manager of the Joint Power Operation, which later served the Reed Shingle Mill, built in 1927.

Pulp and Paper

The other aspect of Reed's plan was building a pulp mill, which would more fully utilize scrap hemlock slabs and ends, and waste from the Reed and McCleary mills. Reed said, "If this industry could be successfully operated on the waste material from our lumbering operations, we would bring about real conservation."

Paper consumption in the United States had doubled between 1914 and 1925, and the number of pulp mills in Washington tripled between 1923 and 1928, ranking the state fourth in the nation in wood pulp production. While the U.S. pulp mill output decreased slightly in 1927, the output in Washington, which had more than a dozen mills, increased by one third. "I feel confident," Reed said, "that the pulpwood industry is going to be a very important factor in the development of the Northwest in years to come."[18]

In 1927, Edward M. Mills, owner of the Washington Pulp and Paper Company in Port Angeles – a sulfite pulp and newsprint mill – was looking for expansion opportunities and needed hemlock fibers. Mills, Isadore Zellerbach, Reed and financier Charles Blyth put up $2 million to build – alongside Simpson's Reed Mill in Shelton – the Rainier Pulp & Paper Company, a sulfite pulp mill that eventually reached a daily capacity of 120 tons.[19]

The pulp mill, the small Reed Shingle Mill and Reed (hemlock) Mill completed what Bill Reed would later call Simpson Logging Company's "developmental stage." Simpson was still, in essence, a commercial logger – and a prosperous one – "but it now had facilities that could utilize the species [hemlock] for which there was little demand in the form of logs." The primary species, Douglas fir, was sold to McCleary and other log-buying mills on Puget Sound. Simpson also received the benefit of its productive investments in the hemlock mill, the shingle mill, its 50-percent interest in the power plant, and its minority interests in Rainier Pulp & Paper Company and Gange Lumber Company, which was run by Ed Gange and financed, in part, by Mark Reed.

Simpson brought 200 million board feet of logs into Shelton in 1928, at a total worth of $3.5 million. The Reed Mill produced 62 million board feet of lumber; Reed Shingle Mill, 53 million shingles; the McCleary Mill, 60 million board feet; and Rainier, 42,000 tons of pulp, which was valued at $2.5 million.[20]

Shelton's emergence as a manufacturing center spurred new growth. With 1,000 employees working for the Reed, McCleary and Rainier mills, Shelton added new housing and a large municipal waterworks system, and paved streets on the north side of town. At the same time, the Northern Pacific Railroad started construction of a branch line, following the route of the Port Blakely railroad from Elma, giving Shelton direct rail connection to national markets.[21]

Hemlock Markets

Besides the local pulp mill, the first major buyer of Simpson's hemlock was Japan, which was still rebuilding Tokyo after the great earthquake of 1923. Having exhausted its own timber, Japan, after World War I, became the principal export market for Northwest lumber. In 1925 alone, Japan bought 600 million board feet from Northwest mills. Simpson held a major share of that business, thanks to Mark Reed's sales trip to Japan, where he secured five years' worth of business commitments for the Reed Mill.[22]

Most of the shipments were rough-cut logs called "squares" – the largest pieces of lumber with sides of equal width that an American mill could cut. Typically, a hemlock square would run from a minimum of 12 x 12 inches up to 24 x 24 inches, and 40 feet long. Cutting to those dimensions was more practical than shipping whole logs to Japan because the squares could be carried more efficiently than logs on the trans- Pacific steamships. The slabs cut from the logs were used to make chips for local pulp mills.

Ultimately, however, the Japanese market dried up, and Simpson began marketing its hemlock on the Atlantic Coast, which had become a new region of opportunity for the Northwest following the opening of the Panama Canal in 1914. The Company had to overcome the prejudice against Northwest hemlock of East Coast buyers who were familiar only with Pennsylvania hemlock, a species that was inferior to the Northwest hemlock. Eventually, the growing scarcity of the other species, combined with the Reed Mill's superior quality, enabled its hemlock to outsell Southern pine, Canadian spruce, short-leaf yellow pine, and Pennsylvania and Wisconsin hemlock, particularly when the Reed Mill hemlock could match the price of the competition.[23]

However, during 1928 and 1929, the East Coast demand for lumber fell and prices tumbled. Coming on the heels of the decline in Japanese business, this put the Northwest lumber industry in a situation that was precarious – and a precursor to the years of the Great Depression. Fortunately, Simpson had kept itself liquid and poised for acquisitions. In 1928, Simpson Investment Company and Agnes Healy Anderson (Alfred Anderson's widow) purchased the interests of Thomas Bordeaux and the Bordeaux Estate Company in the Mason County Logging Company, the Manley Mill Company and the Phoenix Logging Company.[24]

All the expansion moves made by Mark Reed directly influenced his beloved Shelton by bringing a sense of stability to the town and a feeling of confidence in the future – at a time when similar logging-dependent communities were withering away.[25]

The Mark Reed Style

The Mark Reed Style

Mark Reed was, in the words of his son Bill, "a seat-of-the-pants" operator, who ran the Company by force of personality. He didn't use time studies, written reports or professional consultants. Simpson had no operating manual, no organization chart, no formal communication system, not even a monthly balance sheet or profit-and-loss statement. At meetings of directors and stockholders, Reed would often simply dictate the minutes and then have them signed by the people concerned.

"This seems like a dictatorial way of acting, but he didn't ever think of it as such," noted Bill Reed. "He was a warm, strong man and had a great many friends. He was accessible and easy to talk to, but there was never any question about who was running the business."

On a typical business day, Mark walked the few short blocks from his home (known as Colonial House) to the office, trailed by two German shepherds named Baron and Helen, who belonged to Mark's oldest son, Sol. Usually, one of his first stops was the machine shop, where he examined the equipment while chatting with old-time master mechanic Jimmy Frisken. From there, he might tour the boom and sawmills, and on occasion, drive up to the logging camps.

Once he arrived at his office, an hour or two after it opened, "he probably spent no more than a couple of hours a day on what the modern executive would think of as general management," Bill recalled. "He would then read the mail, answer letters by dictation to his faithful secretary, Emma Richert, perhaps confer with someone for 15 minutes, and then go to the barber shop for his morning shave."

Mark often spent the rest of the morning at Smith's Cigar Store, near the Lumbermen's Mercantile, playing the card game Solo with "Father" Pritchard (the town banker), Joe Deer, Frank Fredson, Billy Smith, A. G. Cushman, Jesse Wooster and Joe Weinhart, the butcher. Mark once said that when it came to playing cards, what mattered to him was "the game more than the gain."

After lunch at home and an hour-long nap, he would return to the office to confer individually with the operating executives. He delegated responsibility and authority to those executives and expected them to do their jobs. General Manager Chris Kreienbaum, who would later become president of the Company, recalled that Reed essentially left him alone to manage the operation, and only occasionally would he stop by Kreienbaum's office and politely inquire, "Chris, are you too busy to have a chat?"

This Clark Kinsey photograph was taken during the building of the Oxbow Canyon trestle. It spanned the canyon 190 feet above the Wynooche River and was built without drawings or cranes. "They just stood and looked at where they wanted to go and started building," recalled Dave James. "They were just natural engineers."

A close associate once said that Reed could put people at ease with "a twinkle in his eye that…was always there until he got exercised about something, and then he could look pretty stern." Another former employee said, "When something went against his grain, the sky shook and the lightning was there and the thunder.… But he was a very fair man and a very kindly man."[1]

Alex Polson, a Grays Harbor logger, called Mark "a man of strong convictions. We always know where he stands and, if he is with you, he is a big help. If he is against you, you have a fight on your hands."[2]

Mark could also poke fun at himself. When his girth eventually equaled his prosperity, he ran in the "fat man's race" at Shelton's Fourth of July picnic in 1915.

Sol, Frank and Bill

Mark had carefully prepared for the day when he would no longer manage Simpson.

On the lumber side of the business, he had given more and more responsibility to Kreienbaum, a bright young man from Indiana who had grown up in the business. After serving as manager of Reed Mill, Kreienbaum was appointed general manager of the Mill Division in 1930.

Although there was room for talented outsiders like Kreienbaum, Mark Reed's dream was for his logging interests to be run by his two older sons, Sol Simpson Reed, who was born in the bedroom of the family home in Shelton in 1902, and Frank Campbell Reed, who was born there about a year and a half later.

Mark planned that Sol would manage the timberlands and logging. Sol, a strong-willed leader, was the first of the boys to attend Culver Military Academy in Indiana, where he excelled academically and graduated as a first lieutenant. Sol loved the woods, working in the Simpson camps and studying forestry at the University of Washington. Tall and thin, with round glasses and a prematurely receding hairline, Sol was described by Holbrook as "amiable, hail-fellow and competent," accepted by loggers as one of their own. In 1929, he succeeded the late George Grisdale as superintendent of all the Simpson camps and brought in tractors, then a rarity in western logging. Holbrook credited Sol with originating the practice of sending crews and tractors ahead of the main logging gang to salvage wind-felled timber.[3]

Frank Reed followed Sol at Culver by one year and had an even more outstanding career, graduating as senior captain – the highest-ranking cadet. Frank was an avid sportsman, who favored polo, flying and duck hunting over business. Nevertheless, Mark intended that Frank would oversee sales and lumber manufacturing.

The Mark E. Reed family:
Irene, Sol (behind), Frank
(on his father's right)
and Bill.

c 1914

*Culver Cadet
William Garrard Reed*

*Culver Cadet
Frank Campbell Reed*

*Culver Cadet
Sol Simpson Reed*

47

Log. Co.

The third son, William Garrard Reed, who was born in 1908, recalled that, with his two brothers ahead of him, "it was clearly understood that there was no place for me in the Simpson Logging Company." As a youth, Bill attended schools in Seattle and Shelton, and during this period, he worked as a stock boy in the grocery department of the Lumbermen's Mercantile Company for a couple of summers. He followed his brothers to Culver, but readily conceded that he was "not nearly as compatible with Culver nor as successful there as my brothers." After graduation as a second lieutenant from Culver, Bill entered the University of Washington in the fall of 1925 and was graduated in 1929. He went to Harvard Business School in the fall with the intention of becoming a commercial banker, and was about to accept a job offer from Andrew Price, president of the National Bank of Commerce of Seattle, when his life took a dramatic turn.

On a warm early evening in Shelton on the 23rd of June, 1930, Sol Reed stopped off at the Simpson offices after a full day of inspecting operations in the logging camps. Sol liked to kid with the bookkeepers in the office, and one of his favorite targets was Emma Richert, his father's demure secretary. Emma recalled: "I'd always had unruly hair and never learned how to fix it. Sol came in, pointed to my hair, and said, 'Who have you been fighting with today?'"

Around that same time, Arnold George, an embittered Simpson employee, was coming out of the Shelton Hospital in his wheelchair. George, a World War I veteran from Texas, had spent almost two years in that medical facility, convalescing from a logging accident that cost him one leg and severely broke the other. At the age of 29, George was just a year older than Sol, who considered George his friend; in fact, Sol had often visited George in the hospital.

But Sol didn't know that the mail-order telescope Arnold George had in his hospital room had been trained on the new house on the hill that Sol was building for himself and his bride of one year, Patricia Peterson of Hoquiam. In the confines of his room, George somehow channeled his anger over his fate into a hatred for the Reeds. One day that June, the revolver that Arnold George had ordered by mail arrived at the hospital.

Sol took his time going home that night because his wife was away in Seattle. After leaving the Simpson offices, Sol first stopped at the home of his grandmother, Tollie Simpson, and then at Frank's house, across the street from the hospital. While Sol and Frank chatted on the front porch, Arnold George slowly wheeled down the street.

"Sol, I want to see you," George called out.

Tractor logging was a Sol Reed innovation in the late 1920s, and Simpson was one of the first Washington state logging companies to use tractors for yarding. The Company was yarding logs using high-leads, a technique that employed steam donkeys, large "spar" trees and cables. But with the size of the logs and the density of the underbrush, pulling logs from the woods was too time consuming. Tractors, pulling logging arches, proved to be an efficient solution.

Frank said, "Do you want to see me, too?"

George told him no, so Frank went inside the house. As Frank closed the door, four shots rang out. When Frank opened the door, Sol lay bleeding on the porch; George was slumped over in his wheelchair, his own bullet blown through his forehead. Sol died shortly after arriving at the hospital and Arnold George died about a half hour later.

Mrs. Mark Reed and Bill Reed were in British Columbia when they heard the news. They returned through the fog by flying boat from Prince Rupert to Seattle and then on to Shelton.

A shattered Mark Reed called Sol's death "a most terrible blow," from which he probably never fully recovered. He permanently moved the family to Seattle, declaring, "We've had enough. It is just too awful to contemplate." Sol's murder was not untypical of the rough-and-tumble logging life, where the potential for violence was never far away. On the same day Sol was murdered, a hooktender at one of the camps fell from a log and fractured his skull. Less than a year later, that same hooktender, recovered from his injury, shot and killed the foreman of Camp Three, 24-year-old Joseph Grisdale, a cousin of the Reeds'.[4]

Mark summoned up his strength to move on. He hired George Lincoln Drake, the first professionally trained forester employed by Simpson. Drake was a New Hampshire Yankee and a graduate of the Pennsylvania State College Forestry School. He migrated to Oregon to work for the U. S. Forest Service, where he became an authority on forestry, contracts and legislation. Working for the Forest Service in Portland, Drake had negotiated timber contracts with Simpson. He had never given much thought to going into private industry, but, he recalled, "when I talked to Mr. Reed and sensed some of the possibilities that might be ahead, I was very much interested . . . . Here was a man I'd like to work with and the job that I was offered was such an unusual one. The title was assistant to the president; well that would impress any young punk, wouldn't it?" He quickly discovered that Mark Reed ". . . gave me quite a bit of rope, which was his approach — you are responsible and you pay the consequences."[5] By 1932, Drake had replaced Sol in the woods as Simpson's general superintendent of logging.

Bill's life changed radically with Sol's death. At his father's request, Bill left Harvard, abandoned his banking career and returned to Shelton to learn the forest products business. He spent six weeks on John Rankin's timber-cruising crew and then three months taking a special crash course organized by Dean Hugo Winkenwerder of the University of Washington Forestry School. After he joined the Company on January 2, 1931, Bill interpreted financial statements, analyzed business trends, and sometimes represented his father in financial dealings with customers or competitors. "It was clearly understood that Frank was the senior man and would head the Company someday," Bill recalled, "while I was the one who had 'irrelevant' training in banking, accounting, finance and general administrative theory."

Sol Simpson Reed was murdered in front of his brother Frank's home in Shelton in June 1930. As Mark Reed's oldest son, Sol had been expected to succeed his father as head of Simpson Logging Company.

Sol Simpson Reed   c 1928

Arthur B. Govey started as a skid greaser. He was hired by Sol Simpson in 1891 as camp clerk, responsible for payroll, supplies and, occasionally, feeding the animals and nursing injured loggers. He later became the Company's vice president and a director.

Reed Shingle Mill, a six-machine mill managed by Ashley Drown, was built in 1927 as a Simpson Logging Company customer for the western red cedar it cut along with hemlock, fir and spruce. In 1928, the mill produced 53 million shingles at a profit, but it lost money during the Depression and was closed in 1932.

Henry McCleary (left) and Arnold Glidden (center) stood at the face of a freshly cut Douglas fir log in the McCleary Mill.

(Previous page) By 1928, Reed Mill was producing 62 million board feet of hemlock lumber per year. (The McCleary Mill is shown on the right.)

The Company offices occupied the north and west sides of the second floor of the Lumbermen's Mercantile Company building at Railroad Avenue and Third Street in Shelton. The main line of the Peninsular Railroad ran east and west along the north side of the avenue, with a freight station across the avenue from Bill's office. The machine shop and roundhouse occupied the two blocks on the north side of the avenue west of Third Street. Bill enjoyed watching "the trains of logs as they went through Shelton on the way to the waterfront." He recalled, "This was a more impressive way of keeping track of the quantity and quality of the daily output than any amount of printed statements."

As enthusiastic and ingenuous as a college sophomore, Bill undertook a "Harvard Business School" financial analysis of the Company – complete with lots of charts and graphs – and wrote a report for his father that illustrated Simpson's roller-coaster earnings performance over the previous two decades. The peak return on invested capital had begun to taper off after the middle of the 1920s, even with the Company's investment in manufacturing, and had continued steadily downward after the stock market crash of 1929. The rate of earnings had risen slightly in 1929, but then declined during the Depression. In 1931, when the report was written, Simpson was earning only about a two-percent return on its assets.

"Liquidate the Company!" was Bill's conclusion. He told his father that Simpson could receive "something close to value…then we could make more money by investing half the proceeds in six-percent government bonds, and using the other half to speculate in timber or the stock market or whatever we felt like."

And what was Mark Reed's reaction? "He nearly threw me out the office window," Bill recalled.

As the Depression deepened, it became obvious to Bill that the Simpson Logging Company could not be sold profitably. He began to think differently about the forest products business and decided, "let's expand and make a go of it."

Mark didn't reject all of Bill's recommendations out of hand. In that first year, Bill convinced his father to institute monthly operating statements, which eventually showed that the Company was not operating profitably. Bill recalled that the "projections that my father had me make, based on prices and salary adjustments, gave him the data he wanted, and this was probably a factor in his turning around the operations much sooner than Simpson's competitors did."

The Great Depression

The forest products industry, which was always subject to cycles of boom and bust, had never before in the 20th century experienced anything like the Great Depression. In 1932, Washington produced the smallest amount of lumber since 1904. Between 1929 and 1932, the lumber market was reduced from 7.3 billion to 2.2 billion board feet. Mark Reed readily conceded the effects of the Depression on national and international business, but pointed out that, "measured by the yardstick of money, the people are more scared than hurt." He believed that the real troubles of the lumber trade were due to recent overexpansion in production "far ahead of the development of old and new markets."[6]

During the Depression, Simpson was one of the few operators in the Western Washington forest products industry to operate continuously. The Company strengthened itself through Mark's conservative policy of operating without debt and the willingness of loyal employees to accept cuts in wages, which enabled Simpson to conserve its cash surplus, at a time when most of its competitors were cash-poor.

Mark made sure that Simpson workers could maintain their credit to buy groceries at the Lumbermen's Mercantile. George Drake recalled that sometimes he had to become the "Big White Father" and examine all of the employees' grocery bills. "If I found that a man was buying too much yeast to make beer or buying too many cigarettes, I told him that wasn't in the picture, that we were giving him this credit, but we expected that they were going to pay for it and the less they borrowed, the less they'd have to pay back."[7]

Fears of bankruptcy in the lumber industry motivated talk of merger among operators. Under the leadership of Laird Bell, chairman of the Weyerhaeuser Timber Company, a program was put forth to create two strong companies in the State of Washington: the Weyerhaeuser Timber Company and a new concern, the Washington Timber Company, which would consist of major logging companies such as Simpson, Polson, Schafer Bros., Bloedel-Donovan, as well as smaller operations.

Bill, who represented his father at several of the group's meetings, believed that the program would have succeeded if not for the financial ripples caused by the Bank Holiday of 1933, and the National Industrial Recovery Act, which created the National Recovery Administration (NRA) and authorized individual industries to work with the government to regulate production, prices, hours of labor and wages.

Mark Edward Reed,
December 23, 1866 –
September 5, 1933.

Ever since the first trackage was laid for the Satsop Railroad, steam engines had chugged through the center of Shelton. In 1948, following the completion of a bypass to the town's mills, this was the last load of logs hauled along Railroad Avenue.

By 1928, Shelton's waterfront had been converted from tide flats to an industrial center that included Rainier Pulp & Paper Company (in background), Reed Mill (in the middle), the tall stack of the Joint Power Operation Plant, and the McCleary Mill.

This government intervention was a bitter pill for a lifelong Republican like Mark Reed. Nevertheless, he participated in the development of the National Lumber Code at a meeting in Chicago of the National Lumber Manufacturers Association (despite the fact that he was still recovering from injuries suffered in a fall from a horse). After that meeting, he traveled to Washington, D.C., to participate in the negotiations with the federal government for acceptance of the code.[8]

The industry's work on the code dealt with two fundamental themes. The first, dubbed "soup bowl," allotted precise shares of the national quota to individual operators, and was retained in the final version. The second theme, "birth control," barred the construction of new sawmills. It was eliminated from the final version of the code because it was opposed by Weyerhaeuser and other large firms. The omission of "birth control" doomed the code, which was signed into law by President Roosevelt in August 1933. Stagnating domestic and foreign lumber markets pushed down quarterly production quotas. High, artificially set prices opened the door for the creation of hundreds of new mills across the U.S., which reduced the size of the servings from the "soup bowl." Lumbermen were even more frustrated by the government's inability to vigorously prosecute blatant violators and, led by Weyerhaeuser, they began calling for an end to the code.[9]

Reed's Death

Mark Reed returned to Chicago for another meeting of industry leaders at the Congress Hotel. After the conference, he flew back to Seattle, where Bill met him at Boeing Field. Mark told his son he felt ill, but blamed his condition on a rough flight and lack of sleep. Upon arriving at his home in Seattle, Mark immediately went to bed. He remained there for several days, until he was taken to Providence Hospital in Seattle for observation. As specialists were called in for consultation, Mark grew weaker. The doctors decided that the only way they could find out what was wrong was to remove a section of Mark's intestine for study.

Mark's condition had been misdiagnosed as appendicitis. He had actually contracted amoebic dysentery while eating dinner at the Congress Hotel, where an assistant cook in the kitchen had been carrying the infection. Several other lumbermen who attended that dinner meeting eventually suffered a similar fate. It wasn't until much later that the survivors discovered that attendance at that Chicago gathering was the common thread in the deaths of some of the leading figures in the industry.

As his father lay on his deathbed, Bill Reed, age 25, faced what he called "the most traumatic business decision I ever had to make." On logged-off land in the Wynooche Valley a fire had been ignited by sparks from a Simpson yarding tractor. The fire was spreading and Bill had to take firm action.

Years later, the memories of that night were still fresh in Bill's mind:

Fire weather at that time was very bad, as evidenced by the fact that the huge Tillamook Burn in Oregon was also under way, and the fire on Simpson land spread rapidly to the West. Soon it got close to a large and exceedingly valuable stand of virgin timber owned by the Polson Logging Company. George Drake telephoned me and said that he had been unable to get in touch with Frank Reed. He recommended that I authorize him to set backfires, although he pointed out that if they failed and the fire spread to the Polson timber, Simpson would probably be held responsible for the damage. This timber was as valuable as any in the Pacific Northwest, and I was sure that Simpson would never recover from the impact of having to pay for its destruction. I talked to our lawyer, Frank Holman, and pondered the situation while on vigil at Providence Hospital. After an hour or two I called George and told him to get himself appointed a deputy fire warden by one of the state officials present on the fire line and then to put the fire out in his capacity as a fire warden rather than as a vice president of the Simpson Logging Company. George did so, setting the backfires and stopping the main fire before it reached the Polson timber.

Our father died about 24 hours later, on September 5, 1933, and thus the Mark Reed family existed no more as a single unit.

Bill Reed Steps Forward

5

Bill Reed Steps Forward

Mark Reed's death, compounded by the abysmal performance of the national economy and the logging business, shook the Company to its foundations, and prompted a reassignment of management responsibilities.

Frank Reed took over as president and chief executive of the Simpson Logging Company, overseeing sales, long-range planning and negotiations for timber acquisition. Although the Logging Company's head office was in Seattle, operations were directed from Shelton by the Company's General Manager, Chris Kreienbaum, who was assisted by Logging and Forestry General Superintendent George Drake.

Bill Reed became president of the Simpson Investment Company (a family holding company that owned virtually all of the Reed family stock – representing about 46 percent – of the Logging Company), the Lumbermen's Mercantile Company and the State Bank of Shelton. He replaced Mark as a director of the First-Seattle Dexter Horton National Bank (now called Seafirst Bank), to which he sold the Shelton bank later in 1933, following the legalization of branch banking.

The Simpson Logging Company elected a revamped five-person board of directors made up of the Reed brothers and Govey, and Ed Hillier and Katheryn Wilson, who represented the Alfred Anderson estate, which owned 46 percent of Simpson Logging Company stock. (It was the first time since Anderson's death in 1914 that the interests of his estate were represented on the board by anyone other than Mark Reed.) Hillier was the most experienced director in practical logging and timberland management. He was manager of the Phoenix Logging Company – a partnership of the Andersons and the Reeds – and he became its president after the death of Mark Reed. The formidable Katheryn Wilson, who had been the secretary for Alfred Anderson's attorney, was Agnes Anderson's friend, secretary, business manager and spokesperson.

Beyond the board, the Reeds sought out financial, land-management and forestry advice from Mark Reed's trusted friends, among them Weyerhaeuser Land Manager Minot Davis, Carl Steven (once an associate of noted forester David T. Mason) and Charles Lyford of James D. Lacey and Company.

Simpson logging trains chugged along Railroad Avenue through the center of Shelton, past Mark Reed's office in the Lumbermen's Mercantile, into the Reed and McCleary mill yards on the waterfront.

Bill and Frank needed that help because, in the early 1930s, Pacific Northwest companies were losing market share to southern pine. Simpson was struggling to secure profit at prices that had been set by the lumber code of the National Industrial Recovery Act, and lumber inventories at the Company's sawmills were accumulating at a worrisome rate. In the summer of 1934, the usually optimistic Kreienbaum echoed the sentiments of his frustrated colleagues: "We are playing with a problem in economics that is so far-flung, covering so many operating units, and such a diversity of distribution, I feel the foundation is crumbling by sheer weight of the situation."[1]

Although Simpson was solvent, "we were frightened," Bill recalled. "We maintained a very conservative posture, keeping all the money on hand." That conservatism "meant the missing of enormous opportunities," particularly logged-off lands that could have been purchased for as little as $1 an acre. Nevertheless, "such things as maintaining market position, growing faster than your competitors, and buying equipment to reduce labor costs were not an issue; it was a matter of survival."

In late 1934, Simpson was faced with a grim choice: shut down all sawmill operations or reduce operating time and production (which was the NRA code authorities' recommendation to the industry). Simpson workers, who were already being assisted by the Company through credit accounts at the Lumbermen's Mercantile, could hardly survive on the take-home pay from the shorter hours. Kreienbaum resigned from all his committee memberships with the West Coast Lumbermen's Association and notified the NRA code authorities that, henceforth, the Reed Mill Company was going to abandon the lumber code and sell its lumber at the market price. A Supreme Court decision, which nullified the NRA code price-fixing, spared Simpson the threatened fines and restrictions.

Eleanor Henry Reed

Trees were not the only thing pressing on Bill's mind. In 1934, at a party given by friends on Seattle's Capitol Hill, a comely young woman tripped and fell down near his seat. "I helped her up, introduced myself with an apology for the possibility that my foot had been in her way, and we had a dance," he recalled.

Her name was Eleanor Henry – known as "Nor" to all her friends – and she was the daughter of Mr. and Mrs. Paul M. Henry. Her father was a Seattle businessman and her maternal grandfather, H. R. Williams, was a leader in the construction and operation of railroads in the Pacific Northwest.

William Garrard Reed once recommended to his father that the Company be liquidated. In 1933, following the death of Mark Reed, Bill, then 25, and his older brother, Frank, took charge of Simpson.

Chrysogonus H. "Chris" Kreienbaum was hired by Mark Reed to assist Edward Gange, who was the first general manager of the Reed Mill. He was elected to the board in 1942, where he served until long after his retirement in 1959 as a close adviser to Bill Reed.

George Lincoln Drake, the Company's first professionally trained forester, was hired following the death of Sol Reed. Drake became the Company's apostle in the woods and in Washington, D.C., and, along with Bill Reed and Chris Kreienbaum, fathered the Shelton Cooperative Sustained Yield Unit (CSYU) in 1946.

In a day when few women ventured far from housekeeping, Katheryn Wilson aspired to a business career, and she became a valued adviser to the Reed brothers. In 1933, along with Edward Hillier, she became a Simpson director, and represented the Anderson interests on the board until her retirement in 1960.

64

"Within a year or so, my love for her had grown so great that it far exceeded any feelings I had ever had," Bill recalled. "Fortunately, she was responsive to this feeling and we were married on July 11, 1935, at the Florence Henry Memorial Chapel near her father's Seattle home in the Highlands."

Over the next few years, three children were born: Susan Henry, William Garrard, Jr., and Mary Irene Simpson.

A New Confidence

The Reed brothers were buoyed by a slight upturn in the national economy from 1934 to 1936, and, perhaps more important, an increasing confidence in themselves. At a time when most companies were in severe financial straits, Simpson was literally without debt and, Bill recalled, "the executives not only took pride in staying out of debt, but they even paid all the current liabilities as of December 31 each year so that the annual balance sheets showed zero liabilities."

Simpson began making acquisitions, first buying the Anderson Estate Company's 50 percent interest in the Peninsular Railroad Company and merging that company and the Reed Mill Company (which ran the Reed Mill in Shelton) into the Simpson Logging Company. The Company converted the railroad from a common carrier to a private operation so it no longer had to carry the logs of competitors.

At that time, Simpson owned only 30,000 acres of mostly cutover timberlands. The Reeds launched a campaign to purchase more lands, mostly second growth, which was economically feasible to buy and hold, thanks to the 1931 Washington state legislation that awarded special property tax status for logged-off land, which was assessed at an annual rate of $1 an acre during the regrowth cycle. When the timber was harvested, it was taxed at 12.5 percent of its sales value. In exchange for that favorable classification, Washington timberland owners were required by a 1933 state law to plan for conservation under a timber management program designed to achieve sustained yield, which was spelled out in the National Industrial Recovery Code. The law stood until 1984, when the state legislature phased out the special tax status.

Simpson held its cutover lands as a way of supporting Mason County through taxes, and the possibilities of reforestation grew along with the trees that were generated by natural reseeding. George Drake estimated that, at the time, 90 percent of reforestation in Western Washington came from seeds from trees passed over by loggers who wanted only the biggest and best trees.

The Reed and McCleary sawmills and the Rainier Pulp mill required the output of more timberlands than Simpson had ever owned. Kreienbaum asked the Simpson board for $250,000 to buy – for reforestation – the harvested land that had been allowed to revert to the county, and lands from other operators. This was an opportune time because it was a buyer's market for cutover land.

Simpson's first major purchase of cutover timberland was the 20,000 acres in northern Mason County of the Phoenix Logging Company, which had completed its cutting and closed. Acting for the Anderson Estate Company, Katheryn Wilson and Ed Hillier intended to sell the Phoenix land to the state (in exchange for revenue bonds at the rate of $1 an acre), and they had asked Bill Reed to supervise the negotiations. When Bill said Simpson would buy the property, Miss Wilson told him that he was throwing away his money on worthless property. "It will be a hundred years or more before there's another stand of timber on that land," she said. "Who is going to care about what happens a hundred years from now?"

Bill Reed did. He was beginning to believe that timber really was a crop and that Simpson could just let the land grow trees for the next generation while it used its operating capital to go into business elsewhere. And on a strategic level, Bill knew that if Simpson could secure a dominant position in north Mason County, it could control rights-of-way, especially to the southeast portion of the Olympic National Forest, near Simpson's railroad.

In 1936, wanting to find a new source of logs, as well as a new market for Simpson's existing inventory, Simpson Investment Company joined a syndicate that organized the Malahat Logging Company, which harvested Douglas fir and hemlock on the west coast of Vancouver Island in British Columbia. The syndicate was composed of W. C. Butler, president of the First National Bank of Everett; the Howarth family of Everett, who were the principal owners of the Everett Pulp & Paper Company; and the H. C. Henry Investment Company, the investment arm of the family of Eleanor Henry Reed.

Bill Reed became the chief executive and managing director of Malahat Logging Company, which harvested timber that the provincial government classified as "Crown Grant." This made the timber exempt from the provincial restriction on the export of logs and allowed it to be sold on either side of the border. It was an unusual situation, because only 10 percent of the timber in British Columbia was Crown Grant. Malahat sold hemlock to pulp mills in Port Angeles, and fir to Weyerhaeuser's Mill B in Everett and sawmills in Vancouver and as far away as Australia. From 1937 to 1941, Reed made many trips to British Columbia, and hoped that eventually Simpson would build a major Canadian operation if Malahat succeeded.

In 1936, with the first glimmer of hope that the Great Depression was ending, Simpson acquired the Anderson Estate Company's interest in the Peninsular Railroad, which it converted to a private carrier, thus eliminating the line's obligations to service competing logging companies.

Fighting for Survival

The economy's mid-1930s comeback was brief. The log market was so devastated that Simpson discontinued logging for several months in early 1938. Plans for expanding the power plant at Shelton were suspended, with the materials and equipment left unassembled at the site. The Reeds and the Company's newly-elected Executive Vice President Kreienbaum questioned whether Simpson could ever profitably resume production and, again, they contemplated liquidating the Company. Bill recalled, "Our hopes of reestablishing it as a leading and low-cost producer had been severely shaken."

Kreienbaum felt that Simpson's best opportunity to earn an immediate profit lay in cutting its highest-quality, lowest-cost Douglas fir timber, which was located on a level, easily accessible 200-acre tract in the Wynooche Valley watershed known as the "Le Valle claim" (named after an early homesteader in the area). Kreienbaum was correct. Simpson recovered some needed income and, he recalled, "the picture began to brighten." The ensuing resurgence of the hemlock market, which reactivated hemlock pulp mills, provided "the lift that the Company needed, which allowed George Drake and me to do more long-range planning."

First Thoughts of Sustained Yield

In 1938, one of Kreienbaum's tasks was to solve the problem of the dwindling supply of good timber. He and Drake were both intrigued by the forest management theory of sustained yield, which was being promoted by David T. Mason, a respected Portland forester, who had helped draft the lumber code of the National Recovery Administration. Mason's premise was that joint management of adjoining federal government timber and private timber could produce a sustained yield. Another prominent spokesman for sustained yield was William B. Greeley, who was the manager of the West Coast Lumbermen's Association and a former chief of the U.S. Forest Service. Kreienbaum and Drake often traveled to Washington, D.C., for legislative hearings on the subject, especially those chaired by Oregon Senator Charles L. McNary, one of the most influential architects of forestry-related legislation.

Kreienbaum was convinced that "within a few years, we were going to get some kind of legislation that would allow for cooperative management of national forest and private lands.... If there was going to be a law passed to make cooperative sustained yield possible, it was time for us to start buying this land while it was available."[2]

In 1945, Ted Kallberg, who was known around Camp Five as the "Swedish Sawing Machine," bucked logs for a living with a hand-powered crosscut saw called a "misery whip." His tools consisted of an axe, a wedge, a 20-pound mallet, a saw and a bottle of kerosene-based "saw oil" for lubricating the saw blade.

After making a study of all the available lands that had reverted to the counties for taxes and that the counties were trying desperately to sell, Simpson picked out 20,000 acres that Mason County officials were delighted to put back on the tax rolls. The sale was so large that a public hearing was required, and at the hearing, an oyster grower named Herb Nelson charged that Simpson wanted the land "because there was oil under it." Kreienbaum smiled and said, "We're very agreeable to leaving all the mineral rights with the county."

Kreienbaum, Drake and Walter Snelgrove, Simpson's logging engineer, did not wait for the new forest-management legislation. Drake and Snelgrove drew detailed maps that showed watersheds, the natural areas for Simpson's next half-dozen years of logging and the Forest Service timber that Simpson should acquire. Simpson was cutting too much of its own accessible timber, and eventually Company logging operations would be right up against the Forest Service land. "If we lost the bid on the Forest Service timber," Kreienbaum recalled, "we'd be out of business."

In 1940, Simpson presented Drake and Snelgrove's map and program to the Forest Service and indicated that it was prepared to reduce Simpson's cut if it could continue acquiring Forest Service timber. Kreienbaum recalled that, at the time, Forest Service officials were "really bearing down on the cut-out-and-get-out bunch. So, we wanted to present a program that would prove to the Forest Service that this wasn't the situation with Simpson."

Simpson was not looking for protection against any timber sale that might be made to a third party. Rather, the Company wanted to ensure that its gradual reduction in cut and, subsequently, in manufacturing would be done in a manner that would not bring too much disruption to the "Shelton Working Circle" – Simpson's designation for its logging and manufacturing facilities.

Forced Integration

Simpson had no plans to integrate beyond hemlock lumber and cedar shingles.

Logging and lumber sales continued to improve, boosted in part by the outbreak of war in Europe in 1939. After the United States entered World War II, Congress established the Office of Price Administration (OPA), which froze the prices of logs when they were low and the prices of plywood and lumber when they were high. This turn of events unintentionally altered the character of the Pacific Northwest forest industry: commercial logging became unprofitable, while manufacturing became very profitable.

"Our customers were getting rich and we were getting poor," Bill Reed lamented, and for a long time he had questioned whether Simpson was capable of becoming an integrated forest product operation. He voiced those concerns in a letter to his cousin Dr. Thomas Reed Ingham:

> *In lumber…it is exceptional for one concern to attend to more than one stage of the whole process of converting standing timber into usable wood products. Thus, for the first 30 years of its existence our Company had no other function than to cut trees into logs and put them in salt water, and even now we go no farther than to convert about 20 percent of the logs into lumber, most of which requires considerable remanufacturing. This set-up is typical of the industry.*

This condition in the industry is probably not haphazard, but is a result of the fact that in dealing with wood products, specialization seems to yield greater returns than diversification. That is, a logger can make money logging, but usually loses it in a sawmill; a sawmill operator in turn can make money in a sawmill, but probably loses his shirt if he goes in heavily for remanufacturing; and so on down the line.

As a result of this situation, a company like ours and its personnel are totally incompetent for meeting the problems involved in the successful manufacture and promotion of a finished product...[3]

Some loggers, including Polson Logging Company, shut down operations, stating that they would not start up until prices were again determined by the marketplace. Other logging companies were sold to sawmills or consolidated through merger. Katheryn Wilson and Ed Hillier recommended that the Simpson Logging Company liquidate its holdings. Hillier, experienced in such matters, had been the liquidating trustee of the Mason County Logging Company. Bill Reed and Kreienbaum took the opposite position. They wanted to acquire manufacturing facilities aggressively. Frank Reed took a middle course. Bill recalled: "Frank was emotionally inclined toward my view but was not very interested, either financially or personally, in the prospect of getting more deeply involved in manufacturing. However, he finally sided with us and the board authorized continuation of the business, although it did not specify the means of doing so."

The Company immediately took a hard line with its mill customers, who were informed that Simpson would sell them no more logs but would, instead, negotiate to purchase as many of their mills as Simpson could supply with its own logs. The only old customer that Simpson continued to supply was the Gange mill in Tacoma, which cut logs that were too small for the Reed Mill. At the same time, the Company began negotiations for the purchase of the Springer Mill Company in Olympia, and the Clear Fir Lumber Company, the Gange Lumber Company and the Wheeler-Osgood plywood mill in Tacoma. Before any of those deals were consummated, Kreienbaum received a telephone call on the morning of December 31, 1941, from Montesano attorney W. H. Abel. Abel numbered among his clients many forest products corporations and individuals, including Henry McCleary, the colorful octogenarian owner of the fir lumber, plywood and door-manufacturing operations that bore his name – in the town that likewise bore his name. Henry McCleary was ready to sell – but there was a catch.

A Company or a Town?

Earlier, in the summer of 1941, Carl Macke, manager of the Olympic Plywood Plant, told Kreienbaum that McCleary intended to sell or junk his operations before the end of the year. Kreienbaum was interested in acquiring them and keeping them going because Simpson and the Shelton economy had grown dependent on the McCleary properties. The McCleary Door Plant used green stock lumber shipped in from Shelton, and the McCleary Mill was a partner in the Joint Power Operation Plant.

Acquisition of McCleary's plywood mill and door plant would allow the Company to integrate its entire operation. Simpson could utilize its fir logs for plywood or door-plant cuttings or sell them on the open market. The purchase would give Simpson a large manufacturing payroll in eastern Grays Harbor County, enlarge its Shelton Working Circle, and add what Kreienbaum described as "6,000 acres of beautiful, restocking, cutover land." It would also bolster Simpson's chances for working out a sustained yield arrangement with the Forest Service because it would move Simpson holdings farther into Grays Harbor County and justify more Forest Service timber for the Company in the Olympic National Forest.

The board approved Kreienbaum's recommendation, provided that a reasonable deal could be struck with McCleary. At several meetings over the course of the summer of 1941, little progress was made. Simpson was interested only in the door and plywood plants in McCleary and the sawmill in Shelton. McCleary wanted to sell the entire town, including the houses, the utilities, the hotel and the community church — which he also owned.

Kreienbaum already knew that the three plants were in "terrible condition because McCleary hadn't spent a nickel on them for a long period. They were all run down. The houses were in deplorable condition; the streets were all dirt (dusty all summer and muddy all winter) and there were no sidewalks in residential areas; the hotel was empty, and a bunch of bums were sleeping there at night."

When the talks broke down, a relieved Hillier told Kreienbaum that Simpson was "damn lucky you didn't get hold of that junkpile."[4]

On the morning of December 31, 1941, attorney Abel phoned Kreienbaum with the news that Henry McCleary intended to sell out that day, and if Simpson didn't buy him out, he would just "junk out" his operation. For a variety of reasons, including income tax purposes, the decision would have to be reached by midnight that night, New Year's Eve.

Bill Reed immediately drove down from Seattle to Abel's office in Montesano for the negotiations. After much haggling about such matters as plant inventories (which were worth almost as much as the plants themselves) and supplies, the agreements were signed and Bill handed over a check for $600,000 (covering the first payment for the plants) to Henry McCleary at 11 p.m. — one hour before the deadline. In a matter of hours, the Simpson Logging Company had grown from a few hundred employees to 1,400.

Alas, Henry McCleary had little time to enjoy his retirement. He became ill and died a few months later at the age of 82.

McCleary built his door plant in 1910. This picture was taken in 1928, when the plant was the largest producer of doors in the nation.

Henry McCleary was an 1890s millman who established the town of McCleary, Washington. In December 1941, Henry sold to Simpson Logging Company his land, door plant, log inventory, plywood mill, sawmill and the town.

Along with McCleary's other holdings, Simpson acquired a run-down town. McCleary needed a new water and power system, and its main road was more chuckhole than street. Simpson made the necessary improvements, then sold the town to its 1,200 residents. Simpson Logging Company had no interest in becoming a landlord to McCleary residents, and the Company arranged for titles of homes to be transferred to those who had been Henry McCleary's tenants as soon as they had paid 18 months' rent.

Simpson's first tree farm
foresters, Bill Looney (on left)
and Oscar Levin, watched
Company Planting Foreman
Leo Quinn buy Douglas fir
cones from a picker. Cones were
bagged and air dried, then
threshed. Cone gathering was
one means of earning a little
extra money, and cone pickers
were paid by the estimated
average number of seeds in
their harvest.

The McCleary Operations

Kreienbaum quickly discovered that, more than a plywood mill and door plant, Simpson was actually running a town – and a ramshackle town at that. The winter of 1942 was one of the coldest in memory, wreaking havoc on water lines, telephone lines and electrical wiring. With the municipal problems piling up, Hillier suggested that Simpson sell the town to the 1,200 citizens of McCleary, who would incorporate it and run it. Simpson placed all of the vacant property in the town with a real estate agent in exchange for the agent's arranging the transfer of ownership of the houses and lots to Henry McCleary's tenants as soon as they had paid 18 months' rent.

Simpson repaired McCleary's water system, which originally had been located in the door plant itself. Kreienbaum recalled, "The people in the town were drinking the same water that we were afraid to drink when we were down there." Simpson arranged for the town water system to be cut off from the plant, and built a new reservoir, cleaned out the creek, enlarged and improved the dam, and put the plants and the town on their own separate chlorinated water systems. The water system was sold to the town for less than the cost of the improvements. The Company repaired the light system, installed a large transformer station and constructed a new power plant, which it also sold to the town. In order to provide a stable tax base for the newly incorporated town, Simpson requested that the plywood and door plants be included within McCleary's boundaries.

The purchase marked a rebirth for McCleary and a turning point for Simpson, which launched an unprecedented era of improvement and expansion. In November 1943, Simpson acquired the Olympic Plywood Company, in Shelton, the Company's former shingle mill.

Tree Farming

"As the value of timber increased, so did the interest of lumbermen in forestry," wrote historian Robert Ficken. In 1941, the West Coast Lumbermen's Association directed the organization of 2 million acres of cutover land into private tree farms. That year, the first symbolic seedling was planted on the Clemons Tree Farm near Montesano, in eastern Grays Harbor County.[5]

Simpson Logging Company was one of the most enthusiastic supporters of the "Tree Farm" movement because the Company's vision of the future included developing ways to protect and scientifically regrow and manage its timberlands. In 1943, Simpson, along with other Shelton-area timberland owners, including Weyerhaeuser and the Milwaukee Railroad Land Company, formed the cooperative South Olympic Tree Farm Company at Shelton. The Tree Farm Company foresters oversaw the gathering and threshing of selected seed, which was sold to the Forest Industry Nursery at Nisqually, on

Puget Sound, and they managed the planting of seedlings (mainly Douglas fir). By the end of World War II, the Forest Industry Nursery was annually growing more than 6 million seedlings. Later, the Tree Farm became part of a nationwide program of management, fire prevention and regrowth called the American Tree Farm System. (By 1990, the program had grown to 70,000 members.)

Simpson's foresters recorded the growth rate of new plantings, the factors that aided or delayed growth, the probability of further natural restocking from nearby seed sources, and the quality of the lands in order to evaluate each particular area for the farming of trees. Simpson encouraged small landowners in the Shelton area to participate in the Tree Farm Company for the purpose of protecting and managing all of the lands in the region. Kreienbaum said, "We hope and believe that the small owner will derive as much benefit from his lands as we expect from ours."[6]

In 1958, the South Olympic project was taken over by Simpson and renamed the Simpson Olympic Tree Farm.

Passing of the Matriarchs

In the spring of 1940, within a period of six weeks, death came to the matriarchs of the Simpson Logging Company – Mary Garrard Simpson, 84; her daughter, Irene Simpson Reed, 63; and Agnes Healy Anderson, 81, the widow of Alfred Anderson. The three women collectively had owned 94 percent of the stock of the Logging Company. The balance was held by Bill and Frank through inheritance from the Mark Reed estate and by gifts from their mother and grandmother. Mrs. Simpson and Mrs. Reed left their stock in the Simpson Investment Company to Bill and Frank.

Bill was the sole executor of the estates of Mrs. Simpson and Mrs. Reed and was coexecutor of Mrs. Anderson's estate. Mrs. Anderson's interest in the Logging Company was divided among 16 friends and relatives around the country.

After the death of her husband in 1914, Agnes Anderson, who was one of the largest shareholders in the Seattle-First National Bank, devoted much of her energy to philanthropy and social, cultural and civic leadership. In 1929, she donated $50,000 for a forestry research fund to grant scholarships and fellowships to students in the University of Washington College of Forestry. It was, at that time, the largest endowment for the promotion of scholarship and research ever given to the school. In 1923, she contributed $250,000 for the construction of Anderson Hall, the university's forestry building.

In 1937, Irene Simpson Reed sat for this photograph with Frank and Georgine Reed's children: Mark E. Reed, age 6; Frank C. Reed, Jr., age 4; and Thomas Milburn Reed, age 6 months. Irene Reed died in the spring of 1940. She was 63.

Agnes H. Anderson, the wife of Alfred H., controlled 46 percent of the Simpson Logging Company, although she left the stewardship of her interest to Mark Reed, and later to Katheryn Wilson and Bill Reed. She contributed $250,000 for the construction of Anderson Hall, the forestry building on the University of Washington campus, as well as money for scholarships and fellowships in the University's College of Forestry. She died in 1940 at the age of 81.

Mary Garrard "Tolle" Simpson, who married Sol Simpson in 1875, died in 1940, at the age of 84, within six weeks of the death of her daughter Irene.

The Call to War

Bill Reed, then 34, volunteered to join the United States Army after the Japanese attack on Pearl Harbor on December 7, 1941. (He had been an inactive reserve officer in the Army following his ROTC service in college.) At the same time, he also wrote a letter to the Navy, suggesting that his experience in sailing and power boating might qualify him to serve aboard a naval vessel.

To Bill's "astonishment," the Navy responded before the Army and he was commissioned as a lieutenant, junior grade, in the Naval Reserve, assigned to a training unit at Bremerton, Washington, under the command of a regular Navy lieutenant commander, Jack Frost. After completing his training, Bill was sent to a naval base in Maryland for a six-week course in defense against gas attacks. He then returned as "gas defense officer" on the staff of the 13th Naval District in the Exchange Building in downtown Seattle. "Incredible as it may now seem," he recounted, "my job was to prepare the district for survival in case the Japanese launched a chemical warfare attack against Puget Sound." Nevertheless, being stationed in Seattle allowed Bill to lead an essentially normal life.

Frank Campbell Reed

Frank Reed, "a gregarious and attractive man," in the words of his brother Bill, had the most outgoing personality of the Reed brothers and was popular with a wide circle of friends. He loved the outdoors – particularly duck hunting – and was active in clubs and sports. He organized a Seattle polo team, operated a ranch in Central Washington, near Ellensburg, and enjoyed flying. When Will Rogers, the legendary cowboy humorist, came through Seattle on his last flying trip, he went horseback riding with Frank.

Business was not Frank's primary interest, and he delegated most of the day-to-day management responsibilities of the Logging Company to Kreienbaum. He did, however, enjoy his associations with Seattle's business leaders, and in 1935 (much to Bill's dismay) he became a director of the National Bank of Commerce, the primary competitor of the First-Seattle Dexter Horton National Bank, of which Bill was a director. This move led to one of the few serious disagreements that Bill and Frank ever had.

Frank Campbell Reed became president of Simpson Logging Company following the death of his father in 1935. He died in a 1942 house fire, which also took the lives of his wife and three sons. He was 39.

Bill recalled: "We had some fairly bitter discussions on the subject. Although Frank enjoyed being with his fellow directors, he agreed to resign if I insisted; but I then decided this would cause a permanent rift between us and accepted the status quo. I explained the situation to the executives of the First-Seattle Dexter Horton and canceled all of our business relationships with the National Bank of Commerce. These had, in fact, been quite substantial as a result of, first, our relationship with the Capital National Bank of Olympia (later the Olympia branch of NB of C) and, second, the pleasant personal association I had with Andrew Price, Sr., head of the bank. Although relations were somewhat strained because of this situation, Frank continued as a director of the NB of C and the First-Seattle Dexter Horton benefitted by receiving practically all of Simpson's business."

On an October night in 1942, after a party at their Seattle home, Frank and Georgine Reed and their three young sons went to sleep, unaware that a fire was burning in the library fireplace. A spark must have hit the sofa, which began to smolder. The smoke blew upstairs through the ventilation system.

Bill and Eleanor, who lived next door to the Frank Reed family, were awakened by the sound of sirens. They looked out the window and, to their horror, saw Frank's house on fire. "We immediately dressed and went there, finding firemen and their equipment deployed throughout the dwelling," Bill recalled. "They asked me to go upstairs to identify the bodies, and the firemen led me to where lay my brother, his wife and all three of their children. To my horror, they had all been suffocated by the smoke." The three young sons were Mark E. Reed, 11; Frank C. Reed, Jr., 9; and Thomas Milburne Reed, 6. Frank Reed was 39, Georgine, 35.

In an 18-month period, Bill had lost his mother, grandmother, brother, sister-in-law and nephews, "a succession of tragic events hard to believe and much harder to accept."

A "Go-Go Woodsman"

Bill Reed, the surviving family standard-bearer and the last adult descendant of Sol Simpson, had precious little time for grief.

Bill was in the Navy, and the forest products industry was as uncertain as at any time in its history. Production had gradually been moving from Washington into Oregon, which had large untapped stands of timber. This switch gained momentum in the early 1940s because of the increasing integration of Washington timber owners and mill owners who had no timber resources in Washington. The result was a reduction in the volume of logs available in Puget Sound and Grays Harbor. The war effort briefly boosted national lumber consumption to its highest point since the early 1920s, but that resulted in industry-wide overcutting.

In late 1942, Bill, who succeeded Frank Reed as Company president, decided to take bold action. No longer the fresh-faced boy out of Harvard Business School who recommended liquidation of the Company, he had become, in his own words, "a go-go woodsman" who was going to make Simpson a more integrated company and an industry leader in return on assets. But he needed to acquire more timber, as he knew "the end of the Shelton operations was not many years ahead of us because we were going to run out of old growth, and there was no place to get more except from the Forest Service." He targeted the Puget Sound Pulp & Timber Company, which owned a pulp mill, 200,000 acres of second-growth lands near Bellingham, and a large tract of high-quality timber on the north end of Vancouver Island. George Drake had already examined the tract and given his okay.

Bill learned that Transamerica Corporation owned a 25 percent interest in Puget Sound Pulp, which was virtually equal in value to Simpson's ownership of the Seattle-First National Bank. He also knew that Transamerica was interested in establishing a banking-affiliate relationship in the State of Washington. Jack Agnew, Bill's friend and fellow naval officer, went to San Francisco to negotiate with Transamerica, which agreed to a deal if Simpson paid an additional $2 million in cash. Bill didn't flinch. He was so confident about the opportunity that he bought a 5 percent interest in Puget Sound Pulp on the open market and, at the same time, cultivated the support of the heirs of company founder Ossian Anderson.

Reed convened the Simpson Logging Company board of directors and asked for the authority to make the exchange. Kreienbaum enthusiastically supported the proposition. To Bill's surprise, he was turned down by the majority of the board – Katheryn Wilson, Ed Hillier and Thomas F. Gleed, president of Seattle-First National Bank, whom Bill had put on the board to replace Frank. They argued against expanding so fast.

Deep in the Grays Harbor County forests, Douglas fir and other trees grew along the Wynooche River. Pictured is Pat Caldwell, personnel supervisor at Camp Grisdale.

After simmering for a couple of weeks (and reflecting upon the power of his 52 percent interest in Simpson), a determined Bill Reed called another board meeting. This time he meant business. After almost nine years of politeness and acquiescence to his elders on the board, Bill asserted his power and position, telling the board members, "I want your affirmative vote or your resignation." Stunned, they approved Bill's motion, unanimously. That confrontation forever altered the relationship between Bill and the board. From then on, he ran meetings in his father's benignly autocratic style. "Sometimes," he later recalled, with a smile, "it's hard to argue with the majority stockholder."

Bill had something to prove on the Transamerica deal and he was determined to come back with better terms than the board had authorized. "It was just a crazy, self-image type of thing," he later conceded. Transamerica refused to come down in price and then negotiations were held up because of a slight rise in the stock market.

Bill asked the Navy for a six-month leave of absence in order to discharge the affairs of the Frank Reed estate, restructure Simpson management and conduct the negotiations with Transamerica. His request was turned down, but the naval commandant said that he could arrange for a complete and honorable discharge. This was unacceptable to Bill, who "thought my higher duty was to serve the Navy during the War while [Kreienbaum] ran the Company until I could come back in peacetime."

A few months later, the commandant in Seattle retired and was replaced by Vice Admiral Frank Jack Fletcher, who had been a commander on the *Coral Sea* in the Solomon Islands. Reed and Fletcher became friends, and the admiral tabbed Bill to be his aide at the naval station on Adak, in the Aleutian Islands.

While stationed at Adak, Bill received a letter from Simpson official Charles "Chuck" Rowe concerning the Transamerica deal. Transamerica executives had told Rowe that market conditions were forcing them to sell the north Vancouver Island timber tract. Although they already had received an offer from another logging company, they still wanted to sell the tract to Simpson – provided that Reed would up the ante. Bill recalled, "I thought, oh God, here I am worrying about the Navy and the last thing I want to do is fight with the Simpson directors again by correspondence."

Bill instructed Rowe to forget the deal. Years later, he called it "the worst mistake I ever made." Canadian Forest Products Company acquired the timber tract and became one of the biggest British Columbia companies, and the Bellingham holdings became one of the top assets of Georgia-Pacific.

Bill Reed was granted a discharge from the service in 1945 and decorated with a Bronze Star.

Returning to Shelton, Reed had the Simpson directors elect him chairman and treasurer in charge of long-range planning and financial policy. Kreienbaum was elected president and chief operating officer of Simpson Logging Company, and continued to be responsible for operating the Shelton-area properties. Under Kreienbaum, Simpson ended the war years with strong earnings and a large cash reserve. On the other hand, Simpson, like most other Puget Sound and Grays Harbor loggers, had overcut its timber for war purposes, and its remaining supply was steadily dwindling. Bill estimated that four or five more years of the existing harvesting policy was tantamount to liquidating the Company.

Sustained Yield

With the end of the War and a return to the realities of a peacetime economy, many foresters, led by William B. Greeley and David T. Mason, pushed hard for legislation on the sustained yield management of public and private forestland, which would ensure that the cut of timber would not exceed the growth of new trees.

The Pacific Northwest became the center of sustained yield proposals because it embraced the country's most extensive stands of national forest timber. Although their objectives differed, both industry and Forest Service leaders continued to give broad support to sustained yield proposals through the early 1940s.[1]

Congress – with the cooperation of legislators from the Northwest and the Southeast forest regions – passed The Sustained Yield Forest Management Act of 1944 (Public Law 273), which made it possible to combine federal and private lands into sustained yield units and to form similar blocks of timber on federal land in areas dependent upon federal stumpage.

The objectives of the 1944 Act were stabilization of communities and employment, preservation of forest industries and taxable forest wealth, guarantee of an uninterrupted and substantial source of forest products, regulation of water supply and stream flow, prevention of soil erosion and preservation of wildlife.

Simpson developed a forest management plan to combine its fee timber with federal timber for a sustained yield operation in the Shelton Working Circle, an area now consisting of all Company operations in Mason and Grays Harbor counties, including its lands within the South Olympic Tree Farm.

Before the agreement could be signed, public hearings were held in Shelton and McCleary. Drake and Kreienbaum worked on persuading the unions, local businessmen and small logging companies in the area that the agreement would not be against their interests. This was part of an ongoing campaign by Simpson management to gain the confidence of the Forest Service and to convince trade and professional groups such as the National Lumber Manufacturers Association, the West Coast Lumbermen's Association, the Western Forestry and Conservation Association and the American Forestry Association of the value of "community preservation."

Greeley continued to be an advocate and cheerleader for sustained yield. In 1946, he wrote, "Failure to organize our forest-using industries on a timber crop that is maintained steadily would lead to the same migratory forest industries and often ghost towns that have been characteristic of the great forested regions of the East."[2]

But despite Greeley's and Mason's efforts, most sustained yield proposals failed. The Western Forest Industries Association, which represented mill owners with little or no timberland of their own, complained that big operators were being subsidized at the expense of smaller ones.

After the dust settled, the only cooperative agreement established under Public Law 273 was between Simpson and the United States government. Called the Shelton Cooperative Sustained Yield Unit (CSYU), the historic pact was signed in Washington, D.C., on December 12, 1946, effective January 1, 1947. The terms of the agreement included

1. Unifying approximately 160,000 acres of Simpson-owned land and 112,000 acres of Forest Service land under a forest management plan
2. Providing for continuous harvesting and restocking, so that the supply of timber on these lands would be perpetual
3. Stabilizing employment in Shelton, McCleary and adjoining communities

The agreement was for 100 years, which was the period of time that foresters then considered necessary for Douglas fir to reach harvestable age. (In recent years, the harvesting age for Douglas fir has dropped dramatically through new sawmill techniques and intensive forest management. It is now profitable to cut Douglas fir timber as young as 40 years. This accounted for the larger volumes of fee second growth that, beginning in the 1980s, Simpson harvested in the CSYU.)

At the time, the Forest Service had 4 billion board feet of old-growth timber but almost no second-growth forests. Simpson had 1 billion board feet of old-growth stumpage on 50,000 acres plus over 110,000 acres of young forests, mainly in the 30-year age class. By combining Simpson's young forest with the government's old-growth timber, it was possible in 1946 to expect a sustained production for the next century of 90 million board feet a year.[3]

George Drake noted, "If the national forest timber allowable cut had been dependent entirely upon the government timber in the unit, they could sell a certain amount per year. But if you added second-growth lands, then you could justify an increase in cut on the old growth, which was in need of being cut, because the second growth would take up the slack and there wouldn't be any hiatus of timber

The original Shelton CSYU contract, which was signed on December 12, 1946, included 160,000 acres of mostly second-growth Simpson land, and 112,000 acres of U.S. Forest Service (USFS) old-growth land. Signing the agreement at the Forest Service headquarters in Washington, D.C., were (from left) C. M. Granger, assistant chief forester; Lyle F. Watts, chief of the USFS; and L. S. Gross, division of timber management.

Chris Kreienbaum (left) served one term as president of the West Coast Lumbermen's Association (WCLA). Kreienbaum and Col. William B. Greeley (right), a former chief of the U.S. Forest Service worked successfully for passage of Public Law 273, which authorized formation of the historic Shelton CSYU in 1946.

In 1947, to fulfill part of the CSYU agreement, Simpson hired Dave James, who had been editor of the Shelton Independent, to edit the Company's first employee magazine, The Simpson Lookout.

for the operation. We had the perfect picture of a balance of old growth (ours and the government's) and all this vast acreage. In the long run, when the old growth is gone, the cut will probably go up on the second-growth lands because the old-growth lands aren't growing any more timber; they're stagnated, going back, while your young timber is growing just like a field of mature wheat. You're not growing anything on old growth; it's just sitting out there waiting to be cut; it's your young wheat that's producing the crop."

Keeping the public informed was an important part of Simpson's fulfillment of this public agreement. In 1946, Simpson hired consultant Roderic Olzendam to look at the overall relationships between Simpson Logging Company and the two communities, Shelton and McCleary. Olzendam recommended that Simpson regularly report its activities to the employees and the local communities. Journalist Dave James, who had been editor of the weekly Shelton *Independent* in 1936, was hired in 1947 to edit Simpson's new monthly employee publication, called *The Simpson Lookout.* The small tabloid, which was widely circulated in communities dependent on the Shelton Cooperative Sustained Yield Unit, reported on how Shelton and McCleary were growing along with the Company. (*The Simpson Lookout* was succeeded by the *Simpson Diamond,* and later, *Simpson Magazine,* which had a combined life of 35 years.)

In 1954, James took over from Drake the editorship of the seven-year-old *People, Land and Trees,* which summarized goings-on in the CSYU for a readership that included the local communities, the U.S. Forest Service and the U.S. Congress. It became the only report of its kind issued by a company that purchased government timber. Kreienbaum's instructions, James recalled, were short and direct: "Present the facts in a regular, readable way. We have a good story to tell. Tell it." James wrote and edited Simpson's in-house publications in the same straightforward manner. The Company's public relations policy became, "Tell the truth, be accurate, tell the bitter and the sweet. Tell Simpson employees first."[4]

With the CSYU, Simpson was able to make bold long-range moves, including

1. Establishing the new forest community of Camp Grisdale in the south Olympics, 48 miles west of Shelton
2. Closing Camp Three and transferring those workers to either the new Insulating Board Plant in Shelton or to Camp Grisdale
3. Modernizing the McCleary Door Plant and Plywood Mill
4. Renovating the Reed mills
5. Initiating truck logging to replace railroad logging
6. Expanding executive and sales offices in Seattle and establishing sales outlets across the country for the distribution of products from Shelton and McCleary
7. Increasing employment in Shelton and McCleary from 1,350 to about 1,800

Camp Grisdale was opened in 1946. Housing was constructed for 52 families and bunkhouses for single men. The most popular buildings in camp were the cookhouse and the recreation hall, which included a bowling alley. The camp also had a Lumbermen's Mercantile store, school and barbershop.

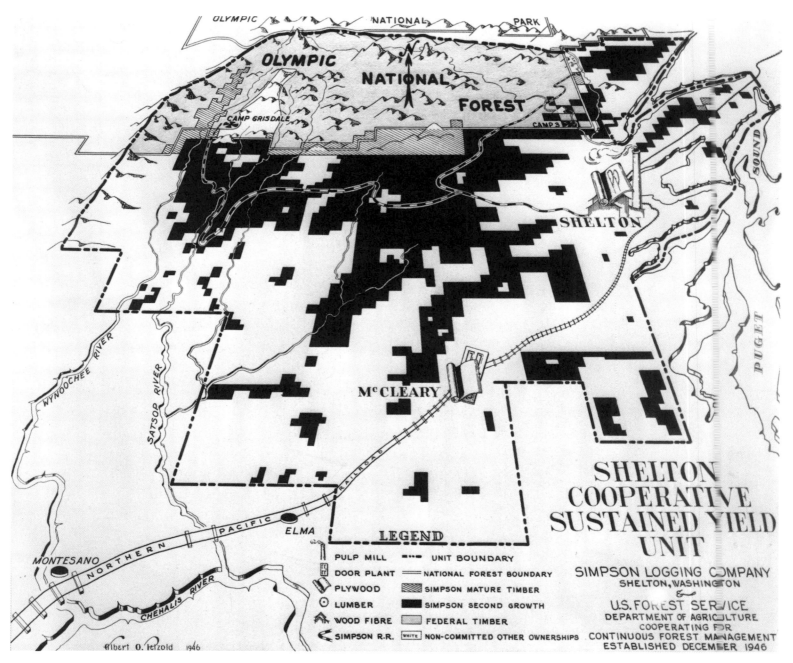

The Shelton Cooperative Sustained Yield Unit in 1946.

With the expansion of sales outlets, Simpson hired its first real lumber salesman, Robert E. "Bob" Seeley, who had worked with Kreienbaum at the Dempsey Lumber Company in Tacoma. Jess Cook, working out of St. Louis, handled midwestern plywood and door accounts, George Melville, in Los Angeles, southwest accounts and George Osgood, in McCleary, the rest of the country.

With the establishment of the CSYU, Simpson knew it had a future in Shelton. Symbolic of its commitment was the construction of a new executive office building, which centralized management under one roof. The new structure created a bit of a stir because it was made of brick rather than wood.

Part of the jump in employment came from Simpson's opening in March 1947 of the 66,300-sq.-ft. wood-fiber Insulating Board Plant, which was built to further improve utilization of the forest resources, and was part of the Company's commitment to the CSYU. The plant was then the only one in the nation that produced insulating board, ceiling tile and allied building products entirely from "leftovers" from Company mills, which had formerly been burned as waste or used to fuel the Joint Power furnaces. In the plant, chips from the sawmills were pulped and shaped into a flat, wet insulating board, which was run through a lengthy drier, sawed off into desired sizes, finished and packaged for shipment.[5]

Simpson had a strong incentive for developing a process that would utilize small timber. Kreienbaum recalled, "We had purchased large acreages of restocking second-growth lands, and the proper management of these lands called for a thinning of the growing young timber. There was no visible or foreseeable market for such material." (Nevertheless, thinnings never became an important part of the Insulating Board Plant chip supply because the chips from sawmills were so abundant.)

Camp Grisdale

With the establishment of the sustained yield agreement, Simpson Logging Company in 1946 opened Camp Grisdale, named after brothers George and Will Grisdale, who were Sol Simpson's nephews. Camp Grisdale was the successor to Camp Five (1925 to 1946) and Camp Three (1930 to 1947).

Camp Grisdale was called, by Holbrook, "that shining beacon in the dark of the forest" and "the last word in logging camps." Drake wanted Grisdale to be a true forest community that would be attractive to the logging families who would endure the 160 to 180 inches of annual rainfall in north central Grays Harbor County. Chief carpenter Charlie Mead laid out the sites for 52 one-, two- and three-bedroom houses, all heated by oil, which then was much cheaper than cutting high-value fir logs for firewood. They rented at $20.50 to $29.50 per month, including garage, water, electricity, garbage service and repairs. A special feature, an "undressing room" where a man could strip off his wet clothes before entering the house, was a big hit with the housewives. Drake believed, "To keep a good man, you've got to please his wife."[6]

Single men slept four to a room in 38 two-room bunkhouses, which included steam heat, Simmons mattresses, hot and cold running water, card tables and mat carpets. Each single bed had its own reading light. For all this, loggers paid 20 cents a day. At the 300-seat cookhouse, they paid 90 cents a meal for heaping helpings of all the T-bone steaks, vegetables, potatoes and salads they could devour. The men also availed themselves of a laundry service, and a recreation building, Frisken Hall (named after a Simpson master mechanic, James H. Frisken), which included a barbershop, pool tables and the first bowling alley ever installed in a logging camp.

Drake was manager of the Grisdale Division, Herman Otto "Bud" Puhn was superintendent and Herb Brehmeyer, Sr., was foreman of the camp. Puhn was a camp-trained man with native managerial abilities. He and his wife, Alice, had lived in logging camps for 28 years before he was promoted to live in Shelton as general manager of the Shelton Working Circle in 1951. He was responsible for building effective relationships with the U.S. Forest Service in the CSYU, and for timberland acquisitions and plant operations until he retired in 1964. He was succeeded by Max Schmidt, Jr., who was born and schooled in Simpson camps and served as Northwest resources manager until he retired in 1984. Both men were leaders in Northwest forestry organizations.

Grisdale was destined to be the last and longest-running of Simpson's forest communities. Its closure in 1985 marked the end of logging camps, which had operated across the U.S. since the 18th century. (In that same year, Simpson also closed its truck-operating center, Camp Govey, which had no family homes or bunkhouses.)

Truck Logging

Another product of the sustained yield era was truck logging. In 1947, Simpson's first fleet of trucks (including three new Kenworth diesels) hauled logs to the Grisdale railhead, where the logs were lifted onto railroad cars and hauled 42 miles to Shelton. Rails were safer and more direct than the winding roads between Grisdale and Shelton.

The impetus to the development of truck logging, particularly in the Douglas fir region, came from advancements in trucks and the fact that most logging operations had reached terrain that was too steep for railroading. "You couldn't get high enough on the hills," said Drake. "With trucks, you could get places you couldn't dream of getting with a railroad."

Over the years, truck design and equipment became standardized. Drake recalled, "As we began to know what we wanted, we specified the type of transmission, gear ratios and so forth, so if anything happened, we could shift the parts from one truck to another. We found out what kind of gear ratios we needed for our particular country, and it was helpful for drivers, too. They were familiar with every truck.... We were in the lead in trying to build up good, efficient repair facilities."

95K. FLEET o PIONEER Logging TRUCKS in UTALADDY, WASH, in 1920. Darius Kinsey Seattle

Truck logging began in the Pacific Northwest with fleets of hard-rubber-tired trucks that afforded little traction and even less comfort. Simpson built railroad spurs to its logging sites until 1947, when it built roads and began truck logging in the newly established CSYU.

Perched on the trunk and stump of a newly felled redwood were (on the log from the left) Bob Puhn, assistant chopping boss; Sam McDonald, chopping boss; Fen Riley, Klamath operations manager; and Leon Jones, logging superintendent; (on the stump from the left) Hokie Hokonson, Klamath-Arcata industrial relations director; Chris Kreienbaum, vice chairman and manager of Simpson Redwood Company; Hank Bacon, vice president of operations, stood behind Bill Reed, chairman; Tom Gleed, president of Simpson Logging Company; Jack Sheppard, logging engineer; Harry Wheat, chopper, stood behind Reuben Green, chopper. With only saw and axe, choppers and two buckers could fall two trees and buck one into logs between breakfast and the dinner bell. This tree was 10 feet at the butt and contained enough lumber to build several homes.

Simpson surveyors and logging engineer crews built spur lines off the main roads and widened and renovated the truck roads (including some of the old main railroad grades) to form a permanent network in the harvesting of the Shelton Working Circle. Simpson had to plan far ahead of actual cutting. Fred Snelgrove, who succeeded his father, Walter, as logging engineer, said that, "Roads that started in one section of the Working Circle had to be designed to tie in with a system of roads that might not be completed for 20 or 30 years." In the 1950s, Snelgrove and Simpson engineers Jesse Daniels, Bud Brigham and "Foggy" Fagergren helped direct the building of Forest Service roads using Simpson's own topographical maps and aerial photography.

Into the Redwoods

Although the CSYU created stability in the Shelton Working Circle, Simpson's only means of growth at that time was to get more products out of its log supply. The need to grow and compete with other forest industry companies spurred Simpson to expand into other areas and to search for timber stands in more distant parts of the country and the world.

Bill hired college friend Fenwick Riley, a top timber cruiser, and assigned him to explore timber tracts and potential sites for new operations. Riley began in Juneau, Alaska, and worked his way south through Canada and southeastern Oregon and into California. He found that the most promising stands were in the redwood region, a narrow strip along the coast of Northern California that extended inland only as far as the summit of the Coast Range. (Dependent upon special conditions of climate, redwood was considered one of the most limited commercial forest species in the world.)

Riley continued down through Central America and northern South America. He rejected that timber because of excessive amounts of hardwood and the fact that the great diversity of species would hinder manufacturing. He was, however, optimistic about the timber in Chile, particularly the alerce forests to the south.

Simpson management decided to pursue acquisitions in Northern California's Redwood Region: primarily old-growth redwood and Douglas fir, mostly in their virgin state (not previously harvested), as well as cutover lands in various stages of reforestation. Riley headed for an area near Crescent City and Klamath, on the western slope of the Coast Range, where heavy stands of mature redwood timber had reverted back to Del Norte County for nonpayment of taxes. The tract was virtually isolated from any road systems; the nearest railroad connections were 60 to 70 miles away at Grants Pass, Oregon, or Arcata, California.

In 1945, Simpson secured an option to buy from the Requa Timber Company about 1 billion board feet of virgin timber in Northern California – 75 percent redwood and 25 percent Douglas fir on 18,000 acres. (Requa, a corporation created by the Hobbs-Wall Lumber Company to settle the claims of its bondholders, was managed by Dean Witter & Company.) At the same time, Simpson secured an option

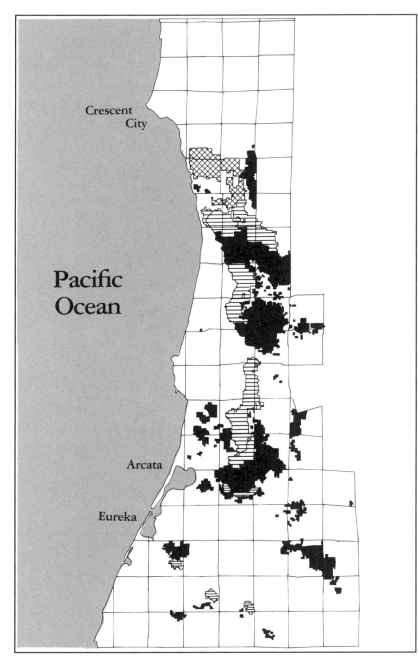

Crescent
City

Pacific
Ocean

Arcata

Eureka

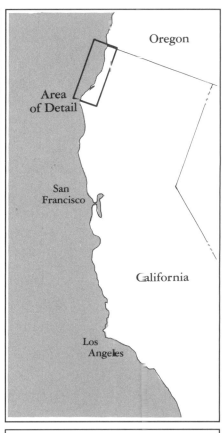

Oregon

Area
of Detail

San
Francisco

California

Los
Angeles

Simpson
Redwood Timberlands
1990

1948 Purchases

1956 Purchases

Other Purchases

to buy the Elk River Timber Company, on the west coast of Vancouver Island, an area that Bill Reed knew well from his days with the Malahat Logging Company. Both deals appeared equally desirable. The difference was that the California transaction included title to the land, whereas the British Columbia purchase would have been limited to cutting rights because most of the timberland was owned by the provincial government.

Simpson chose the Requa deal, paying $750,000, an amount based on a value for the redwood of $1 per 1,000 board feet. No value was attached to the Douglas fir within the acreage, which Simpson then decided could not be marketed competitively with the superior Douglas fir in Washington and Oregon. Simpson built truck roads to reach the timber, but did no harvesting.

Kreienbaum called the Del Norte purchase "an investment in an area that had potential.... For many years, the large old redwood lumber operations had been located from mid-Humboldt County southward, and the redwood-timbered area in Del Norte County was the last of the undeveloped timbered areas in the country."

Although the other Simpson directors were not enthusiastic about expansion, Bill Reed planned for Simpson to spend five to 10 years acquiring redwood-type forestland before deciding whether to log commercially in California, or become a seller of stumpage or an integrated manufacturer. The Company began a decade of selling, trading and replacing timber tracts to consolidate operations and holdings in the redwoods.

The most troublesome of the large redwood timberland holders was the M&M Woodworking Company, a colorful family-owned (and argued-over) firm based in Portland. M&M controlled the right-of-way into several of the most logical entrances to the Requa parcel. Bill sensed that owner James Malarkey was receptive to the idea of selling some land, but his son, Herb, "the rising star in the company," decided to hold on to the property, and negotiations ceased.

In early 1948, Simpson opened a Redwood Division and named Riley as its manager. The first headquarters was modest – a 15-ft. by 15-ft. cubicle over a service station in downtown Klamath that "contained an oil heater, three desks, six chairs, two steel filing cabinets, occasional piles of construction supplies and an acute air of congestion," according to an article in *The Redwood Cone,* the division's newspaper. [7]

Simpson's loggers, accustomed to Washington state Douglas fir harvesting methods, were determined to take it slow in Northern California, where they were faced with a different species of tree. Old-growth redwood logs, the biggest of all, could reach 140 inches in diameter at the butt end. They were covered with tough, fibrous bark that had to be stripped away with peeling bars and burned. A stringent tree-selection procedure was designed to retain as much usable wood as possible during the felling of the trees, and allow for the recovery and transportation of the logs with a minimum of breakage and waste. (Redwood trees are brittle and prone to splitting upon impact when felled improperly.) By selectively logging the holdings in Del Norte and northern Humboldt counties, Simpson could buy time to research the characteristics of the redwood between the seedling stage and the harvesting stage, the soil in which it grew, the processing problems and the end-use markets before going into product manufacturing.

During that period, Bill Reed proved his fallibility. He had offered a friend, Stephen B. Moser, the job of running the Canadian operation if the Elk River Timber Company deal had gone through. When it didn't, Robert Slaughter, owner of the Cascade Lumber Company of Yakima, offered to sell Moser half of Cascade's stock. Moser asked Simpson to buy 40 percent of Cascade Lumber for $100,000 and finance Moser's purchase of the other 10 percent. Bill declined.

Bill called that decision "one of the worst mistakes of my career. I did not even bother to look at the company because, as I told Steve, I was not interested in becoming a minority owner in any enterprise. Later, this company became a part of the Boise Cascade Corporation and its owners, including Steve, received a substantial amount of Boise Cascade stock."

Coast Redwood Company

In 1948, A. K. Wilson, a mill owner from central Oregon, was the primary active logger in the Klamath Basin, which was located 30 miles south of the Oregon border and 60 miles north of Eureka. The holdings of Wilson's firm, Coast Redwood Company, were concentrated mostly south of the Klamath River, but the company also held a 7,500-acre tract north of the river near the Requa land in Del Norte and Humboldt counties.

Simpson wanted to purchase the property but not Wilson's antiquated Klamath-area sawmill, which could cut 80,000 board feet per shift. Wilson would not make a deal unless the sawmill was included, so Simpson found itself involved in manufacturing in California. As part of the contract, Wilson agreed to continue taking lumber from Klamath, but within a few months he canceled orders, claiming that the lumber was inferior. Simpson was forced to shut down the mill for several months until it could find new customers.

Reed responded by reorganizing the redwood operation. Don Clark, operations manager at McCleary, was named Klamath sawmill manager, reporting to Kreienbaum. A sales staff was hired and production resumed. Eventually, the modernized sawmill proved to be a good investment, producing about 30 million board feet of rough green lumber annually. (The Klamath Mill was closed in January 1989, following Simpson's acquisition of Arcata Redwood Company, including a large-log sawmill at Orick, California.)

Despite the early sawmill setbacks, Reed's plan for Simpson was on target. The Company possessed magnificent commercial timberlands, which had the growth capacity to maintain the resource base and prolong the communities that were dependent upon it. Integration had become Bill's chief ambition. While his timber holdings increased in Northern California, he also set his sights on the pulp and paper business.

Aggressive
Acquisitions

7

Aggressive Acquisitions

The Reeds' first interest in pulp and paper dated back to the mid 1920s, when Mark Reed invested in Rainier Pulp and Paper Company in Shelton, which used hemlock chips from the Reed Mill Company and steam and electricity from the Shelton Joint Power Operation. Rainier survived the Depression when majority owner Edward M. Mills teamed up with the Du Pont Company to develop a process for making rayon from dissolved hemlock pulp. (Up until then, rayon had been made only from cotton fibers.) The new pulp product was given the brand name "Rayonier," a union of rayon and Rainier. Du Pont became the mill's biggest customer. [1]

In the 1930s, when the mill was threatened with permanent closure, stemming from charges of pollution, made by local oyster growers, Mark Reed organized the "Pulp Mill Retention Fund" and raised $250,000 (about $50,000 from Simpson), which kept Rainier and its jobs in Shelton, and allowed Mills to settle the lawsuits and buy oyster beds in Oakland Bay. This was a satisfactory compromise for Reed, who was a partner in the Olympia Oyster Company, along with the Dr. George Ingham family (Mrs. Ingham was Mark's half sister). In the late 1930s, Mills' successors, David Zellerbach and Charles Blyth, merged Rainier Pulp's three Washington pulp mills (in Shelton, Hoquiam and Port Angeles) with one in Florida to form Rayonier, Inc., a publicly traded company whose largest stockholders were the Zellerbach family and the Hammermill Paper Company.

In 1948, when Bill Reed was on the acquisition trail, he learned that Rayonier, which had recently acquired timberland in the West and the South, had offered to buy the Polson Logging Company, a family-owned business in Grays Harbor that had been Simpson's biggest competitor on the southern Olympic Peninsula, and owned most of the land between Simpson's operating area and the Pacific Coast, north of Grays Harbor.

Learning of Polson's interest in selling, Bill dashed down to Grays Harbor to talk to Arnold Polson, like Bill a third-generation company president. Polson told Bill that Rayonier already had made an offer of $18 million. "I gulped a bit," Bill recalled, "and said I would sign a note for $18 million and put up our redwood operation as collateral, with the understanding that if Simpson could not pay off the principal in 10 years, Polson would get our redwood plus his own company back again." Those terms were acceptable to Arnold Polson, whose family owned 50 percent of the stock.

Following Bill Reed's blunted attempt to acquire control of Rayonier, Inc. he acquired Everett Pulp & Paper

The other half of Polson, however, was owned by The Merrill & Ring Company, whose chief, R. D. Merrill, insisted on an all-cash transaction, which meant that Simpson would have to borrow the $18 million from a bank. Merrill, whom Bill liked and respected, believed such a move was too risky for Simpson, and told Bill that because of his high esteem for Sol Simpson and Mark Reed, he did not want to live with the responsibility of causing the bankruptcy of Simpson Logging Company. Bill appreciated Merrill's concern, but the loss of Polson was "a very serious blow to my plans," because the most logical direction for Simpson to expand on the south Olympic Peninsula was to the west, "so that we would dominate the timber ownership between Grays Harbor and Puget Sound."

The Quest for Rayonier

Bill Reed went after bigger game – Rayonier itself. He had already decided that Simpson would replace the Insulating Board Plant with a pulp mill, and he reasoned that if Simpson acquired a percentage of the Rayonier stock equivalent to the ratio between Simpson's total production of hemlock chips and Rayonier's total consumption of chips, "we could be in the same position as if we were fully integrated with a pulp business of our own."

Bill added to Simpson's interest in Rayonier and soon had acquired more than 10 percent of Rayonier's stock, which legally required him to make that information public. When he did, Rayonier president Edward Bartsch invited him onto the board, and he was elected in February 1949.

Over the next year and a half, Bill saw a rift develop between two factions of the board – Bartsch and some of the eastern stockholders on one side; J. D. and Harold Zellerbach, Charles Blyth, Norman Wilson and Don Leslie on the other side. (Wilson and Leslie were, respectively, the chairman and president of Hammermill Paper Company.) Both sides cultivated the support of Bill Reed, who knew "I could not remain neutral."

To Bill, Bartsch himself was the issue. If Bartsch stayed on the board, there would surely be a fight between the two factions. Bartsch flew to Seattle to meet with Bill, but before he did, he met with their mutual friend William Edris, a substantial stockholder in Rayonier. The next morning Edris submitted Bartsch's handwritten letter of resignation to Bill, who was "astonished and delighted."

In October 1950, the board hastily convened in New York City for a meeting that was presided over by Bartsch, who asked to withdraw his letter of resignation. Legal counsel, however, informed him that the resignation was unconditional. After it was accepted by a 3-2 vote, the majority faction asked Reed to succeed Bartsch, but he refused, citing his obligations to Simpson. Following a heated, bitter discussion, a compromise was reached: The presidency was left open, and an executive search would be

In 1950, the Oakland Bay waterfront was a beehive of manufacturing activity. Simpson owned the Olympic Plywood Mill, the Insulating Board Plant, Reed Mill One and Reed Mill Two, and it was a substantial stockholder in Rayonier, Inc., which operated the pulp mill in Shelton.

Though profits from Simpson's insulating board manufacturing were slim, the products were successful. Shown is Plant Manager Gil Oswald (on left) with customers from R. W. Frank & Company of Salt Lake City, Utah

Thomas F. Gleed succeeded Chris Kreienbaum as president of Simpson Logging Company in 1951.

launched to fill the position. Meanwhile, Bill agreed to move to New York to run the company as executive vice president – on an interim basis – until a successor was found.

With Reed in New York, Simpson was left without a direct operating head because Kreienbaum had suffered a heart attack that January and Bill had, ostensibly, named himself to replace Kreienbaum. He was forced to commute back to Seattle every few weeks in propeller planes, which was, he recalled, "a pretty tough life."

In the meantime, Samuel Gottesman, a Bartsch supporter who had been trying to acquire controlling interest in Hammermill, agreed to stop buying Hammermill shares if Wilson and Leslie would buy back his shares. Apparently, they didn't have the money to make the transaction, so they asked Reed if he would purchase Gottesman's substantial minority interest in Hammermill. "It was an intriguing possibility, but I said, 'No, thanks' because my life was already complicated enough, and also I did not want to put additional financial strain on Simpson."

Finally, an able and qualified candidate was found to run Rayonier. He was Maxwell D. Bardeen, president of the Lee Paper Company, a small, efficiently run firm based in Vicksburg, Michigan. Bill approved "with enthusiasm" the selection of the knowledgeable, energetic Bardeen, who accepted the job. A board meeting was called for the purpose of Bardeen's election.

Until the meeting, the board seemed secure on the Reed side, which included Blyth, the two Zellerbachs, Wilson and Leslie from Hammermill and Carl J. Schmidlapp, the executive vice president and second-ranking man at the Chase National Bank. (Dave Zellerbach was absent from the meeting. He had been appointed Ambassador to Italy by President Eisenhower and was living in Rome.) On the other side were Gottesman, investment banker William A. Parker and Morton H. Fry, partner in a New York stock brokerage.

On the eve of the meeting, Wilson and Leslie invited Harold Zellerbach and Bill Reed to dinner in New York. Wilson and Leslie then revealed that they had made a deal with Gottesman, who had agreed to sell them his shares in Hammermill if the Hammermill executives would vote according to his wishes at the Rayonier board meeting. They would, therefore, vote to elect Bardeen as scheduled, but would also vote to remove Charles Blyth and Bill Reed as officers and members of the executive committee.

"Harold and I counted noses," Bill recalled, "and found that the switch of the Hammermill votes would give them the margin to achieve their plan by one vote because our supporter, Dave Zellerbach, was in Rome. So Harold telephoned Dave to see if he could get to New York in time for the meeting, but a schedule could not be worked out for Dave to get there in time."

The next day, Blyth and Reed were fired by one-vote margins. Bardeen was unanimously elected president, but he felt uneasy. "I talked to each member of the board," Bardeen recalled, "and the longer I talked, the deeper the schisms appeared to be. This was not a mess that I wanted to get into." Bardeen declined the job.

Bill was fed up with Rayonier. Despite the urgings of both allies and adversaries, "I simply returned to Seattle, declined to run for reelection to the Rayonier board and looked for other investment opportunities for Simpson in the pulp and paper business."

Everett Pulp & Paper Company

That first opportunity was found close to home, in Lowell, Washington: Everett Pulp & Paper Company, which was owned by the Howarth family, former partners with Reed and others in the Malahat Logging Company, in British Columbia.

Built in 1892 by interests of John D. Rockefeller, the Everett Mill still contained some of its original equipment, although at the time of the purchase it was in the midst of a $3 million expansion and efficiency program. Using cottonwood chips or leftover fir chips from plywood, the 650-worker mill produced 90 tons daily of high-grade lithographic paper, book paper and school tablets and manufactured a substantial volume of label paper used for canned goods and fruit boxes in the western United States.

On December 1, 1951, Simpson purchased the mill for $9,049,000 – much of it from liquidation of Bill Reed's Rayonier stock.

Reed had no intention of barging in and making changes in an industry that was new to him and his company. A few weeks after the purchase, detailing the immediate impact of the new ownership on the Everett Mill, he laid out the Simpson philosophy of assimilating a new company in a new business: "Any changes which may be made in the future will be handled carefully and slowly over a long period of time and only after we in Simpson have an opportunity to become well acquainted with the individuals and the process in Everett."

In 1954, at Max Bardeen's invitation, Bill personally purchased about 15 percent of the stock in Lee Paper Company from a shareholder who wanted to liquidate. He acquired the stock – in his own name, because Simpson Logging Company was in a slump – in order to get a working knowledge of the paper business in the Midwest. He thought, "This knowledge...eventually will be of value in determining whether Simpson should ever expand into that area; and if so, what property it should attempt to acquire."

Thomas F. Gleed

In 1951, on the heels of the Rayonier escapade and Kreienbaum's illness, Reed named Thomas F. Gleed president and treasurer of Simpson Logging Company. Gleed had been a Simpson director since 1943 and president of Seattle-First National Bank since 1945.

Gleed's father had run logging and milling operations in Wisconsin and later in Bonners Ferry, Idaho. Young Tom worked in the mills and woods of his native Idaho during summers, and did everything from counting logs at the decker and driving a four-horse team to piling lumber to working on the greenchain. His first job in Seattle was pumping gas in a service station.

Tom Gleed was an outgoing, urbane figure, a connoisseur of Cuban cigars, a man who was as comfortable in boardrooms and wine cellars as he was in mess halls. Kreienbaum once marveled that Gleed "knew most lumbermen in the area. He could probably call more men in the State of Washington by their first name than anybody." A profile story in *Fortune* magazine described Gleed as "a friendly, heavy-set man with a somewhat imperious air that makes him seem much taller and more imposing than his five feet eight inches."[2]

Gleed was a wily financier of the first order, and his ability to create innovative funding stirred Simpson's aggressive expansion.

Schafer Brothers Logging Company

The 1950s were a golden opportunity for the acquisition of timberlands. Timber company shareholders who were liquidating their stock fell into two major groups – short-term investors who wanted to take advantage of high prices, and major stockholders, many of whom were nearing retirement and wanted to cash in. Several family-owned timber companies looked to sell their holdings before inheritance taxes eroded their worth.

One of those companies was Schafer Brothers Logging Company, a pioneer operator in Aberdeen, Washington, that hauled logs over Simpson's railroad in Grays Harbor County. Schafer held substantial acreage of mature timber in Lewis County as well as considerable amounts of well-stocked second-growth timber on its Grays Harbor County lands, which intermingled with Simpson's. They also had a timber contract with the U.S. Forest Service, a sawmill in Cosmopolis, and a railroad from the Wynooche watershed to Grays Harbor.

Back in the late 1940s, Bill Reed had written a letter to John Schafer, then president of the company, expressing Simpson's interest in acquiring Schafer Brothers if the family ever decided to sell. Nothing further was ever discussed and John Schafer eventually retired because of ill health. In 1955, his brother, Edward, found the letter in John's desk, contacted Bill and worked out a deal.

The acquisition of the Schafer timberlands strengthened Simpson's sustained yield position in Washington state, consolidated its land holdings, and simplified land management. Six months later, Simpson further solidified its holdings through a series of land and timber transactions with Weyerhaeuser. Bill rather enjoyed the acquisition process. "I went through all of our original redwood purchases very carefully with the cruisers, sometimes on foot, sometimes on horseback," he recalled. "And when we bought timberland in other places, I always looked at it. I can't remember buying any without looking at it."[3]

Redwood Acquisitions

In 1956, the combination of Bill Reed's stiff backbone, Chris Kreienbaum's vision and Tom Gleed's creative financing resulted in new acquisitions in California that made the industry take notice

One of the "appetizers" was Sage Land & Lumber Company, primarily a nonoperating holding company that had once been in the sawmill business. In order to consolidate its ownership north of Eureka, and to fill in gaps in its holdings, Simpson Redwood Company, which was formed in 1954, acquired from Sage about 12,000 acres of virgin timber in the Usal region near the Mendocino coastway, as well as Sage's cutting rights and rights-of-way on a valuable 45,000 acres near what was called the "Requa tract," which ran south along the Klamath River.

Bill made it clear that if Simpson sold or traded any timberlands, they would have to be replaced by tracts near Simpson holdings. The Usal tract, which was too far from Simpson's operations, was sold for a profit that nearly paid for the entire Sage transaction.

At about that same time, Simpson acquired for $1.3 million what was called the "Sweet timber tract" – about 14,000 acres of young-growth timber along the main Mad River. Henry Trobitz, Simpson's California land and timber manager (and later resources manager), called it "a highly significant acquisition. It gave us more time for our earlier cutover timberland, which was harvested in the 1950s, to get of age and to sustain the necessary volume.... Selling people on buying young growth was not an easy thing to do at that time because all eyes were turned toward the purchase of old growth."

In February 1956, Gleed arranged Simpson Redwood's acquisition of Northern Redwood Lumber Company, a 70-year-old firm located in Korbel, 12 miles east of Arcata, in Humboldt County, California. Negotiations had been difficult and, ultimately, the property was put up for bid. Simpson's offer, which was less than one percent over the next-highest bid, "was a great tribute to the accuracy of Mr. Gleed's judgment in determining what he though the competitive market would pay," said Reed.

To manage the CSYU, frequent meetings were held between U.S. Forest Service (USFS) officials and Simpson managers. Shown in the early 1950s on the steps of Colonial House in Shelton are: (front row from left) Dave James, Ten Gled, Lloyd Gilmore (USFS), Herbert Stone (USFS), Bill Bryan (USFS), Chris Kreienbaum, Walt Lund (USFS), Bud Puhn; (second row from left) L. Jorgenson (USFS), Hal McClery, Hank Bacon, Jr., Lee Flower (USFS); (third row from left) Max Schmidt, Jr., Gib Rucker, Archie Adams, CSYU Committee Chairman Roy Dunn, Chuck Funacres, Jr.; (fourth row from left) Fred Snelgrove, Bob Hutchinson, Harvey Warnaca, Bill Looney; (fifth row from left) Albert Petzold, Oscar Levin, Bob Sedl, Richard Brewer and Hugh McKay.

George L. Drake, shown with secretary Emma Richert, retired from Simpson in 1954, as vice president.

During the 1950s, new faces emerged to manage Simpson operations in Shelton. Among them were Bud Puhn (left) and Max Schmidt, Jr.

M&M was one of the first companies in the U.S. to perfect the manufacture of marine-grade plywood. During World War II, it produced scarf-jointed plywood for military use, including construction of the high-speed PT boats used by the U.S. Navy for patrol in the Pacific. The Albany Mill, acquired by Simpson as part of the M&M purchase, continued to produce marine-grade plywood until it was closed in 1989, due to insufficient sources for peeler logs for plywood manufacturing.

The Northern Redwood properties included a sawmill that was cutting 150,000 board feet daily on one shift, a planing operation, about 30,000 acres of virgin and second-growth timber and the Arcata & Mad River Railroad (also known as the "Annie & Mary," in honor of two office secretaries), which served Korbel and the Northwestern Pacific outbound lines at Arcata. Northern Redwood added 250 employees to Simpson's payroll, which increased the Company's Humboldt County employment to 375. Klamath woods and plant operations supported another 475 jobs in Del Norte County.[4]

Substantial acquisitions were getting harder to find. Simpson had already bought most of the adjacent property held by non-operating owners; the rest was held by operating companies that did not want to sell such potentially useful assets.

M&M Woodworking Company

The most important of these tracts were the Northern California timberlands of the M&M Woodworking Company, which held reserves of approximately 2.5 billion board feet, much of it in locations that controlled access to Simpson-owned timber. M&M, whose stock was listed on the New York Stock Exchange, was considerably larger than Simpson, with 11 operating divisions at nine locations in California and Oregon. M&M operated a veneer mill at Idanah, Oregon, plywood mills in Albany, Lyons and Portland, Oregon, and the only large volume redwood plywood mill in the world, which was located at Eureka, California. It also manufactured glue, resins, flush doors, wood tanks and pipe in Portland, and it operated lumber divisions in Portland and Eureka (once owned by John Dolbeer, inventor of the Dolbeer steam donkey.)

Bill Reed was well acquainted with J. A. Malarkey and other members of the Malarkey family, who were M&M's majority stockholders, because their plants in Oregon were longtime competitors of Simpson's McCleary operations. Bill thought that the only likely way to acquire the California property was to buy the entire company and then to sell off its Oregon timber and manufacturing plants. He assigned Gleed to negotiate with the Malarkeys and arrange financing because, he conceded, "I was never a very good horse trader." Gleed, on the other hand, was a crafty negotiator who, Dave James, Simpson's public affairs director, once noted, "knew when to put on the charm and when to apply the chill." Bill marveled at Gleed's "remarkable facility for establishing close and personal relations with people with whom he was dealing."

M&M's board approved Simpson's offer for M&M, and despite the fact that the price of the stock was about double what it was when negotiations began, Reed went ahead with the deal because the lumber business was booming and the Oregon timber would be attractive to many other operators.

George Drake Retires

In 1954, George Drake retired after almost a quarter century as chief forester. He was instrumental in planning the conservation of timber resources and the replanting of harvested lands, which eventually became trademarks of Simpson, and he set up a fire-control system, which was the first step in managing logged-off land for something besides farming. A pioneer among tree farmers, he headed the South Olympic Tree Farm from its inception in 1943 until 1954. He served as president of the Pacific Logging Congress, Western Forestry and Conservation Association, and the Society of American Foresters, and served on the board of the American Forestry Association, the nation's oldest conservation organization.

Drake preserved much of Simpson's organizational history. He arranged for the Company's first locomotive, "Dinky No. 1," to be exhibited in Camp Grisdale, to commemorate logging since 1884. He honored the memories of respected old Simpson engineers by placing their names under the cab windows of locomotives, and named the Company's biggest tug after Arthur B. Govey and Grisdale's recreation hall after master mechanic Jimmy Frisken. He also directed production of the book *Green Commonwealth,* by Stewart Holbrook, which chronicled Simpson's first 50 years.

George Drake lived to be 89, passing away on April 5, 1979.

In November 1960, Simpson Logging Company and Simpson Redwood Company operations were consolidated and centralized into Simpson Timber Company, which was headquartered in Seattle.

In the more than two decades since the death of Mark Reed, Bill Reed had radically transformed Simpson. He observed his father's allegiance to the survival of Shelton while expanding the Company's horizons in geography, products and philosophy. And he was just getting started.

Remodeling the Company

8

Remodeling the Company

Following the Company's Northern California acquisitions during the late 1940s and 1950s, Bill Reed pronounced Simpson's Pacific Coast geographic expansion "essentially complete." The 1960s were a time of consolidation and for strengthening Simpson's balance sheet.

C. H. "Chris" Kreienbaum

Chris Kreienbaum retired in 1960, after 35 years with the Company. He had developed new sales, marketing, research, promotion, forestry and public relations programs. The *Simpson Lookout* memorialized his career, which "spanned a half-century of the greatest development in the western forest products industry. His contributions to Simpson and to the forest products industry were monumental. His 'CHK' became a recognized stamp of approval on every phase of the Company interests."[1]

Kreienbaum, like Mark Reed, was a visionary. He comprehended the importance of new forest products, such as the use of wood fiber in paper, wallboard and other insulating materials and, eventually, wood plastics, new plywoods and manufactured products that were fire- and decay-resistant. He saw that volume of wood, not the age of the tree or the number of its growth rings, was what mattered. He set in motion Simpson's goal of a quick-growing forest and was a key figure in the creation of the CSYU.

Kreienbaum's value to the Company was best described by Bill Reed in a letter he wrote on the occasion of Kreienbaum's retirement:

> *Your retirement is a real wrench for me. Having worked in Simpson with you for thirty years, more than any other man, I will never get used to having to make decisions without sharing the responsibilities, the disappointments and the satisfactions with you . . . . You have been the main source of strength for the Company and me . . . . In the history of Simpson Logging Company, there have been three great names, three great men: S. G. Simpson, Mark E. Reed and C. H. Kreienbaum.*[2]

Kreienbaum died in April 1983 at the age of 87. Two years before his death, he was elected to the World Forestry Center's Hall of Pioneers, joining Sol G. Simpson, Mark E. Reed and George L. Drake.

Beginning in the late 1950s, competition from Canadian lumber producers and a Jones Act-induced scarcity of U.S.-registered ships cut off Simpson and other Pacific Northwest cargo lumber mills from East Coast markets. Maritime rates climbed, green lumber markets slumped and Simpson evolved into a producer of kiln-dried dimension lumber.

C. Henry Bacon, Jr.

In 1962, Bill Reed named C. Henry "Hank" Bacon, Jr., to succeed Tom Gleed as president of Simpson Timber Company. (Gleed continued to serve Simpson as chairman of the finance committee until his retirement in 1965, and he remained a director until 1970.) Bacon, a friend and fraternity brother of Reed's at the University of Washington, had served the Company since 1945 in many roles, including vice president of operations and vice president and general manager of Simpson Logging Company.

Simpson was severely leveraged following its redwood and M&M acquisitions in the 1950s. The Company's plan to sell its Oregon timberlands and mills was stalled by a severe downturn in the market. In order to generate some sort of cash flow, Simpson accelerated the cutting of its Oregon timber. The Company, said Bacon, had "hit bottom. Operations were reduced to stop-and-go…and Simpson damn near could have gone broke."[3]

Simpson's bread-and-butter product at Shelton was green cargo commodity lumber, which was barged to Puget Sound lumber ports and transported by the shipload to regional and national customers. The industry was on the down side of its price and production cycle, suffering from overcapacity, and facing the new challenge of domestic and imported non-wood building products, particularly aluminum siding, windows and doors, which were being peddled by an army of door-to-door salesmen, dubbed "tin men." Steel, concrete and plastics also represented growing threats to traditional wood markets.

Another threat to Simpson was competition from western Canadian lumber. The Canadians owed their cost advantage, in part, to a U.S. maritime trade law, commonly known as the Jones Act, that banned the shipping of goods in a foreign vessel from one U.S. port to another. Canadian lumber could be shipped from Vancouver, B.C., to the U.S. East Coast at a significantly lower cost on ships of foreign registry.

For two years in the early 1960s, Bill Reed campaigned personally for repeal of the Jones Act, speaking out publicly (uncharacteristic of this private man) and making numerous trips to Washington, D.C., to lobby Congress. "In Canada," he recalled, "I was regarded as a son-of-a-bitch, and the Canadian government even changed the consul in Seattle to get a guy to sweet-talk me into not being so wound up about it."

Despite the efforts of several Pacific Northwest elected officials, including Senators Warren G. Magnuson of Washington state and Maureen Neuberger of Oregon, the act was not repealed. Bill blamed the defeat on the opposition of the Canadian government, U.S. shipping companies, who did not want intercoastal competition from foreign lines, and above all, southern U.S. lumber producers, who had no desire to help their western competition.

(This same situation repeated itself in 1981-1986, when dollar-exchange rates favored Canadian lumber, the Jones Act was still law, and Canadian lumber increased its U.S. market share to about 32 percent – up from an average of about 22 percent in the 1970s. This time, a portion of the U.S. industry was successful in bringing a countervailing duty action through the U.S. Department of Commerce. As a result, a tax was imposed on Canadian softwood lumber exports to the U.S.)

Kiln-dried finished lumber was loaded into boxcars and shipped to midwestern and eastern customers.

With many accomplishments to his credit, including his participation with Drake and Bill Reed in the CSYU, Chris Kreienbaum retired in 1960.

In 1964, Simpson expanded its waterfront acreage with fill and constructed six dry kilns, a dry lumber shed and a planing mill to accommodate its move into the dry lumber business.

C. Henry "Hank" Bacon, Jr., succeeded Tom Gleed as president of Simpson Timber Company in 1962.

Hank Bacon (left), then president of the Douglas Fir Plywood Association (DFPA), showed a DFPA-designed plywood home to President Dwight D. Eisenhower (center) and DFPA Managing Director W. E. Difford. The prototype was designed in response to a growing need for inexpensive housing for the retired.

During the 1950s, Simpson operated three Washington plywood mills: Shelton, McCleary and Olympia. In 1964, the cutting of veneer was centralized at a new plant in Shelton.

Modernizing Shelton

In the early 1960s, after extensive studies of future resources and how best to convert them into profits that would yield the highest return to the stump, Bill Reed ordered a $21 million modernization program for the Shelton facilities, including conversion of Simpson products from green cargo lumber to dry lumber, which would allow Simpson to economically ship overland to any market in the U.S.

Dry lumber was already an established part of the industry – particularly in the Midwest – but companies on the West Coast, who were used to transporting their products by ship, were the last to dry lumber. While this was a new and entirely different market for some western producers, Simpson was not a neophyte – the Company had been marketing and selling dry redwood lumber for many years. However, dry lumber was no panacea for Gus Hubbard, Simpson's traffic manager, who found that overland shipments were beset by problems, including a shortage of freight cars and ceaseless rate hikes.

Supervising the rebuilding of the Shelton complex (which added Sawmill Three in 1961) were Gilbert L. Oswald, vice president of manufacturing – who had overseen the improvements of the Company's redwood sawmills at Korbel and Arcata – and Byrne T. Manson, director of engineering. In 1964, Simpson completed a three-year expansion, including 15 acres of industrial fill along the Shelton waterfront, six dry kilns and an 800 ft. x 100 ft. dry lumber shed with a planing mill. The kilns were used primarily to dry Douglas fir and hemlock, as well as a new product, white pine. Simpson became the "westernmost" United States member of the Western Pine Association, and annually harvested about 2 million board feet of pine in the Shelton Working Circle.[4]

During their planning, Company engineers specified reinforced concrete kilns, but Bill Reed felt they should be built of wood because Simpson was, after all, in the wood business. The engineers argued that wood would rot, and have to be replaced within five years. They lost the argument, but were right about the eventual result.

Reed "was the final committer of the dollar," Oswald recalled, so everyone beat a path to his door. Bill was receptive to a well-thought-out capital proposal that was presented to him with personal conviction. Oswald admired the fact that "you could really slug it out with Bill and there were no personal feelings at stake."

Also during that era, Simpson purchased Rayonier's half interest in the Joint Power Operation. (In 1938, the Company had sold to Rayonier an interest in the power plant, which served Rayonier's Shelton pulp mill until it was closed in 1957.) Simpson also completed a $300,000 program at the power plant that included the installation of cinder collectors, a godsend for Shelton residents, who for years had endured cinders on their line-dried laundry.[5]

In 1964, the Company built the Shelton Central Veneer Plant for peeling and drying veneer for its plywood mills at Shelton and McCleary and the Capital Plywood Mill. The veneer facility helped consolidate the Company's Washington plywood operations. Later, Simpson shut down its obsolete

Shelton Plywood Mill, and in 1967, it closed Capital Plywood and consolidated its operations into the McCleary Plywood operations. (In 1985, all of Simpson's Washington plywood operations were consolidated into a single facility in Shelton.)

Simpson later closed the outmoded Shelton sawmills – Reed Mill One and the McCleary Mill – which were built for old-growth logs. During its lifetime, Reed Mill One cut enough lumber for 250,000 average-sized homes. The Company saved the McCleary Mill's 11-foot band saw, the largest ever installed in a U.S. sawmill, and made it part of a monument on the hillside overlooking Shelton's industrial waterfront.

In 1967, Simpson built the $4.5 million Sawmill Four, the largest – and one of the last – automated large-log sawmills built in the U.S. It was geared to either second-growth logs over 16 inches or old-growth logs from Simpson and Forest Service lands in the Shelton CSYU. That same year, the Company remodeled Sawmill Three into a small-log mill for handling logs five to 16 inches in diameter.

Marketing and Sales

In the old days, the selling of green lumber consisted of one salesperson and an assistant calling on green lumber buyers. But when the Company built kilns and developed a line of dried dimension lumber and a variety of plywoods, it suddenly had many hundreds of accounts – and a need to learn how to market its products. Simpson was, according to Bacon, "a company that grew from tree to customer. Most of our successful competitors grew from customer to tree and they outperformed us in marketing and product lines."

Retired Simpson Lumber Sales Manager Leroy McCormick recalled that marketing "had been something you could do without. It was one of the last things Bill Reed wanted to spend money on."

Reed readily conceded that making and marketing finished products was the least profitable business and "certainly my weakest point, although Kreienbaum was good at it. When we got away from selling logs, I failed to keep up with marketing needs and perhaps never really expanded my own concepts beyond what was needed to sell logs in Seattle, Tacoma, Olympia, McCleary and Shelton."

Jack Robins, vice president of marketing in 1962, felt that Simpson was too susceptible to outside market conditions. "We were convinced that we could establish less vulnerability to our markets by becoming a very strongly market-oriented company. Later, we learned much from our Paper Company people, who showed us how."

It took many years for Simpson marketing to catch up with that of Georgia-Pacific, U.S. Plywood and Weyerhaeuser. Eventually Simpson was able to run plants efficiently and to have sufficient available inventories to serve the customer, regardless of the business cycle.[6]

In the late 1950s, the Company formed the Lumber Wholesale Division, which operated distribution centers at Arcata, Santa Clara and Cerritos, California. In 1964, the Wholesale Division was merged with the Company's Shelton Wholesale Warehouse to form Simpson Building Supply Company, which sold Simpson products through its own wholesale system in regions lacking adequate distribution.

Simpson Building Supply had acquired New Jersey-based Rosen Redwood Company and Walling Sash and Door Company of Wichita, Kansas. By 1965, it had acquired General Plywood Corporation's distribution facilities at Decatur, Illinois; Detroit and Grand Rapids, Michigan; Louisville, Kentucky; and Wilkes-Barre, Pennsylvania; and Great Lakes Distributing Corporation's operations at Ft. Wayne, Logansport and South Bend, Indiana.

The Building Supply Company created anxiety among Simpson Timber's independent distributors, who felt they were competing with Simpson, and in late 1983, Furman Moseley, then president of Simpson Timber Company, began liquidating Simpson Building Supply Company.

Return to the Stump

During the 1960s, the Company was run by managers who had grown up in Simpson and were faced with the problems of a rapidly growing, changing industry. Bacon became a link between the senior managers and a stream of new ideas that were generated by a group of young, professionally trained employees who became the nucleus of Simpson's newly formed Industrial Engineering Group. The Group, which reported to Director of Engineering Byrne Manson, was managed by Edmund N. "Ned" Giles, Jr., and it included future Simpson executives Thomas R. Ingham, Henry P. Sandstrom, Ronald R. Grant, and Allen E. Symington. Simpson Investment Company Vice President Symington recalled the Company's senior managers as being "very supportive of the Industrial Engineering Group, and they were a constant challenge to our thinking."

This Group, which had as its mentor Gil Oswald, reviewed and assessed capital improvement proposals, and studied Simpson's manufacturing processes. As the result of early studies, the Industrial Engineering Group developed a scientific system for maximizing the Company's net return to the stump – a traditional Reed interest. With data collected from mill tests of different sizes, grades and species of logs, the optimum return for each type and grade of log was ascertained. Company technicians were able to determine which logs were best suited for plywood, dimension lumber, chips or sale to other mills. These studies also represented the Company's first use of computers, an advancement that Simpson pioneered in the forest products industry.

William G. Reed, Jr.

Another young executive to emerge during the 1960s was William G. "Gary" Reed, Jr.

In the years after the second world war, family-owned and -controlled forest products companies were becoming a novelty rather than the rule. Simpson was one of the exceptions because Bill Reed had a son, Gary, who he hoped would one day succeed him.

Bill Reed had made a conscious effort not to treat his only son as a crown prince. "He told me I could do whatever I wanted to, but there was certainly a job in the Company for me," recalled Gary, who worked college summers as a choker setter at the logging operations at Camp Grisdale and as a timber cruiser assistant in the Shelton Working Circle.

Because Bill wanted Gary to be exposed to life outside the Pacific Northwest, he recommended that wherever Gary went to college, it should not be within 1,000 miles of Seattle. Gary attended Duke University in Durham, North Carolina, and was graduated in 1961, with a bachelor of arts degree in business, and then served for two years in the United States Marine Corps.

He joined the Company in 1963 and worked in various production and marketing capacities. For a brief period in 1966, he worked for Weyerhaeuser's fine paper division in New York, which gave him exposure to the culture and operations of another company. He earned an MBA degree from Harvard before returning to Simpson Timber Company in 1969 as executive vice president.

Pulping Redwood

Ever since Simpson began amassing its California land base, Bill Reed and Kreienbaum had persistently explored ways to pulp redwood as part of the Company's long-range strategy toward achieving a full-utilization sustained yield program for its lands in Del Norte and Humboldt counties. However, they were environmentally and technically stymied by the fact that redwood is low in density and high in extractives (which decrease yield), and the chemicals inherent in redwood were corrosive to the existing batch-digesting equipment. Compounding these problems, redwood responded poorly to some pulping processes, and it is a very wet wood and its chips are heavy and more costly to transport.

There were dozens of sawmill "teepee" burners disposing of thousands of tons of redwood fiber and causing substantial air pollution around Arcata, Simpson initiated redwood-pulping research with forest products laboratories, including the Forest Products Laboratory in Madison, Wisconsin.

Simpson shipped to Madison for testing about 50,000 pounds of redwood – old-growth, second-growth, stump-sprout and root-sprout material. Because redwood was not the only species in Simpson's California timberlands, the pulp tests also included redwood mixed with Douglas fir and tanoak. The samples of machine-made paper from these woods confirmed that redwood pulping had a future. The tests also showed that fibers from second-growth redwood were superior to fibers from old-growth wood, which added promise for the future. (Later, those initial studies would be useful when Simpson sought to finance its part of the pulp mill it would build at Fairhaven, California, in partnership with Crown Zellerbach.) Simpson became committed to redwood pulping.

Long before the technical problems of pulping redwood were solved, Simpson began a site study for a pulp mill. The site would be determined by its proximity to Simpson's redwood operations and by the availability of a large, dependable water supply. The search for groundwater, which was centered on the area around Eureka, proved negative. Eureka's water supply was held in a reservoir on the Mad River and it

William G. "Gary" Reed, Jr., toured second-growth timberlands near Maverick with U.S. Forest Service Regional Forester Rexford A. Resler in 1971.

During the 1950s, Simpson's redwood operations were toured by Starr Reed, who later became Simpson's vice president, timberlands, logging boss Ed Griffith and Hank Trobitz, Simpson's chief redwood forester.

Robert J. Seidl was hired as the Company's director of research in 1957. Later he became Simpson's vice president of research until 1970, when he became vice president of pulp. In January 1972 he was named vice president and resident manager of the Shasta Mill, and two years later he became president of the Simpson Lee Paper Company.

could not provide sufficient water for a plant. The reservoir was badly silted and its storage capacity was already dangerously low, and the small, old wooden pipeline into the city had been damaged by earthquakes. The city's leaders, not surprisingly, placed their concerns about the water system ahead of their interests in attracting new industry.

At that time, the State of California was planning to capture as much water as possible for rechanneling to its agriculturally rich Central Valley. Kreienbaum and Hank Trobitz, knowing that the state intended to pump the water from the Mad River over the Coast Range and pipe it south, came up with an idea that might solve the water problems of both Simpson and Eureka. In the spring of 1955, they met with officials of the Eureka Chamber of Commerce and the Humboldt County Supervisors and convinced them that the area had potential for industrial development, including a pulp mill, if an adequate water source could be found.

Simpson found a potential pulp mill site on the Samoa Peninsula at Fairhaven, near Eureka, and with no guarantee that the mill would be built, the Company signed a contract for large amounts of future water, and helped form the Humboldt Bay Municipal Water District, which led to the construction of Ruth Dam (now Matthews Dam) and a pipeline about 90 miles up the Mad River. The dam would have the capacity to impound about 75 million gallons a day and Simpson made a commitment to 30 million gallons a day on a 40-year contract at a cost of $22,000 per month.

During this time, the size and cost of pulp mills had risen greatly. Simpson, which renamed the Company's Everett, Washington, paper division, Simpson Paper Company, began to look for a partner, not only to split the $55 million price tag, but also to provide what it lacked – the technical expertise to supervise the design, construction and operation of a pulp mill. Discussions were held with several companies, including Fibreboard, Weyerhaeuser, MacMillan Bloedel, Champion and American Can. Georgia-Pacific, perhaps stimulated by Simpson's activity, liked the idea so much that it decided to build its own mill right next to Simpson's proposed site, and it agreed to participate in the contract for water.[7]

In 1964, Simpson found the partner it needed in Crown Zellerbach, and a new company was born – the Crown Simpson Pulp Company.

Robert J. Seidl

During the 1950s, when the Company participated in redwood pulping research with the Forest Products Laboratory in Madison, Kreienbaum worked closely with Robert J. Seidl, assistant chief of the lab's pulp and paper division. In 1957, Kreienbaum hired Seidl as Simpon's director of product research.

Seidl, who brought to Simpson a scientist's curiosity and a team captain's leadership skills, was asked to create a central research program and direct the design and construction of a central research laboratory. "I was impressed by Simpson's willingness to build a laboratory as part of its long-term approach," recalled Seidl. "The image of big lumber companies was that they were depleting the forests and moving on without much regard for the future, but Simpson was keeping its cutover lands and it had the Cooperative Sustained Yield Unit."

Aided by Simpson Research Center studies and ideas from the industrial design firm of Walter Dorvin Teague Associates, Simpson reduced its number of door designs and increased the number of interchangeable parts used in its line of doors.

In the 1940s, central product research and development had become a hallmark of growth-oriented forest products companies such as Weyerhaeuser and Crown Zellerbach, who invested heavily to find better ways to grow and use wood. As part of the Shelton Insulating Board Plant, Simpson built its first research laboratory in 1947. It was run by Arthur T. Walton. The laboratory developed products such as Forestone®, the first wood-fiber, fissured ceiling material, which enabled Simpson to compete for the home consumer market with large-volume producers such as Armstrong and Johns-Manville.

At Kreienbaum's request, Seidl spent his first year with Simpson visiting all of its 21 plants — the sawmills, plywood mills, door and insulating board plants — gathering feedback on the kind of research support they required.

The Research Center

In 1961, the Company opened the 22,000-sq.-ft. Simpson Research Center. Built with Simpson Douglas fir plywood structural panels and decorative plywoods, the center was located in a wooded 10-acre setting in the Seattle suburb of Redmond — "close enough to corporate headquarters for good communications and yet far enough away to prevent it from being used as a hobby shop," recalled Seidl. Twenty-five research and engineering staff members were housed in the facility, which had nine laboratories, a 9,100-sq.-ft. pilot plant area and a variety of rooms for climatic testing.[8]

Seidl's first concern was how to adapt scientific research to what was primarily a commodity lumber and plywood company. From a practical standpoint, he chose to create departments that covered technologies or products, rather than basic sciences, such as biology, physics or chemistry. The Redmond facility's focus was on wood bonding, coatings, finishes, treatments, overlays, rigid boards, doors and technical services. Research on insulating board was moved from Shelton to Redmond. Expanding on the invention of Forestone ceiling material, the research program developed fire-retardant products (under the name Pyrotect®), better acoustic performance, improved coatings and contemporary designs. The coatings and finishing section created new products that were accepted by the marketplace. The structures section assisted in the development of stress-rated lumber and laminated products.

Major advances were made in specialty overlaid panel technology using a resin-impregnated paper that improved the surface of plywood, particleboard or other panels. Simpson plywood operations, under Hal McClary's direction, had been pioneer producers of "high density" overlaid plywood for the military, which used impregnated papers produced by Kimberly-Clark. Later Simpson began producing "medium density overlay" using Crown Zellerbach paper. (The terms "high density" and "medium density" relate to the amount of phenolic resin impregnated into the paper fiber.)

Research introduced the concept of formal industrial and product design into Simpson, through a long association with the design firm of Walter Dorwin Teague Associates. The Teague group, which noted the door plants' large number of unrelated designs and thousands of parts, designed a series of doors that utilized common parts, which reduced waste and lessened the number of door components in inventory. The Teague group also developed new ceiling tile designs, and later the firm created the distinctive bright red Simpson logo.

The "Glue Plant"

The Research Center also supported the adhesives plant in Portland, Oregon, which was acquired as part of the M&M purchase. The "Glue Plant," as it was called, made phenolformaldehyde glue for exterior and marine-grade plywood, protein glues for interior plywood and urea resin glues for hardwood plywood.

Glue production was an alien business for Simpson, and Tom Gleed had put the plant on the block. But when a major chemical company offered a surprisingly high price, Gleed reversed his thinking. Figuring that there must be more to the glue business than he had thought, he rejected the offer and continued the business. It was run by former Shelton laboratory head Arthur Walton until 1958, when he was killed in an automobile accident en route to Portland from Shelton. His duties were assumed by Seidl, who in turn hired a chemical engineer named Ralph Casselman from the Bakelite Corporation (the first producer of phenolic resin).

Research at the central laboratory, coupled with the resin experience of Casselman and the extensive background of Hal McClary, led to another bold maneuver for a timber company: building a small paper-treating machine in Portland, Oregon in 1966 to make high density overlay paper, in direct competition with Kimberly-Clark's Kimpreg™. Later, the Company began making medium density overlay paper in competition with Crown Zellerbach. Possibly as a result of Simpson's success with overlays, Kimpreg production ceased and Crown Zellerbach sold to Simpson its medium density product, Crezon™, which was used for signs and cabinets. High density overlay products, including FormGuard® and Multipour®, were used in all types of concrete construction. Simpson's other overlay products included Guardian® highway signs, Skidguard® deck and dock panels, and marine and industrial cabinet panels.

Everett Reichman, who was the process-control engineer in the Portland Chemicals Division, believed that the Company's move in the mid 1960s into full-scale overlay production may have been the division's salvation. Price competition from chemical companies had "virtually eliminated the profit margin" for Simpson in making plywood adhesives at Portland. The timing was right on target.

Strengthening the Balance Sheet

In 1965, Simpson acquired 35,000 acres of Northern California timberlands and a plywood mill on the Mad River at Arcata. It also acquired cutting rights to more than 100 million board feet of old-growth timber, mostly Douglas fir, which adjoined existing Simpson California timberlands.[9]

The Company was timber-rich but short of cash and, in one of his toughest decisions, Bill Reed directed Hank Bacon to sell most of its Oregon assets. This was a very unpopular decision with Simpson's Oregon management group, but it was necessary to reduce Simpson's heavy debt load.[10] Bacon recalled, "It was a terrible thing to have to do, but we had to do that to stay alive.... We were very fortunate that U.S. Plywood Corporation wanted to expand in Oregon and scale back in California, so we completed excellent buy and sell agreements with them." Bacon negotiated the sale of the 30,000-acre Avery Timber Tract, which contained about 280 million board feet of timber, and the Lyons Plywood and Idanha Veneer mills to U.S. Plywood for $16.5 million and 3,400 acres of second-growth redwood in Northern California. Simpson booked an $8 million gain and increased its California timberland ownership to more than 248,000 acres. (The Company retained its Albany Plywood Mill, which was run continuously until the lack of available public timber forced its closure in 1989.)

In a second transaction Simpson purchased U.S. Plywood's Mutual Plywood mill at Fairhaven, California, for $1 million – $200,000 down and the balance to be paid over five years with zero interest, and an option to purchase about 40 million board feet of U.S. Plywood stumpage.

Simpson modified Mutual Plywood for production of redwood plywood siding and changed its name to Fairhaven Plywood, and it closed its obsolete Eureka Plywood Mill. With its Mad River and Fairhaven mills, Simpson became the largest plywood producer in California, with annual production of 235 million sq. ft. of Douglas fir, redwood and overlay panels.[11]

The Mad River and the Fairhaven Mills were operated until late 1979 and 1981 respectively, when they were closed due to increased competition in the plywood market and the shortage of logs following the Company's remodel of it Korbel Mill.

Simpson emerged from the 1960s with momentum and money in the bank. Reflecting on those times, Bacon singles out three managers: Raw Materials Planning Director W. E. "Bill" Lawson, Simpson Timber Company Vice President, International, H. W. "Hal" McClary and Director of Timberland Development H. O. "Bud" Puhn. "These men helped bring the Company out of bad times to good, improve Simpson's operating efficiency and ultimately its balance sheet."

Simpson Lee Paper Company

9

Simpson Lee Paper Company

Simpson merged its paper operations in Everett with the Lee Paper Company on August 28, 1959, to create the Simpson Lee Paper Company.

Lee Paper President Max Bardeen wanted to build a new specialty mill on a site on 220 acres in Ripon, an almond-growing community near the Stanislaus River, 10 miles north of Modesto, in the San Joaquin Valley. However, the cost was prohibitive.

Bill Reed, a 15 percent stockholder in Lee Paper, agreed to a joint venture in the new mill with Bardeen. But in the midst of drafting the financing agreement, the two men decided, instead, to merge their paper companies. Both Reed and Bardeen felt that the consolidated company could reap a broader market, offer a greater assortment of products, and enjoy substantial cost savings by combining research, sales and administrative functions. For the future, the new firm would be able to expand the scope of operations in the rapidly growing Pacific Coast states, where competition was then minimal.

Under the terms of the merger, Simpson controlled 60 percent of the stock and the former Lee shareholders 40 percent. Bardeen was named president and chief executive officer, and Reed chairman of the board (a position he modestly described as requiring "only such duties as might be assigned to me from time to time by the directors").

Lee Paper Company

The Lee Paper Company was long on papermaking experience and expertise.

The company was founded in 1903 by a group of Michigan businessmen led by Frederick E. Lee and George E. Bardeen, one of the original papermakers in the Kalamazoo Valley of southern Michigan, where paper had been made since 1866. Vicksburg had been selected as the site for the new mill because of its plentiful supply of clear water and an experienced labor force for making all-cotton fiber writing, printing, text, specialty and technical papers. The first paper rolled off the machines on May 31, 1905, and soon the Lee Paper Company was producing about 35,000 pounds per day.

Lee recruited foremen and managers from the nearby mills and encouraged an influx of immigrants from Poland, England, Scotland, Italy, Sicily and Canada to form a reliable, stable work force, many of them living in company housing built adjacent to the mill.

Lee Paper Company quality control and research laboratory.

Virtually from its inception, the company was led by the Bardeen family. Norman Bardeen, Sr., George's brother, was made general manager in 1911 and eventually became president. Unlike the dozen or so other mills in the valley, Lee Paper Company used cotton rags to produce its paper but, by the mid 1920s, Bardeen conceded that the mill could not build up enough business volume for rag paper grades to maintain full-time production. So, in 1926, the company made a successful transition to the production of a new group of papers – offset, sulfite bonds and other sulfite (wood pulp) grades.

That year, Norman's son, Max Bardeen, joined his brother, Norman, Jr., at Lee Paper Company. Max, who graduated with honors in chemistry from Yale University, was working as a chemist with Procter and Gamble in Port Ivory, New York. When Lee needed a chemist, Max moved back to his hometown of Vicksburg, which "was just like putting on an old shoe – very comfortable." He split his time between the laboratory and the mill, where he assisted the superintendent.[1]

Max found that "the paper industry was changing from an art to a science.... It was the beginning of chemistry in paper manufacturing. I was there for the transition at the Vicksburg mill from a sort of seat-of-the-pants organization to a technically controlled operation."[2]

Bardeen was an independent man, articulate and persuasive, and committed to making high-quality paper. A colleague once said, "Max was never so happy as when his arms were covered with paper stock."[3]

Lee had a poor year in 1926, and a lot of scrap paper (known as "broke") had piled up all over the mill. Bardeen recalled questioning, "How were we going to get rid of all the broke? In the lab, I started making up some handsheets of paper out of the broke. I tried to make various weights, finishes and surfaces, but mostly my objective was to get rid of this mass of color. There were so many colors and so much broke that I segregated it by primary color. If there were 10 tons of one color and 20 tons of another color, I'd use two to one. When I got them all together, they made quite an interesting pastel shade."[4]

The sheets of muted colors caught the eye of a New York paper merchant. Lee ran some paper to the merchant's specifications for an advertising folder, "and it grew and grew," said Bardeen. The line of recycled paper was dubbed "Corsican®" and was the beginning of an extensive family of text and cover products that would later become Simpson Paper's most popular and consistent earners.

In 1932, Max Bardeen, who had spent two years in Chicago selling paper, returned to the mill to become operating superintendent. Three years later, Norman Bardeen, Sr., was killed in an automobile accident and the board of directors named Max general manager. About a year after that, he was elected president. "I was surprised – and challenged," Bardeen recalled, "and a bit scared." One of his first moves was to change the mill's motive power from steam to electricity.

When Lee Paper Company first began making paper in 1905, it used cotton fiber from old rags, which were sorted by hand for purity, then digested and bleached.

Yale chemistry graduate Maxwell L. Bardeen became president of Simpson Lee Paper Company when it was formed in 1959 and oversaw its growth until he retired in 1968.

Early paper machines were small and slow, but they worked on the same principles as those of the 1990s. Shown is a 19th-century paper machine at the Hamilton Paper Company in Miquon, Pennsylvania. (In 1980, Simpson acquired the facility, which is now known as the Valley Forge Mill.)

The Ripon Mill, which opened in 1961, represented the combined thoughts and schemes of Bill Reed and Max Bardeen. The mill, close to both San Francisco and Los Angeles markets, was the first text and cover mill in the West.

Among the Company's important reasons for selecting Ripon as its mill site was the community's interest in having the paper mill. For years after the plant opened, Ripon annually celebrated Simpson-Lee Daze.

When the United States entered World War II, the War Manpower Commission declared the Vicksburg mill's production of blueprint paper essential to the War effort. At least 80 percent of the mill's output during the War consisted of blueprint paper and photographic base paper. (The rest, for high-priority civilian needs, was made from old mattress covers and shavings.)

Photographic base paper was considered the most difficult to produce of all the technical grades made by Lee. Before World War II, all photographic base paper was either made by Eastman Kodak Company of Rochester, New York, or imported from France, Germany or Italy. Those channels were closed by the War and photographic paper went on the ration list. Because it was impossible for Kodak to supply the entire market, several mills tried their hand at it for war use, but only a handful, including Lee, were successful. After the War, Lee was the only paper company to continue to produce that grade of paper, as well as photographic paper for reproduction, X-ray papers and a variety of engineering-type papers that used the photographic process.

Rejected photographic paper produced a new line, called Talisman®. Bardeen recalled, "We had a helluva nice piece of paper, which was fine for reproducing photographic images, but was it any good for anything else? My brother Norman said we didn't have to make it photographically pure for everything, but we should try it. We changed it a little, got the cost down and ultimately broadened the market tremendously. This was the way these kinds of businesses got started – by somebody with a little imagination."

In 1943, Lee's old 100-percent rag Washington Bond was revived under the name Corinthian®. Two years later, a series of new wood-pulp papers was developed. In 1949, one of its machines was modified with new felts and the company began producing Teton® , a textured text and cover paper that quickly grew in popularity. (The text of this book was printed on Teton.)

In the years after the War, the mill completed its transformation from steam to electricity and steadily replaced obsolete equipment. In 1951, Lee Paper Company became the first American rag paper mill in a quarter of a century to install a new paper machine, which made it possible to produce several new text and cover grades, including Coronado®, which has become one of Simpson's largest-selling non-technical papers. Another popular product that was introduced at about this time was Decor,® a duplex paper made by pasting together two sheets of Corsican® in different colors. Also during this era, the company began the first work on photocopy paper for a company called American Haloid, which eventually changed its name to Xerox Corp. This mill was the first to produce paper for xerography, leading to the large quantities used in copy machines today.

Because of his scientific, technical background, Bardeen always put a strong emphasis on research and development: "We recognized the fact that if we were going to live as a small converter paper mill, we had to be innovative and we had to recognize problems and how to solve them. I put together a damn good technical team and we got a reputation for solving people's problems."

Because of its relatively small size, the Vicksburg mill stayed clear of commodity grades, preferring, as Bardeen said, "to stay in the grades that were hard for others to make. The profits were traditionally higher on specialty grades of paper, but the risks were greater, too. If you slipped a little somewhere, the paper was unusable." The company had a policy that, "Any paper we made had to be usable for the purpose for which it was intended or it could be returned for full credit, no questions asked."

In 1955, the year Bill Reed joined the board, Lee Paper Company recorded $9.2 million in sales on production of 36,573 tons, at an average sales price of $265. In 1956, the year the Number Four paper machine was added to the mill, sales were $11.03 million on a production of 39,183 tons, at an average price of $299 a ton.

The Ripon Mill

Ripon was Bardeen's choice for a California mill site because, among other reasons, it was centrally located for West Coast markets, particularly those south of San Francisco and north of Los Angeles. The area also had good transportation facilities adjacent to the main north/south highway from Canada to Mexico, low freight costs, a good labor market, adequate shipping, a waste disposal site and a good source of soft water – melted snow that trickled down from the western slope of the Sierra Nevada Mountains. This water was color-free and low in iron content.

Bardeen recalled one final, significant point, "Ripon wanted us." Simpson Lee returned the favor by working closely with the County Board of Supervisors and keeping them well informed. Simpson Lee asked them to send a designated electrical specialist – at the Company's expense – to the Vicksburg Mill to learn firsthand what was planned for the Ripon Mill and to see if it conformed to the county code.

The 14-acre Ripon Mill site, set within the 220-acre parcel of land, was laid out by Bardeen – to include a landing strip for his light plane – and a technical team of engineers, chemists and physicists from Vicksburg. Because paper is a heavy commodity to handle, the key to holding down the costs was to design the mill so that the manufacturing process economically moved the product. The Company installed a $1.2 million paper machine with a trim of 122 inches that ran at speeds up to 1,500 feet per minute. The mill produced duplicating paper, various light-sensitive papers, blueprint papers and diazo printing papers, and it was also the first text and cover mill in the West.

The mill's October 1961 opening was one of the biggest events in the history of Ripon, which celebrated with "Simpson-Lee Daze" festivities – including a parade, a Miss Paper Doll competition and an open house. The operation provided the biggest payroll in Ripon, starting with 100 employees, with plans to enlarge to about 250 when full-scale production went into effect.

The Ripon Mill production had a difficult time finding its place in the market because the East Coast and West Coast mills that made similar grades of paper were already deeply entrenched. Ripon was too small for commodities and too big for specialties. "We just staggered, trying to find a place in the market that was substantial enough to support our kind of an operation," Bardeen recalled. Foreign competition caused further concern. In 1961, the year Ripon opened, the U.S. pulp and paper business had tariff protection of about seven or eight percent, compared to 18 percent for the Common Market and 22.5 percent for Canada, which gave foreign competitors the upper hand over U.S. paper producers. In the following two years, Ripon brought down Simpson Lee's net income from $1.3 million in 1961 to $734,000 in 1962, recovering to $988,000 in 1963. Bill Reed looked upon Ripon's performance as a source of personal responsibility and frustration, and he often prefaced board meetings of the Paper Company with an apology for the project.

Lee Schoeller Pulaski Mill

The Polaroid Corporation of Boston and the General Aniline & Film Corporation (GAF) of New York were two of the Vicksburg Mill's biggest customers for, respectively, high-grade photographic paper and duplicating paper. Those two companies were also supplied by the Frederich Schoeller Company, which operated a paper mill near Osnabruck, West Germany, and was one of the world's leading manufacturers of technically intricate, high-quality photographic paper.

In the early 1960s, when Schoeller found itself at a competitive disadvantage because of shipping costs, Schoeller accepted Bardeen's invitation to participate in a U.S. mill that would combine Schoeller's technical knowledge and Simpson Lee's access to the U.S. market. In January 1964, the Lee Schoeller Paper Company, a 50/50 partnership, built a state-of-the-art mill in Pulaski, New York, near key customers such as Eastman Kodak, Du Pont, Ansco Corp., Polaroid and GAF.

Unfortunately, the mill faced unusually severe problems even before it began production. The Xerox copying process had just been perfected, and xerographic papers immediately took over the market, which made GAF's duplicating paper obsolete. Suddenly, the mill was left with a market for only 40 percent of its output. The rest of its operating time had to be switched to production of nontechnical papers, which were highly competitive, and for which the Pulaski machinery had not been designed.

Before the problems at Ripon and Pulaski developed, Bill Reed was "euphoric" over the prospects for paper. Unfortunately, his euphoria caused him to commit what he called in retrospect two "unnecessary errors." The first was his decision to turn down a proposal to merge Simpson Lee with the Nekoosa Edwards Paper Company, which would have created a larger firm. The second error stemmed from Bill's conclusion that his original concept about Rayonier "had not been all bad, inasmuch as it would be good for the family not only to have a privately owned company, but also to have a significant interest in a public company." He believed that Simpson Lee would be the logical one to go public with, since it already had several hundred stockholders who had been Lee Paper Company investors. As a public company, Simpson Lee Paper Company could use marketable equity securities for acquisitions of other paper mills – something it could not do as a private company – and it would provide a source of liquidity for family members without disturbing the ownership of the privately held Simpson Timber Company.

Reed asked Blyth & Co. to make a public offering on the open market of a significant percentage of the Simpson Lee stock owned by Simpson Timber. The demand for the stock, which sold at $25 a share, was initially so strong, particularly in Seattle, that purchases were limited to 100 shares per buyer in order to secure the widespread ownership that Reed wanted.

The timing couldn't have been worse. The downturn in the industry caused the Paper Company profits to tumble and the price of its stock fell to about $15 per share.

For Bill, this was a personal embarrassment. He keenly felt a business responsibility to the investors, and a private responsibility to his friends, many of whom had put their money on a company that carried the Simpson name and the Reed imprimatur. He did what he felt was the honorable thing, paying $25 per share to anyone holding shares purchased through Blyth. By the time he was done, he had dispensed $1 million out of his own pocket to repurchase Simpson Lee stock.

Crown Simpson Pulp Mill

In the mid 1960s, after the Simpson Timber Company had acquired what it considered the "critical mass" of redwoods for sustained yield production, secured the water source from the Humboldt Bay Municipal District, and developed workable redwood pulping technology, the long-awaited pulp mill began to become a reality. In 1964, Simpson agreed to form a 50/50 partnership with Crown Zellerbach – called the Crown Simpson Pulp Company. Crown was one of the powerhouse forest products companies on the West Coast and one of the biggest users of pulp. It had a strong commitment to research and development,

The Crown Simpson Pulp Mill was the realization of Bill Reed's interest in utilizing redwood fiber, which had been burned as waste before the pulp mill opened in 1966.

Chips from Simpson and other lumber mills in California's North Coast region provided the resource base for the Crown Simpson Mill.

"Teepee" wood-waste incinerators were common to every redwood sawmill. When the Northern California air was calm, the smoke and ash from the burners covered nearby communities, but when the pulp mill started up, wood waste was converted to pulp and energy and most of the teepees were shut down.

and had perfected new papermaking techniques, including on-the-machine double coating. Crown would build and operate the mill and Simpson would supply the wood fiber. The deal was sealed with a "telephone handshake" between Bill Reed and his friend Crown Zellerbach President Reed Hunt.

In a newspaper interview, Hunt hailed the coming of the new pulp mill as "probably the single most significant consequence of the advent of the pulp industry on the North Coast. Now, for the first time, the region can begin to move in the direction of an integrated forest products economy..."[5]

The waterfront site for the mill was at Fairhaven, on 150 acres near the tip of the Samoa Peninsula, a narrow strip of land separating Humboldt Bay from the Pacific Ocean. The location provided direct access to deep-water shipping.[6]

Simpson Lee was convinced by the results of its own pulping experiments that it could blend redwood and tanoak and/or Douglas fir chips and produce a pulp that, in Bardeen's words, "came very close to achieving what we wanted to achieve." Crown Zellerbach duplicated pilot trials in its central laboratory in Camas, Washington, while the mill was being engineered. By this time, a continuous digester could be built with confidence that it would be large enough to overcome the low density of the redwood and yield high-quality pulp from redwood chips. The digester was lined with stainless steel to overcome possible corrosion.

During the early stages of construction, the Federal Trade Commission almost stopped the project because of anti-trust considerations. The FTC charged that the two paper companies were operating in collusion in building the mill. After much negotiation and a lengthy approval process, the FTC gave Crown Simpson permission to proceed – with one caveat: each company had to market independently its own half of the pulp production.

Simpson was shocked by the decision. "We didn't know how to market pulp," recalled Hank Bacon, then president of the Timber Company. "But it was so important to get this pulp mill in Northern California that we agreed" to the ruling. Simpson Timber Company created a pulp-marketing department and Crown signed a management contract to run the mill and, in turn, paid Simpson an acreage-usage fee, which virtually offset the management fee.[7]

The FTC requirement for independent marketing of the product had a considerable impact because it exposed each company's desires for different products. These differences in direction were honest but significant. Bardeen recalled, "Crown Zellerbach was not interested in printing papers; they were interested in bags, wrapping – coarse papers. Crown was just a mass-production, lowest-conceivable-cost operation. We knew we were dead if we did that."

Nevertheless, the mill, which produced its first pulp at 11 a.m. on Thanksgiving Day 1966, was sophisticated – with a unique eight-stage bleaching process – and it had a yearly capacity of 180,000 tons of very pure bleached kraft (the German word for "strength") pulp.

Earnings from the Vicksburg Mill kept the Simpson Lee Paper Company solvent while it looked fo profits from its mills in Everett and Ripon.

Simpson Lee Problems

Simpson Lee proved to be a company that was very difficult to operate. Within two years of the merger of Lee and Simpson, management was confronted with the problem of designing and building two plants, of finding new national markets, and of resolving the many problems inherent in getting all the mills organized and running efficiently.

At Ripon, the Company was unable to keep the machine supplied with profitable orders in sufficient volume. Bardeen expended an enormous amount of energy traveling from mill to mill and market to market, and he managed to keep the Company operating in the black. Simpson Lee's net earnings in 1965 were up to $1.3 million from $1.02 million in 1964. However, both Ripon and Pulaski continued to show losses; the latter mill in 1965 lost $1.6 million (much of that blamed on the lengthy advanced training of workers). In 1966, net earnings moved up to $2.2 million, but the good year was offset by losses at Pulaski, which required an additional investment of $975,000.

The financial problems of the Paper Company were endemic throughout all of Simpson. But Bill Reed showed patience. He was determined to do what needed to be done to create the kind of enduring business legacy that his grandfather and father had first begun.

"The Longest Timber Company in the World"

10

"The Longest Timber Company in the World"

Bill Reed's mind seemed always to be on strategic expansion, on moving ahead. Opportunities in Northern California were limited and, with the exception of some logged-off land still owned by A. K. Wilson, all of the major redwood tracts were owned and operated by companies too large for Simpson to acquire. So, Bill turned his sights to the rest of the Americas and beyond.

Fenwick Riley's report in the late 1940s on Chilean timber had stuck in the back of Bill's mind. In 1962, he flew to Chile, for some fly-fishing and prospecting – specifically for a minority stock position in a major Chilean lumber manufacturing company. (This was typical of how Bill Reed chose to learn about a new industry or country.) He was most interested in Bosques E Industrias Madereras, S.A. (BIMA), a well-managed firm with a large supply of floating capital stock.

Perhaps most important, BIMA owned the world's largest remaining stand of alerce, which is a member of the cypress family. Chilean alerce was introduced to Spain and Italy by the conquistadors and was in great demand in the Mediterranean countries.

BIMA President Antonio Fernandez welcomed Bill's acquisition of about 10 percent of the company. Within a year, Fernandez came to Seattle to offer Bill a large block of company-owned stock in exchange for capital for financing BIMA's expansion in Chile. Bill agreed. Although he was not interested in controlling the company, he thought Simpson might eventually increase its holding in BIMA to as much as 40 percent. Simpson agreed to provide technical and managerial expertise and to pay some BIMA personnel to work in the redwoods, where they could learn Simpson's logging and manufacturing practices.

Furman Moseley

Bill designated his son-in-law, Furman Colin Moseley, Jr., to represent Simpson's interests on the nine-person BIMA board of directors.

Moseley, a South Carolina native who was born in Spartanburg in 1934, was married to Susan Henry Reed, Bill and Eleanor Reed's first child. Moseley, a light-framed but aggressive football player, won a scholarship to attend Elon College, in North Carolina, where he became president of the student body. After graduating in 1956 with a bachelor of arts in history, he became an infantry officer in the United States Marine Corps, and two years later he married Susan Reed.

Simpson faced the challenge of adapting to new environments when it expanded beyond U.S. borders in the 1960s. During the Saskatchewan winters, local farmers, using teams of horses, were employed to skid logs from the forests to truck-loading sites.

Moseley was ambitious and methodical about his path to success, although working for his wife's father was not one of his goals. He and Susan moved to Seattle, where he took a position with the investment banking firm of Blyth & Co., but his father-in-law kept talking about his joining Simpson. Eventually, he acquiesced, and for very logical, sound reasons.

"What got me over the stigma of working for my in-laws," Moseley recalled, "was the realization that I didn't have a capital base. I had to work for somebody and I figured that whoever I was going to work for, I was going to be reasonably good. If that were the case, I'd prefer to work for the benefit of my family and my children a lot more than for an anonymous group of shareholders."

Susan noted that Furman's strengths were quite different from the Reeds'. "He was a nice counterbalance to both Gary and my father. My father recognized this and provided Furman, and us as a family, opportunities that weren't duplicated in Gary's experience."

Moseley characterized Bill as "probably the only father-in-law I could have ever worked for. He was a good man. He was smart. He was fair. He was honest. And he was willing to work and take risks when he didn't have to."

Moseley joined Simpson in 1960, spending his first year in an array of production jobs, beginning in the logging camp at Korbel. "Those were the days when they still had cookhouses in the logging camps," he recalled. "We went in to have lunch and I sat down with my tray at the first available seat which – as I soon discovered – was where crusty Ed Griffith, the logging boss, always sat. He came in, saw where I was and abruptly sat right down next to me. I was nervous, and as I reached for my milk, I knocked it over. Ed looked at me, got up, picked up his tray, said 'Shit,' and then moved to another table.

"I later worked closely with Ed in Chile and got to know him well. He was just as tough as he seemed at the time."

For a year, Moseley and Susan lived in Shelton. He later worked as a mill representative at the wholesale yard in Tacoma, selling lumber, plywood and doors. After that, he was transferred to Southern California to sell Simpson specialty products, including redwood lumber, plywood, designer doors, insulating board and acoustical tiles.

When Bill offered him the opportunity to go to Chile, Moseley was initially reluctant because he was still unsure of his niche within Simpson. But upon reflection, he and Susan chose to take up the challenge. In August 1962, while a pregnant Susan remained in Seattle to have their baby, Moseley arrived in Chile, where he soon became chairman (and the only non-Chilean) of the BIMA board.

Puerto Montt

One of BIMA's principal assets was a tract of alerce in the Pichicolo area, which was located among a group of 9,000-foot volcanic mountains, 500 miles north of Cape Horn and 700 miles south of Santiago. Although part of the mainland, the tract was one of the most isolated areas on the South American continent and could be reached only by boat or plane. In fact, it was so isolated that some of the Chilean investors in BIMA disapproved of the project. Bill half-joked, "the reason our ownership in BIMA got so close to 49 percent is that we bought out some of the objecting stockholders."

Simpson dispatched a couple of representatives to the area to make a preliminary investigation of the economic atmosphere and the people with whom Simpson would be dealing in Santiago. That first Simpson group was followed by Company foresters, who cruised by air the high mountainous timber. Bill Reed, Starr Reed (no relation to Bill), Simpson's vice president for timberlands, and Moseley later visited the region to review the findings, the preliminary economics and the feasibility of the project.

Starr Reed recalled, "We knew there was going to be a considerable amount of defective timber. Some of the local operators who were logging alerce at that time had found rot in the trees. But the big bulk of the timber that we had anticipated using did not seem to display the defects." Simpson cruisers reported a total stand of about 1 billion board feet – the last billion feet, they believed.

During that period, Bill was put in contact with Jorge Ross, a Chilean businessman who was running a sugar company in Santiago. Ross recalled, "Mr. Reed told me that he was interested in developing an operation in the southern part of Chile in an area where most people don't even go. The intention was to cut timber and develop markets for Chilean lumber in Portugal, Spain, Italy, and to some extent in England and northern Europe. He asked for my help. His proposal represented a constructive plan to develop wealth in our country, so I joined him." Ross purchased a block of stock and succeeded Moseley as chairman of BIMA's board of directors. Moseley later became BIMA's president.

The project was beset with delays. Simpson had its loggers cut some of the fringe timber, which was hauled by oxen to a little Chilean mill to be sawn and assessed. To get further data about the timber quality, Bill intended to send a shipment of alerce logs from Pichicolo to Arcata, California, for manufacturing but the shipment was delayed by transportation difficulties. Simpson found itself up against the deadline on the governmental financing agreement that was essential to its development of Pichicolo.

Bill returned to Chile to review the timberland and confer with Moseley, Starr Reed and Bill McCredie, the Simpson cruiser who headed the timber-stand study. Bill recalled, "After a few days in the woods, we all came back to Puerto Montt to make the awful decision. I was very uncomfortable with it, for there were some signs of defect in the timber, but I had to decide whether to go ahead with insufficient information or to give up the project. I thought it over, and then told Moseley to proceed, and we started work on the mill site on Pichicolo Bay."

Simpson committed about $1.5 million to the project; the U.S. government Agency for International Development and the Chilean government each put up several million dollars more. BIMA's cost for the potential billion board feet of alerce (which it had purchased 10 years earlier) was about $5,000. With the support of the U.S. and Chilean governments, Simpson began to construct logging roads and a sawmill.

Meanwhile, the Company cruised the timber a second time. Because there were no roads or trails, all travel had to be done on foot, usually in the pouring rain. Cruisers pushed through the brush at a rate of perhaps 50 feet every half hour. After the trees were counted, measured and tested, the original estimate of a billion feet was reduced by about 250 million board feet.

While preparation for construction of the Pichicolo sawmill was under way, Bill received a call from Maurice Hitchcock, owner of the White Swan Lumber Company of Yakima, Washington. Hitchcock wanted to sell his Chilean operations, which included a sawmill he had recently built at Fundo Contao, on the beach south of Puerto Montt, and a timber stand adjoining the Pichicolo tract. When Bill told Hitchcock that BIMA was not interested in such a large investment, Hitchcock replied "Make me any kind of an offer." With Bill's approval, Moseley offered Hitchcock $150,000 for the property and, to Bill's astonishment, Hitchcock accepted it.

"I was delighted to have the mill," Bill recalled, "not only because it gave us a beachhead, but also because it allowed us to get into production much faster and at a smaller cost than anticipated." Satisfied with the yield and quality of Hitchcock's timber, Simpson abandoned its site at Pichicolo Bay and built a new mill, called the Contao Mill, alongside Hitchcock's mill. The Pichicolo timber was to be brought to the Contao Mill over a logging road that Hitchcock had built.

Simpson closed Hitchcock's mill for a month to study the facility, take inventory, transfer people from Pichicolo, and make plans for the consolidation and development. Unfortunately the sawmill burned down under suspicious circumstances before Simpson had an opportunity to familiarize itself with it.

Starr Reed recalled, "If that sawmill had not burned, I think the project would have looked different. We would have tested the trees and found out how good they really were, and subsequently designed something other than what we did. Or perhaps we would have come to the conclusion that we were overrating the stands of alerce."

Simpson then experienced yet another setback. While rebuilding the Reed Mill in Shelton, the Company decided to move its surplus Shelton machinery to Contao. But the Chilean government would not allow the importation of secondhand equipment. Simpson was forced to buy new machinery. The result was a powerful high-speed mill as good as most North American operations – but at a cost much higher than anticipated.

The Company intended to apply traditional old-growth redwood harvesting technology – cable systems and road building – for logging on steep ground. In order to accomplish this, Simpson shipped to Chile standard Pacific Northwest logging equipment – shovels, bulldozers, portable spars, power saws and trucks. Moseley recalled, "We started building truck roads suitable for the Kenworth trucks up into the Andes to get access to the timber." Maintenance on that equipment proved to be a major problem. Starr Reed said, "It was terribly difficult to get parts, to get permission from the government to bring them in, and to keep them flowing in. Often, we had to cannibalize equipment to keep something else running."

For the first two years in Chile, Simpson had to log the timber purchased from Hitchcock because it took so long to build a road through very mountainous backcountry into BIMA's timber, which

Soon after the purchase of what the Company believed was the "last billion feet" of alerce in Chile, Simpson timber foresters began lowering their estimates of the available timber. By the time the Contao Mill was completed, the estimated size of the alerce stand had been reduced to 75 million board feet.

Inspecting the Contao Mill with Bill Reed (left) were Don Roder, from the Shelton timberlands office; Bill Lawson, Company forestry specialist; Barney Elking, Contao Mill's manager; and Ed Griffith, redwood logging boss.

Built from the ground up in the mid 1960s, the Contao Mill, which could cut up to 8,000 board feet an hour, was considered to be the most modern sawmill in South America.

The mill, which employed 290, included a power plant, an elementary school, Company housing and a medical dispensary.

In 1962, Furman Moseley (right), who thirsted for management responsibility, was sent to Chile to oversee Simpson's investment.

142

the Company expected would be of much higher quality than Hitchcock's. "We could hardly wait until we got over the mountains into our beautiful stand in the heart of the Pichicolo tract and all would be well," said Bill.

As it turned out, nothing was farther from the truth. Simpson foresters discovered that the heart of the big virgin alerce was full of rot and that the merchantable timber now was projected to be no more than 75 million board feet, only a tiny fraction of the original estimate of a billion.

Exiting Chile

By 1969, after seven years, Bill was ready to abandon Chile and to chalk up the whole thing to experience. In retrospect, Bill thought Simpson built the wrong kind of mechanized logging operation. "We should have logged like the Araucanian Indians, who were still using oxen. Perhaps we just tried to make too big a jump; probably we would have been smarter if we had replaced the oxen with horses rather than with what worked most efficiently in the sophisticated economy of North America."

Moseley, who by this time had been elected president of BIMA, and Jorge Ross arranged for the government to purchase Simpson's investment in BIMA for a nominal sum. BIMA was taken over by an agency of the Chilean government, which paid off BIMA's loans from U.S. and Chilean agencies, the Export-Import Bank and the Morgan Guaranty Bank.

As if the alerce problems weren't enough, the situation in Chile grew murkier by the day because of oncoming clouds on the political horizon. Presidential candidate Salvador Allende Gossens, a self-avowed Marxist-Leninist, stood a good chance of assuming power in the 1970 election, and if he did, he would nationalize the industries.

Simpson had other holdings in Chile, including a drying yard and remanufacturing plant in Santiago and a plantation of radiata pine. At the request of the government, Simpson sold the plantation to it in August of 1970 in exchange for some promissory notes. The next month, Allende was elected president with 36.3 percent of the popular vote in a three-man race.

While Allende set in motion his campaign to communize the country, the government continued to pay off on schedule the promissory notes as well as the BIMA loans – even re-evaluating them for inflation and interest. However, the government would not let Simpson transfer its last remaining money, about half a million dollars, out of Chile. "We could have taken the money out using the black market, where it was worth only about $55,000," Moseley recalled. "So we had $55,000 worth of purchasing value in U.S. terms."

Alarmed by the government takeovers, many businesses sold off their assets at reduced value and left Chile. Simpson, on the other hand, chose to take advantage of the buyer's market, and Moseley (who by this time had transferred back to Seattle) returned to Chile to look for alternative investments for Simpson's funds. Consulting with Jorge Ross, Moseley narrowed the choices to two. The first option was to buy 10 ski lodges at $5,000 apiece at an exclusive ski area within commuting distance of Santiago. "I figured there would always be skiers, whether they were Communist or not," Moseley recalled.

Nevertheless, he chose the other option: shares of a Chilean pulp and paper manufacturing company named Compania Manufacturera de Papeles y Cartones S. A.(CMPC). CMPC was one of the few remaining corporations that had not yet been nationalized, and was the last independent supplier of newsprint to the last independent newspaper in the country.

The government was about to buy up the remaining CMPC stock, buy out management and nationalize the company. CMPC did not have the funds to buy its own stock nor could it borrow the money from any of the remaining private corporations left in Chile. Ernesto Ayala, the beleaguered general manager of CMPC, called Jorge Ross and said, "We can't hold the fort any longer. Do you have any rich American friends who could help us?"

Ross phoned Moseley in Seattle, apprised him of the situation, and asked him if he had any thoughts on the matter. Moseley asked if $100,000 would help. "In those days, on Chile's black market, that was an enormous amount of money," recalled Ross. "I told him that $100,000 would be spectacular."

Allende's communizing of Chile within the framework of the existing laws was a very slow process. And when word spread that a "rich American" was buying CMPC stock, the government stopped its securities acquisitions, a move that prompted other capitalists, who were emboldened by Simpson's efforts, to invest in CMPC. "The spirit developed and on we went," said Ross.

Simpson eventually bought up about 3.7 percent of CMPC stock, and by 1980, the listed value of the shares purchased had risen enough to more than offset the cost of the BIMA venture. Simpson remained close to CMPC management, and in 1987, long after Allende had been overthrown, the two companies began collaborating on the construction of a large pulp mill in Chile.

To Ross, who is now a director of the Simpson Paper Company, Simpson's purchase was not only a good investment but also a "patriotic contribution. It is too much to say that Simpson saved CMPC in the Chilean Marxist years, but, boy, was it helpful. Simpson did that because it had faith in the country and it stood by its political beliefs."

Hudson Bay, Saskatchewan

Simpson's interest in Canada was partly motivated by the inequity of the Jones Act. After the attempts to repeal or change the law failed, Bill Reed decided that if he couldn't beat the Canadian competition, he'd join them.

In the early 1960s, Simpson and two Canadian businessmen, brothers Robert and Alf DuMont, entered into a joint venture to construct a sawmill in the town of Hudson Bay, 240 miles northeast of Regina, and to purchase timber, which would be provided in sufficient supply by the Saskatchewan provincial government.

C. E. "Chuck" Runacres, Jr., Simpson's corporate secretary and long-range planner, investigated Saskatchewan and found it feasible. Simpson and the DuMonts agreed to a joint venture, and Runacres became president, in 1965, of a new Canadian subsidiary, Simpson Timber Company (Saskatchewan), Ltd. Simpson later acquired the DuMonts' interest.

Simpson entered into a harvest license agreement for a 6,000-sq.-mi. timbered area with the Saskatchewan government, which was then controlled by the Liberal party. Simpson and the province also signed a timber-reserve agreement for exclusive development of all presently uncommitted timber in the areas of Hudson Bay and Flin Flon, which was 200 miles north. The logs were to be moved by truck and rail to Hudson Bay.

Bill used to quip that, "although Simpson may not have been the biggest timber manufacturer in the world, we sure were the longest – from Puerto Montt to Hudson Bay."

Simpson's first look at Hudson Bay, population 2,000, was reminiscent of Chris Kreienbaum's inspection of the Town of McCleary in 1941. Hudson Bay, which dated back to the fur trading days of the 18th century, was dotted with buildings that were small, old and dilapidated. All of the streets were gravel. There were no sewers and the municipal well-water supply was limited. But the town perked up with the arrival of Simpson and MacMillan Bloedel, which started up a waferboard plant at around the same time.

Simpson built a $2.5 million stud mill three miles south of Hudson Bay. The mill – equipped with the first Chip 'N Saw machinery in the province – was slated to saw and dry 55 million board feet annually of white spruce, black spruce and jack pine studs, nearly equaling Saskatchewan's entire previous lumber output. The studs were marketed under the name "Simpson Red Diamond Studs" and sold primarily in Canada and the U.S. Midwest.

The new operation was not without its problems. The task of providing raw materials was far different from typical West Coast logging. Because the flat timberlands of Hudson Bay are boggy throughout the summer, the best time for logging was during the subzero winters, and Simpson had to learn how to harvest wood in that kind of weather. Hauling was stopped for several weeks during the spring thaw in order to protect the roads. Some of the early Simpson logging was done by farmers with teams of horses, because they were available to work in the wintertime.

The smaller Saskatchewan trees and the manufactured products were new to Simpson, which learned on the job how to run a cost-efficient plant and how to develop international markets for quality studs. The Canadian National Railway transportation costs to U.S. markets – primarily the Midwest, south to Louisville – were comparable to Simpson's costs from the West Coast.

The Hudson Bay Mill was a profitable operation, but the picture changed in 1967 when the voters returned to power the socialistic New Democratic party, which had most often dominated the government since 1944. (In fact, Saskatchewan was considered the cradle of Canadian socialism, which was born in the midst of the Depression of the 1930s.) When the New Democrats took over the government, they unilaterally broke the contract with Simpson.

The government requisitioned all of the large diameter logs for a provincial plywood plant that it built adjacent to Simpson's mill, and diverted other logs to a sawmill that the government had constructed at Carrot River. Rather than leave, Simpson rallied its grass roots support and the goodwill of the people of Hudson Bay and local Simpson employees to lobby the government. From the beginning, the Company had worked closely with the community, including hiring local Indians, and had good relationships with the provincial foresters. Hank Bacon recalled, "I think we would have been kicked out of there if we had not had the support of the people in the local community."[1]

Simpson was forced to retool its mill in order to accommodate smaller logs. Eventually, Starr Reed recalled, the government "kept backing off a little bit at a time and eventually compensated us for some of this loss."

In 1971, Simpson Timber Company (Saskatchewan), Ltd., and the Saskatchewan Department of Natural Resources established a 40,000-acre wilderness reserve in the Wildcat Hills, northwest of Hudson Bay, the first reserve of its kind in the province. In early 1989, Simpson announced that the lack of available timber would force it to close its Hudson Bay Mill in June 1990, after operating steadily for 25 years.

Whitecourt, Alberta

Despite its problems with the New Democratic party government in Saskatchewan, Simpson could see opportunities in the Province of Alberta, where the government was more encouraging to private enterprise. In 1973, the Company won a bidding competition with several other firms and negotiated with the provincial government a long-term timber harvest agreement that covered 1.1 million acres in the Whitecourt Forest. The pact also included a Simpson commitment to build a sawmill at Blue Ridge, near Whitecourt, a town of 3,200 people located 110 miles northwest of Edmonton. The overall package also contained an obligation to build a fiber-conversion plant to make either pulp or particleboard.

Simpson entered the Canadian woods in 1955, when it purchased the majority interest in the DuMont brothers' Hudson Bay logging operations.

Because of the remote location of Hudson Bay's timberlands, portable logging camps were built for Native Canadian loggers.

In October 1972, Simpson purchased the DuMont brothers' interest in the Hudson Bay operation. Shown at the signing were (seated, from left) Robert DuMont, Gary Reed and Alf DuMont, and (standing, from left) Simpson Vice President, Finance Robert Hutchinson; President Gil Oswald; and Vice President, Resource Manager Starr Reed.

147

The Hudson Bay Mill was designed to cut small logs into 2" x 4" studs. The mill could annually cut, dry and plane 55 million board feet of spruce and pine lumber. Shown is the Hudson Bay Mill yard in 1979.

In a scene reminiscent of early days of logging, the entire crew posed for a photo in July 1976, when the first shipment of lumber left the newly completed Simpson sawmill at Blue Ridge, Alberta.

Sometime later, the government exercised an option in the agreement to allow the Alberta Energy Company, a quasi-public group, to acquire 40 percent ownership of the project. Simpson retained the remaining 60 percent.

The Company again found itself involved in a Canadian joint venture with a partner that had different financial capabilities and objectives. "Alberta Energy Company was looking for immediate profitability because they were partially owned by the public," Starr Reed recalled. Simpson discovered that profitability was difficult to achieve for two reasons: log-processing costs were higher than anticipated, and the training of inexperienced workers was more complicated and time-consuming than expected.

"But all of that would have been resolved if we had not been faced with a second phase of investment (building a pulp mill) that would have cost millions of dollars," added Starr Reed. "When it came time to make that very difficult decision, we did not see eye to eye. There was too much investment and too much risk, and we just couldn't bring ourselves to do that." In 1981, Simpson Timber Co. (Alberta) Ltd. was sold to Alberta Energy Company Ltd.

Though well-intentioned, Simpson's forays into Canada and Chile ultimately diverted attention and substantial financial resources from timber acquisitions in the U.S. Soon, the price of stumpage, particularly in the South, was so high that investments there became impractical.

Moseley's Future

Simpson, like other forest products companies that tried to develop foreign timber properties, discovered how difficult it was to successfully transfer North American logging and manufacturing techniques to South America – and still make a profit. Consequently, Moseley, who had become Simpson International foreign development manager in 1966, recommended that Simpson de-emphasize business outside the U.S. because he didn't believe that such efforts would bear fruit.

The Chile experience was a severe disappointment personally and professionally for Moseley, who had his own questions about his future with Simpson. He considered his duties in Simpson International a "make-work job," he recalled. "And I don't like make-work."

In 1968, Moseley was named director of corporate planning for Simpson Timber Company. The job was the by-product of Bill Reed's interest in developing an entrepreneurial atmosphere that encouraged Simpson executives to come up with ideas not directly tied to the forest products resource. As a result, the Tank and Pipe Division was expanded into fiberglass-reinforced plastics; molded plastics and extruded plastics companies were acquired; door manufacturing and distribution were broadened; and real estate development was intensified. Moseley's task was to coordinate these businesses, all of which were competing for capital. In addition, Moseley continued to be responsible for Simpson's interest in BIMA, and served as corporate secretary of Simpson Lee Paper Company.

Still, he felt, "I wasn't carrying my weight and I thought I should leave the Company."

Moseley was also frustrated by Bill Reed's company rule for executive succession: only a descendant of Sol Simpson could be Simpson Timber Company chairman. In other words, that position was Gary Reed's – and the only job for which Gary was eligible. Bill reasoned that Company executives would be less hesitant to provide assistance to Gary if they knew he wasn't competing for their jobs. Conversely, the one job that would never be filled by a family member was Simpson Timber Company president because Bill wanted to vest that job with sufficient responsibility and authority to make it attractive to talented executives outside the family. This edict rankled Moseley, a family member by marriage. If he merited the presidency, he did not want to be automatically ineligible. He explained his feelings to his father-in-law.

In the spring of 1969, Bill asked Hank Bacon to convene a meeting in New York at the University Club with Moseley and Gary, who was about to get his master of business administration degree at Harvard. The purpose of the meeting was to lay out future assignments for the two men, and to "convince Mo that he should stay with the Company," Bill told Bacon.

The meeting did not completely convince Moseley that his future was with Simpson, so upon returning to Seattle, he sought the advice of former Company president Tom Gleed. "It was the only time I ever consulted with Mr. Gleed on anything," Moseley recalled. "And I did it because I was told he was a sage person. He advised me to keep my head down, follow through and see what happens. I decided to do that."

Expand and Diversify

11

Expand and Diversify

Furman Moseley finally found his opportunity in the Simpson Lee Paper Company, which in 1969 hardly seemed the place for it. Changes in personnel and a foundering financial performance by the paper group made its direction uncertain.

In 1967, Bill Reed stepped down as chairman of the board of the Paper Company, although he continued as a board member and majority stockholder. One year later, Max Bardeen retired after 42 years in the paper business, 32 of them as president of Lee or Simpson Lee.

Bardeen was succeeded as president by Malcolm McVickar, a former paper executive with Weyerhaeuser. McVickar inherited a company that was barely breaking even, if that, and saddled with old, slow and inefficient equipment.

Also, the single-machine, unintegrated Ripon Mill and the Lee Schoeller Paper Mill in Pulaski, New York, were big losers. Ripon, which was operating primarily in support of Everett and Vicksburg, was failing. Lee Schoeller had been unable to secure a profitable position in the photographic business and, in 1968, Simpson sold its 50 percent interest to Mead Corporation. This left Simpson with three mills (with a total annual tonnage of 109,700), including tired old Everett, which was sputtering, near obsolescence and losing its markets.

Only Vicksburg, with three old and small paper machines, was still profitable. It produced text and cover papers, technical and specialty papers, xerographic papers, direct-process engineering papers, photographic papers and several designer papers.

In 1969, Simpson's market share in the West, including the Mountain States, consisted of 23 percent of the business of coated one-side label, 12 percent of uncoated offset and 16 percent of writing paper. [1]

Nationally, a downturn in the economy slowed the consumption of printing and writing paper, which closely parallels the performance of the Gross National Product. The nation's purse was strained by inflation due to outgoing President Lyndon B. Johnson's "guns and butter" fiscal policy, which called for simultaneously fighting both the Vietnam War and the War on Poverty.

Paper Checker Kay Rains precision trimmed paper on a 110-inch trimmer at Simpson Paper Company's Ripon Mill.

151

Strategy

Moseley recalled that he had raised "so much Cain" about the poor performance of the Paper Company that Bill Reed essentially told him, "if you think you're so smart, why don't you figure it out?" Moseley said he would. In June 1969, he was elected chairman of the board of the Paper Company – a move that signaled Simpson Timber Company's switch from passive investor to hands-on manager of the Paper Company.

Simpson's limited financial resources prevented it from competing in large-scale commodity papers with the likes of Crown Zellerbach and Boise Cascade, whose paper mills in the West were dedicated to specific, cost-efficient run sizes, and who were dominant producers in the industry. Simpson could succeed only by growing large enough to achieve economies of scale in production, and the flexibility to match the right grade mix of paper with the right machinery.

At a time when most paper companies were building ever wider and faster machines, Simpson focused on specialty products adaptable to small machines. Moseley had discovered that machine limitations are more mental than physical, noting, "You can make tremendous differences in machinery if you are willing to spend the required time and money."

Consequently, Simpson's plan was to buy existing paper mills and hardware that could be integrated into its product line. In 1969, the Company pursued mills owned by Kimberly-Clark, Potlatch Forests, Inc., and Hammermill, but none was immediately available. That year, the Paper Company finished with a net loss of $362,000 on sales of $43.7 million. Business grew worse during the recession of 1970, when profit margins were squeezed by depressed paper prices and rising labor and raw materials costs. Sales fell to $39.6 million, with a net loss of $1,344,000. In January 1971, Moseley replaced McVickar as president of Simpson, while continuing as chairman.[2]

To Buy or to Sell

Simpson Timber Company was at a crossroads. Should it continue to pursue mergers or completely abandon the paper business? Bill Reed left it up to Gary and Furman, telling them that they would "have to live with the consequences of their decision."

The Paper Company had no luck selling itself. Only MacMillan Bloedel Ltd. presented a legitimate offer, but just before an agreement was finalized, fate stepped in. On August 15, 1971, President Richard M. Nixon, who was fighting inflation and rising unemployment, announced an immediate 90-day freeze on wages and prices. MacMillan Bloedel then dropped its offer by 25 percent, which was unacceptable to Simpson. The decision was made to hold on to the Paper Company and make it work.

The very next day Simpson switched from seller to buyer. Moseley immediately contacted Kimberly-Clark to resume the pursuit of K-C's Anderson Mill, near Redding in Shasta County. That mill, built in 1964, ostensibly to supply *Life* magazine, made coated paper for high-quality printing and color reproduction and had the finest off-machine coater in the West. Daily capacity was 150 tons of kraft pulp and 155 tons of printing paper. Located near the Sacramento River, close to large forest reserves, the mill got its primary supply of residual chips from Kimberly-Clark's adjacent lumber operations.[3]

The Anderson Mill, in spite of significant recent investments by K-C (including a new pulp digester for $2 million), had never been profitable, losing millions each year. Its small groundwood-type pulp process was uneconomical, fixed costs were high because it had only one paper machine, and production was limited to coated paper. Despite those drawbacks, the mill fit into Moseley's strategy because its products and location would enhance Simpson Lee's market position. And Anderson's $18 million in annual sales would expand Simpson Lee's total sales by almost 50 percent.

By the winter of 1971, Kimberly-Clark, dearly wanting to rid itself of the mill, reached an accord with Simpson Lee, which agreed to purchase the fixed assets for $5 million. Simpson Lee also purchased $2.5 million of raw material and paper inventories and pledged $2.5 million toward modification and transition expenses. In addition, the Company committed $3 million to a reserve for losses it expected to incur during the mill's transition from Kimberly-Clark to Simpson, and, Moseley recalled, "We spent every dime of it."

But first, Moseley had to sell the idea to the Company's board of directors, which – along with virtually the entire paper industry – questioned how Simpson could succeed where Kimberly-Clark had failed. Before voting on the proposal, the board flew to Anderson to see the mill firsthand. When Hank Bacon, "the old scrap dealer," laid eyes on the plant, he marveled, "There's more than $5 million worth of scrap metal here."

To which Moseley replied, "And if we can't make it work, Hank, I'll give you the responsibility of scrapping the damn thing."

Simpson Lee officially took ownership of the Anderson Mill on January 4, 1972.

Seidl, who was then vice president of pulp for Simpson Timber Company, was named vice president of western manufacturing. His operating responsibilities included the Ripon Mill, the new mill at Anderson and Everett Pulp & Paper, until it was closed later that year. Teodoro E. Reinhardt, formerly production manager at Everett, was transferred to the new mill to become production manager for paper. Moseley, who was elected president of the Paper Company in 1971, took on the responsibility of marketing the Company's pulp. Simpson Lee renamed the facility "Shasta," in honor of the nearby mountain, thus establishing a Company tradition of naming mills after local landmarks that lasted for most of two decades.

The Shasta Mill purchase was made with the complete support of Bill Reed, who had been stoic and steadfast in the wake of the Paper Company's losses. Bill had "an unbridled conviction that Simpson was going to be a better company if we had a strong pulp and paper side," Moseley recalled. "He was the only person in Simpson who had a clear commitment to the pulp and paper side, which permitted the Paper Company to exist."

Bill Reed Steps Down

Bill resigned as chairman of Simpson Timber Company on June 29, 1971, and was succeeded by the fourth generation of management, Vice Chairman Gary Reed, then 31.

In his farewell message to the men and women of Simpson, Bill wrote, with typical modesty, that he was "happy and proud to have had the privilege of being an active member of your organization for the last 40 years." He added that he was confident that his successor, "will perform his duties competently, for he is an able man and you have given him good indoctrination."[4]

In March 1973, Bill brought down the curtain on his active working relationship with the Company when he reached Simpson's mandatory retirement age of 65. Although he remained a member of the board of directors, Bill moved his base of operations from Simpson's corporate offices in the Washington Building in Seattle to the Exchange Building – the same building in which he had worked 30 years earlier when he was on the staff of the 13th Naval District – where he devoted most of his time to family business, particularly the family investment arm, Simpson Reed & Company.

Bill was motivated to move his offices because he didn't want to appear to be looking over the shoulder of his successor. He had enormous confidence in Gary Reed and Furman Moseley, executive vice president of the Timber Company and chairman and president of the Paper Company, and he knew that it was time for them to earn their spurs.

Reed and Moseley were assisted by a group that blended several generations of Company management: Hank Bacon, vice chairman; Gilbert L. Oswald, who had followed Bacon in 1970 as president and chief operating officer of Simpson Timber Company; and Robert B. Hutchinson, vice president-finance and secretary.

Hutchinson represented Simpson continuity. He was a home-grown Company executive who was raised in Shelton, where his father was an engineer on the Simpson Railroad. As a boy, he delivered newspapers to the Reed family, including Tollie Simpson, and shopped at the Lumbermen's Mercantile. He was graduated from the University of Puget Sound in 1944, and, after two years in the military, he returned to Shelton and Simpson, where he spent six months in the purchasing department before he was

Bill Reed (left) remained on the Timber Company board as director emeritus until his death in 1989. Others pictured in 1971 included (left of Reed) Vice President, Finance and Secretary Robert B. Hutchinson; Executive Vice President Furman C. Moseley; Chairman Wm. G. Reed, Jr.; President Gilbert L. Oswald; directors Chapin Henry and Eleanor E. Reed; and Vice Chairman C. Henry Bacon, Jr.

On June 29, 1971, Bill Reed was succeeded by 31-year-old Gary Reed as chairman of the board of Simpson Timber Company. The gavel, which was presented by Bill to his son, had been handed down by Mark E. Reed, who served as Speaker of the House of the Washington State Legislature.

Following the retirement of Bill Reed, the Company was managed by (from left) Gil Oswald, Furman Moseley, Gary Reed and Bob Hutchinson.

155

In 1972, Simpson Lee Paper Company turned from a seller to a buyer when the Company purchased the Kimberly-Clark mill in Anderson, California. Simpson renamed it the Shasta Mill.

Q. A. "Sandy" Narum came to Simpson, along with the Shasta Mill, from Kimberly-Clark. Narum later became the Company's first corporate director of environmental protection.

David J. Moeller, who came to Simpson with the acquisition of the Shasta Mill, later became vice president of engineering for Simpson Paper Company.

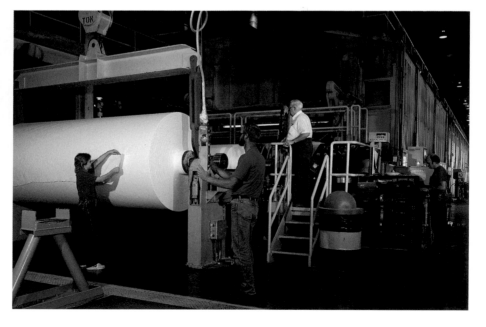

Furman Moseley recognized the inherent worth of old equipment. When Everett Pulp & Paper was closed in 1972, he put its best paper machine into storage. It was rebuilt and installed as Shasta Two in 1974.

transferred to the Seattle office as an accountant. Hutchinson recalled that, at the time, the Company required that all employees work on Saturdays and men wear suit coats in the office at all times. He kept his coat on and became a skilled financial manager and trusted adviser.

Consolidation

In 1972, Simpson chose to shut down the Everett Pulp & Paper Mill rather than keep it running with costly, sorely needed improvements. The mill had become a weak player in its two primary businesses, printing and writing paper and school supplies. In fact, Simpson had dropped the school-supply paper, Simpson Tablet, which had been losing its market share.

The closure of the mill was spread out over a 10-month period, and special programs were developed to assist the Everett employees. The mill was kept running during the transition period so that the Company could maintain its markets until 60,000 tons a year of printing and writing paper could be shifted to the Shasta and Ripon mills.

After Simpson took it over, the Shasta Mill was retooled, the paper machine's speed was accelerated from 1,300 feet per minute to 2,000, paper quality and economy were improved, and by the end of 1972, Shasta was running full-time and making a profit.

Operating time and profit were helped by the Company's success in developing coated one-side label paper, an Everett Mill product, on Shasta's big modern coater. Ted Reinhardt, who had come from Everett, and Dave Moeller led the way on product and mill improvements, which were big factors in Simpson's turnaround. In a short time, Simpson became a major producer of label paper by building on its experience with the small equipment at Everett.

In spite of this momentum at Shasta, the Company needed to make more changes. It was cumbersome to produce both coated and uncoated paper on a single machine, known as "Shasta One," and it was clear that economics and product flexibility could be greatly improved with a second machine. Moseley recognized the inherent value of old equipment, and when the Everett Mill was closed he put its best paper machine into storage. Along with other stored surplus machinery, it was moved to the Shasta Mill, where it was completely rebuilt and renamed "Shasta Two," adding 50,000 tons per year capacity. Eventually, the Shasta Mill emerged as the Paper Company's "flagship."

The Ripon Mill became more important because it could take some of Shasta's excess pulp, help with finishing responsibilities and, because it was strategically located, serve as a distribution center for Shasta papers. As specialty paper volumes increased, grades were transferred between Vicksburg and Ripon as dictated by market fluctuation. This, along with new papers such as Sundance®, greatly improved Ripon's operations and earnings.

"Ripon was suddenly the right size for specialty paper, and also fit some grades that couldn't be economically made at Shasta, which was too big," said Bob Seidl. "Before Shasta, Ripon was at the mercy of the pulp market. If the pulp market was down, Ripon was forced to make any paper just to use pulp."

Ripon did record some of its own accomplishments, including setting new standards in recycled paper, which was not a widely available product in the early 1970s. In fact, Simpson was one of the first paper companies in the nation – and the first in the West – to make completely recycled white paper. By the end of 1971, the Company had recycled almost 5 million pounds of paper, earning commendation from the San Francisco chapter of the Sierra Club and mention in the *Congressional Record.* [5]

Fine-Tuning

In 1973, after four years of losses, the Paper Company registered a net profit of $2.3 million on sales of $55.8 million, thanks to increased penetration in its western markets and a Company record output of pulp. In 1974, sales jumped 32 percent to $73.4 million and profit soared 174 percent to $6.3 million. Nationally, paper companies were running close to 100 percent capacity, which allowed the industry to raise prices and earn a higher rate of return. [6]

Simpson was buoyed by its financial performance and encouraged by projections that the West was going to outpace the rest of the country in population growth, a trend that would translate into greater demand for paper. Simpson could pick up a larger portion of the western market because it was able to produce both coated and uncoated paper, and market a complete product line, from offset to text and cover to coated paper. Competition was much keener in uncoated paper, but Simpson still was able to maintain its market share against the likes of Crown Zellerbach, Boise Cascade, Hammermill and Potlatch.

Although Simpson was maintaining its business with smaller paper merchants, larger merchants were another story. The Company needed to land a major customer to show the rest of the market that Simpson was a legitimate supplier of coated paper products. Zellerbach Paper Company was that merchant, and its decision to take on the new line helped launch the new-look Simpson Lee Paper Company. The gradual acceptance of the Shasta Mill in the market also dramatically increased the Company's production of coated-one-side label paper for canned and bottled goods and coated-two-side stock for sales brochures and corporate annual reports.

Shasta's success was a corporate watershed. The quality of the paper established the mill and the Paper Company, and, "For once," Seidl recalled, "we could stand up straight and say that we have a first-class mill that is making some money. We could build around that. If Shasta had not succeeded, Simpson would probably not be in the paper business today."

Simpson Timber Company demonstrated its confidence by paying $14 a share for remaining outside common stock in Simpson Lee, and, by the end of 1973, it owned 98 percent of the common stock.

In 1974, Seidl was elected president of the Paper Company, succeeding Moseley, who continued as its chairman. Robert G. Millard replaced Seidl as vice president and general manager of western operations. Millard, who had been vice president and general manager of eastern operations, was replaced by Kenneth A. Perkins, the former manager of the Ripon Mill.

The Company was not yet out of the woods. The recession that began in the fourth quarter of 1974 and continued through 1975 was the longest and steepest economic decline since the early 1930s. Mill shipments fell off drastically, and operating volumes for paper mills dropped to the lowest point since the Depression. Simpson, although hard hit, stuck to its plan to emphasize coated paper for the western market, and the Company succeeded in being able to produce and market these grades economically, which kept the Shasta operation in business during the recession.

Earnings rebounded strongly over the next couple of years as the Company shuffled and reshuffled its product mix among the mills, and searched for the ideal combination of products, facilities and markets to make it a significant paper company in the West.

Emboldened by its success, Simpson poured about $30 million into Shasta, including $4 million to improve and expand the mill's primary and secondary water-treatment facilities, and a $10 million recovery boiler for clean air. Shasta was the first pulp mill in the U.S. to use treated mill effluent to irrigate crops for livestock feed. Shasta One was speeded up, which brought its annual capacity up to about 75,000 tons.

By 1977, the Paper Company had bought out the remaining outside stockholders, the Lee name was dropped, and Simpson Paper Company was born.

Beginning to Grow

"If we're going to become more important to our customers, we're going to have to get larger over time," Moseley stated in the late 1970s.

Following Moseley's dictum, Simpson continued acquiring mills that had not been profitable — a direction that was 180 degrees away from the conventional wisdom of the time. Inherent in Simpson's approach was the view that often those mills were unprofitable because their owners were not making the right paper on the right machines. Also, because of the rising inflation of the 1970s, it was cheaper over the long term to buy used machinery than to build new machinery. "Replacement cost ultimately was going to express itself in the end-product price," Moseley noted. "If we could raise our efficiencies and keep our capital costs low, the margins would open up."

Moseley's confidence came from an intimate knowledge of the effects of spiraling inflation, which he had seen firsthand in the 1960s in Chile, where it averaged three percent a month over four years. "You can't feel inflation unless you've lived it," he said.

The fact that Moseley was able to capitalize on what he learned in Chile was sweetly ironic because for a long time he believed it had been "a lost experience." Instead, the period from 1975 through 1980, when the U.S. was racked by an intensive period of skyrocketing inflation, "was the only time that I felt that I was ahead of my peers."

Moseley had been playing catch-up because, simply, he had never worked in a paper mill, and his technical experience consisted of on-the-job training, much of it provided by Bob Seidl.

He did, however, have an understanding of financing. "I learned at Blyth & Co. not to be afraid of zeros, because the numbers work just the same no matter how many zeros there are behind them." And he enjoyed strategic planning, particularly analyzing the competition. "You've got to know more about the thinking of your competition than your own organization's because you respond to the actions of the competition. When we were trying to merge with those mills in 1969, we learned a great deal about their operations. Many of them were selling the same kinds of paper to many of the same customers that we were selling to."

San Gabriel

One older mill that Simpson had been eyeing since the late 1960s was owned by Potlatch Forests, Inc., in Pomona, California. The mill had a fascinating history of its own. Founder Erik Fernstrom, a paper importer and exporter with operations in Sweden and England, built the mill – the first in the Pomona Valley – in 1925 to manufacture citrus-wrap paper for the large fruit-packing houses such as Sunkist and Pure Gold, and later tissue wrap for packing new shirts. The California Fruit Wrapping Mill, as it was named, was unique because it was not near a lake or a river; all water came from underground wells. In 1952, Fernstrom and his brother, Fritz, sold the mill, which by then had three paper machines and a production capacity of 100,000 tons per year, to Potlatch, which used it as an outlet for the excess pulp from its mill in Lewiston, Idaho. The Pomona mill continued to make citrus wraps until the middle of the 1960s, when box liners became the preferred means of preventing mold in fruit. The mill then branched out into uncoated offset, writing paper and copy roll grades, as well as napkins.

In 1978, Potlatch's strategy of concentrating on paperboard and household papers – towels, toilet tissue and napkins – called for building a new tissue machine next to its Idaho pulp mill. That decision, which meant a de-emphasis of printing and writing production in the West, made the Pomona mill expendable.

In 1979, Simpson purchased the Potlatch Forests, Inc. mill in Pomona, California, and renamed it San Gabriel Mill. The mill came with deinking facilities used for recycling waste paper into white pulp. Deinked pulp from this process later was used in a new family of Simpson papers (including Evergreen, which is used in this book).

When Simpson first entered the pipe business in 1967, its annual production was 20 million pounds, not enough to be profitable. In 1977, Simpson began acquiring other companies, and in 1985, its name was changed to Pacific Western Extruded Plastics Company, with James K. Rash as its president. By 1989, the diversified producer of plastic pipe had increased its annual production to over 350 million pounds.

Pacific Western Extruded Plastics Company senior managers (shown from left) John R. Cobb, vice president production; James K. Rash, president; and Norman M. Stickel, vice president marketing.

In 1990, PWPipe acquired polyvinyl chloride resin production facilities from Air Products and Chemicals, Inc. Included in the acquisition were two plants: one at Calvert City, Kentucky, and another (shown) at Pace, Florida.

Simpson bought the mill on January 31, 1979, at a time when the mill had been shut down by an industry-wide strike for seven months. It was renamed "San Gabriel" for the mountain range on its horizon.

San Gabriel was a neat fit. Its line of uncoated papers, especially writing paper and copy grades, increased Simpson's total annual production capacity by 50 percent to 300,000 tons. The mill was located in the populous Los Angeles market, where it had an existing and rapidly expanding customer base. Its 54,000-sq.-ft. warehouse space, shipping facilities and recycling proficiency strengthened Simpson's customer service capabilities in Southern California and solidified the Company's position as the only manufacturer of printing and writing paper in the State of California. San Gabriel became the largest supplier of 8-1/2-inch by 11-inch cut-size papers to the western market.

With this new acquisition, recalled Walter A. Duignan, vice president of sales for Simpson Paper, "We were able to restructure the products within our three California mills to make each facility a little bit stronger."

In less than 10 years, the Simpson Paper Company had grown from an organization on the verge of liquidation to one that rang up sales of $200 million in 1979. But Simpson's leadership was not going to restrict itself to the West. Moseley had been planting seeds around the country, and as Simpson Paper Company entered the 1980s, those seeds began to bear fruit.

Pacific Western Extruded Plastics Company (PWPipe)

Bill Reed saw aluminum (siding) and plastic (pipe) eating into what had traditionally been markets for wood. He viewed the aluminum industry as capital-intensive and very competitive, but the plastics industry offered Simpson a means to diversify into a new market.

In 1967, the Timber Company purchased the Gil-Wel Manufacturing Company, a small Eugene, Oregon, manufacturer of extruded thermoplastic pipe – primarily used for irrigation – and operated it as the Plastics Division. Simpson established the Specialty Products Group, which was managed by Jack Haney, to oversee plastics operations in Eugene, Oregon, the Portland-based Fabricated Products Division (doors), the Tank and Pipe Division and the Chemical Division. (The old Portland door plant was closed in 1973, and all work operations were transferred from Portland to Vancouver, Washington, where the new Columbia River Door Plant produced 8,000 flush doors a day as a complement to the panel doors produced at McCleary. Columbia River Door was sold to Jeld-Wen in 1987.)

The Plastics Division's annual volume of 20 million pounds was too small to make a sufficient profit selling commodity products. Despite periodic modernization of its extrusion technology and a move into gasketed pipe production, profits remained small. "The market was growing and we were not keeping up with it," recalled James K. Rash, who became manager of Specialty Products in 1976. He recommended that Simpson either expand to achieve an economy of scale or abandon the pipe business.

The decision was made to expand and Simpson did so, dramatically, over the next decade. The Company acquired the Robintech, Inc., plant in Sunnyside, Washington, in 1977 and Gifford-Hill Company, Inc., plants in Visalia, California, and Spokane, Washington, in 1982. (The Spokane plant was shut down and its assets redistributed.) The capacities of all three plants were gradually expanded and, by the end of 1985, Simpson was producing about 100 million pounds of extruded pipe a year, about 80 percent of which was used for agricultural and turf irrigations. Pipe sizes ranged from 1/2-inch diameter up to 24 inches.

The agricultural business cycle turned down in the early 1980s, prompting Simpson's decision to diversify its pipe business into the municipal water and sewer and electrical conduit markets. In 1985, the Company doubled both the number of facilities and its production volume, from 100 million to 200 million pounds, when it acquired three Western Plastics Company plants, one in Tacoma, Washington, and two in California – at Union City and Downey. These acquisitions transformed the Company by elevating it to a major position in the businesses of electrical, sewer and potable-water pipe, and firmly established it in California, which represented half of the firm's market. In order to take advantage of Western Plastics' superior name recognition in California (and to separate it from Simpson's image as a wood products company), the Company's name was changed to Pacific Western Extruded Plastics Company, with Rash as its president. The trade name PWPipe was adopted to identify the Company's plastics business.

In January 1987, PWPipe made further inroads into California with the purchase of Certainteed Company's pipe plant in Cameron Park, east of Sacramento; another plant at Perris, California, was acquired in 1989. Simpson became the largest plastic-pipe producer on the West Coast and one of the top three nationwide, with annual capacity of about 400 million pounds. Today, the pipe business represents close to 10 percent of Simpson's sales volume.

In 1990, PWPipe took another step to ensure the supply and price of plastic resin when it acquired two polyvinyl chloride resin production plants from Air Products and Chemicals, Inc. One plant was located in Pace, Florida, and the other in Calvert City, Kentucky.

A Major League Player

12

A Major League Player

Simpson roared into the 1980s with a master plan to become a major national producer of specialty paper products. By the end of the decade, the Company owned five and a half more mills, each enhancing Simpson's resource base, expertise, capabilities, product mix and distribution. It would produce more than 1 million short tons (1 short ton = 2,000 pounds) of pulp annually and nearly 1 million tons of paper by 1990.

John J. Fannon

It was fitting that the Simpson Paper Company began the decade with a new president, John J. Fannon, who moved up from vice president of marketing when Seidl became vice chairman of the board of directors. Fannon, a graduate of the University of Notre Dame and the University of Chicago School of Business, had held sales and sales-management positions with Champion International in Chicago before joining Simpson in 1973. He worked closely with Seidl in the early 1980s, making changes in products, distribution and the Paper Company's machinery. Seidl observed, "John has a respect for the balance between marketing and manufacturing, which is important, but not common."

Fannon did not have the technical background of his predecessor. He was not an engineer nor an accountant, but he was "uniquely gifted in being able to understand the markets," according to Moseley. "He was a well-schooled marketer and an experienced manager who had a knack for seeing potential in every market, anticipating problems and fixing them, and developing new products."

The Reed/Moseley Dynamic

The Tacoma Kraft Mill, which was acquired by Simpson in 1985, had a required daily diet of 2,200 dry tons of wood chips. Some of the chips arrived by truck from area mills, some from Central and Eastern Washington were transported by rail, and others were barged in from mills around Puget Sound and from the Company's Shelton mills or British Columbia, Canada.

Over the years, Gary Reed and Furman Moseley developed a complementary relationship by blending their individual talents and temperaments. Moseley was an aggressive entrepreneur and strategist, Reed a contemplative investor, the steward of the family interest, the decision maker as chairman. Susan Reed Moseley observed that her husband and brother understood early on that "they would always be affiliated in some way. Both men have a commitment to family. I think they have worked at keeping communication refreshingly open. It's sometimes combative – perhaps necessarily – and I think we've all been enriched by that."

Moseley has noted that neither he nor Gary "makes any major decision that we don't interact like a tennis volley at the net. We make pretty good decisions because we each pick apart the other's positions. We never let it become personal."

Bob Seidl described Gary Reed as being "a lot like his father – mild-mannered, modest, hardworking and devoted to the Company. He is personally conservative about new actions, but is quite prepared for risk when it is there." Simpson Vice President and Chief Financial Officer J. Thurston Roach described Gary as "reflective, almost philosophical. He asks detailed, crucial questions and thinks several moves ahead on the chess board."

Moseley became a student of the industry, well versed in the competition's products, performance and facilities. He committed Simpson to aggressive expansion by his belief that older mills, which were available at very favorable capital costs, could be improved by careful reinvestment and removal of obsolete parts, and that their product development and marketing programs could be tailored to accommodate the scale of the improved equipment.

Moseley developed a talent for identifying possible acquisitions, figuring their worth, and creatively financing them. Simpson Paper Company Director Jorge Ross described this proficiency as "partly intuitive. Mo can put together figures very rapidly. He stores a lot of information in his head and it comes out through his pencil."

He also had the patience to wait for the right time. "Mo will tell the owner of the mill what his intentions are," said Gary. "Almost all the acquisitions we have made have been projects we have talked about a year or two in advance."

Once a mill was earmarked for acquisition, the Company dispatched a team of specialists to assess every aspect of the operation. The team included Bob Seidl (still active as an adviser even though he officially retired from the Company in January 1980) and a roster of vice presidents, among them Bob Millard, operations; Thurston Roach, finance; Jon Irwin, controller; David Moeller, engineering; Walt Duignan, sales; Gary Snider, business planning; Joseph Breed, legal; Joseph Leitzinger, public affairs; and Cynthia "Cindy" Sonstelie, human resources.

"By the time we sign the acquisition papers," said Fannon, "we know what we want done with the products and the mill, how we are going to work with the customers, which people we want to keep, and whether there are any environmental liabilities."

The psychology of building morale in a newly acquired operation, particularly one that had problems, was as important as the mechanics. Because Simpson management believed that good housekeeping and safety go together, the premises were almost immediately cleaned and painted. (After the Company did just that at the San Gabriel Mill in Pomona, a returning mill worker was heard to marvel, "It looks like Disneyland!")

In most cases, the Company replaced only the manager of an acquired mill with an experienced Simpson employee. Rather than cut wages, Simpson made the "conscious choice that we'd rather have cooperation than resentment," Moseley noted. Change often brought out the best in the people who came

Shown (from left) is J. Thurston Roach, Simpson Investment Company vice president and chief financial officer; and Simpson Paper Company's 1990 senior managers, which included Vice Presidents Jon W. Irwin, controller; Gary L. Snider, business planning; Walter A. Dungnan sales; Robert G. Millard, operations; and Simpson Paper Company President John J. Fannon. (Not shown, David J. Moeller, vice president, engineering.)

In 1990, the Paper Company's board included (from left) Whitney MacMillan, chairman of Cargill, Inc.; John J. Fannon, Simpson Paper Company president; H. G. "Pat" Pattillo of Pattillo Construction Co.; Jorge Ross, a Chilean businessman; Gary Reed, Simpson Investment Company chairman; Bob Seidl, retired president of Simpson Paper Company; and Furman Moseley, Simpson Paper Company chairman.

Furman Moseley assumed operational responsibility for Simpson Lee in June 1969. Since then he has become the principal architect for rejuvenation and expansion of Simpson's paper business.

Simpson Paper Company executives, mill and sales management gathered frequently for performance review meetings. This 1989 meeting at the Shasta Mill included (from left) William A. Schul, operations manager – Valley Forge Mill; Roger L. Huckendubler, operations manager – Ripon Mill; William J. Turgeon, Jr., western sales manager; Robert F. Haiduk, southwest sales manager; Keith R. Anderson, marketing manager, international; Walter A. Duignan, vice president, sales; Gary L. Snider, vice president, business planning; Robert G. Millard, vice president, operations; Furman C. Moseley, chairman; John J. Fannon, president; Jon W. Irwin, vice president, controller; Aaron L. Gettel, operations manager – Humboldt Mill; Teodoro Reinhardt, operations manager – Shasta Mill; Claus Globig, manager, research & development; E. Guy Lalouche, operations manager – San Jacinto Mill; Dan T. Paulucci, product development manager; J. Thurston Roach, Simpson Investment Company vice president & chief financial officer; (not shown) Raymond P. Tennison, Jr., operations manager – Tacoma

Kraft Mill; Peter W. Lowe, operations manager – Vicksburg Mill; R. Bryce Seidl, operations manager – Plainwell Mill; William Ernst, general manager – Centennial Mill; John M. Sommers, plant manager – Burlington Mill; David J. Moeller, vice president, engineering; David DeYoung, operations manager – San Gabriel Mill; Frank D. Watters, director, management information systems; Richard P. Gallagher, general sales manager, domestic; and Donald W. Nay, east sales manager.

Located near Rittenhouse Town, Philadelphia, the birthplace of the U.S. paper industry, the Valley Forge Mill was acquired from

Weyerhaeuser Company in 1980.

to Simpson with each acquisition. Their ideas and suggestions were encouraged because the Company had found that among the hidden assets in its new mills were capable people whose talents had not been tapped.

The Shasta Mill, for example, produced three standouts, who rose to important positions: David Moeller became vice president of engineering and was responsible for hundreds of millions of dollars of capital spending; Quintin A. "Sandy" Narum became the Company's first corporate director of environmental protection, and an industry environmental leader; and Aaron L. Gettel became operations manager of the Humboldt Pulp Mill.

Each acquisition triggered refinement of the product lines of all the other Simpson mills. No plant benefited more from this than Ripon, which had consumed a lot of red ink throughout most of its existence because it was often used as a buffer for other mills and had to make papers that didn't fit its machines. Seidl recalled, "What we needed, and got, from Bill, Gary and Mo was patience. We asked them to understand that although Ripon was having a tough time, it was accomplishing useful things for the Simpson Paper Company." By the start of the decade of the '90s, Ripon had found its place as a producer of specialty papers.

Valley Forge

One of the major competitors of the Vicksburg Mill in text and cover papers was Weyerhaeuser's mill in Miquon, Pennsylvania, a suburb of Philadelphia on the Schuylkill River. It was founded in 1856 by William C. Hamilton and Edwin R. Cope, who began operations with one 62-inch Fourdrinier paper machine. It was known as W. C. Hamilton & Sons from 1875 until 1956, when it was renamed Hamilton Paper Company. Over the years, the mill expanded to eight machines, and was capable of producing 260 tons of paper per day – including writing, book and specialty papers, text and cover and reproduction paper. Hamilton was purchased by the Weyerhaeuser Company in 1961. (Coincidentally, in 1966, Gary Reed was working for Weyerhaeuser, where he first became familiar with the Miquon mill.)

Simpson acquired the plant on March 2, 1980, and renamed it "Valley Forge" for the nearby site of the 1777 winter encampment of George Washington's Revolutionary Army. The transaction, which marked Weyerhaeuser's exit from the text and cover business, gave Simpson access to some of the finest wholesale merchants in the East. Valley Forge, combined with Vicksburg outside Chicago, and Ripon outside San Francisco, put Simpson in the best national position for supplying high-quality text and cover papers.

Because some of the product lines and distribution outlets of the Valley Forge Mill overlapped existing ones in Simpson, much time and effort was needed to select those lines that would best fit the overall Simpson text and cover business.

Humboldt Pulp Mill

At times during its growth years, Simpson was either pulp-rich or pulp-poor, and found it difficult to balance paper capacity and pulp sources. In the early 1980s, the Company sought greater pulp capacity in order to fully integrate its wood products and pulping operations into its paper facilities, to increase paper production and to strengthen its base for exporting pulp to world markets. The Company was able to achieve its pulp requirements with the acquisition in 1982 of Crown Zellerbach's half of the Crown Simpson Pulp Mill on Humboldt Bay, which it renamed the Humboldt Pulp Mill.

"It was no time to be buying a pulp mill," Thurston Roach recalled. "But, because we take the long-term view – and we have confidence in our asset base – we bought Crown Simpson and expected to carry it at a loss or no better than break-even for several years, which is what happened."

Harding-Jones

By 1983, the industry was operating near capacity and other paper companies emulated Simpson's policy of purchasing existing operations rather than building new ones.

That year, Simpson acquired the 118-year-old Harding-Jones Paper Company mill, on the Miami River in Excello, Ohio, near Middletown. The tiny specialty mill was known for its fine bond and ledger papers and premium high-quality writing papers made from cotton and wood fibers. Harding-Jones' distinctive, individualized line of watermark papers employed a process used for over a century for identifying manufacturers, preventing counterfeiting of currency and important documents, and providing a personalized name or trademark for the user.

Unfortunately, Harding-Jones, with its small 1896-vintage single machine, was not able to operate at a profit, and in 1989 Simpson announced plans for its closure in the spring of the following year.

Tacoma Kraft

Simpson was interested in the Tacoma kraft pulp and paper mill long before its owner, Champion International, put it on the market in 1985, a year after it purchased St. Regis Paper Company, which ran it from its inception in 1931. (The mill was built – but never operated – by Union Bag & Paper Company of Savannah, Georgia, which sold it to St. Regis.) Simpson, which was already selling pulp to the Pacific Rim and was looking for more pulp capacity, was attracted by the mill's ability to produce 1,250 tons per day of commodity-grade unbleached and semi-bleached kraft papers and linerboard. The mill also had the advantage of its location on Commencement Bay, one of the West Coast's major shipping ports. The Company could easily barge in its own chips from Shelton to provide much of the raw material base of the Tacoma mill, which consumed more than 2,200 bone-dry tons of wood each day.

Moseley was in New York when he learned that Champion was ready to make a deal. He made an offer and, to his astonishment, Champion accepted quickly – so quickly, in fact, that he could not immediately confirm the agreement because Gary Reed was traveling in Europe. Moseley finally tracked

Tacoma Kraft Mill was constructed in the late 1920s by Union Bag & Paper Company, but it was not put into operation until it was acquired by the St. Regis Paper Company in 1931. Champion International bought St. Regis in 1984, and sold the Tacoma mill a year later to Simpson. Simpson recognized the mill's liabilities and its assets. By 1990, the Company had committed more than $143 million to production and environmental improvements.

(Next page) Paper production at Simpson's Vicksburg Mill in 1990.

With the aid of an electron microscope and other research and development equipment, research assistant Rick Peterson worked to develop new papers and improve existing pulps and grades at the Maxwell D. Bardeen Research Center.

The Maxwell D. Bardeen pulp and paper research laboratory at the Vicksburg Mill.

Dr. F. Claus Globig, manager of research and development for Simpson Paper Company.

down his brother-in-law by phone in the middle of the night in Munich, West Germany. "I apologized," Moseley recalled, "because I never like to be forced to make a fast decision."

Gary conceded that the Tacoma mill decision "was a scary one for me. Mo was primed to go. I simply said, 'If you think it's a good deal, let's do it.'"

The mill's urban setting on Tacoma's tide flats – in full view of the city – was a liability. The purchase brought up serious environmental and public relations issues, which were addressed by a Simpson team of legal and technical specialists and Joe Leitzinger, Simpson's vice president of public affairs, who had lived and worked in Tacoma for 17 years before joining Simpson in 1974. Early in the 1980s, the ASARCO smelter in Ruston, near Tacoma's Point Defiance Park, was closed for environmental reasons, and Simpson had to make sure there was not a public agenda to shut down the pulp mill, which had contributed to air and water pollution. The Company was able to ascertain before buying the mill what environmental improvements would have to be undertaken and at what cost.

Simpson assured the Tacoma community of its intention to build a healthy business and be a good corporate citizen. In its first five years of ownership, Simpson invested or committed $143 million in production and environmental improvements at the mill, including completion in 1988 of the first Superfund cleanup in Puget Sound, the award-winning St. Paul Waterway Remedial Action and Habitat Restoration Project. Equally important to the community was the Company's reduction of pulp mill odors.

Patrick J. Hassett, who had served as operating manager at Crown Simpson and then at the Humboldt Pulp Mill, was named executive vice president and manager of Tacoma Kraft. In 1989, Hassett was named by the Company to oversee its interest in the Celulosa del Pacifico Mill, a 900-metric-ton-per-day Chilean pulp mill scheduled for start-up in 1993.

The pulp business in 1985 was, in Fannon's words, an "unmitigated disaster," because a strong dollar and high inventories throughout the world caused a severe depression, which did not begin to improve until early 1986. However, by the end of that year, Tacoma Kraft was a contributor to pulp and paper sales, which accounted for 58 percent of Simpson's total sales, compared with 24 percent in 1978.[1]

Maxwell D. Bardeen Research Center

Max Bardeen preached a doctrine of research, and in recognition of his scientific approach to papermaking, the Simpson Lee laboratory at Vicksburg, which was constructed in 1965, was renamed the Maxwell D. Bardeen Research Center following his retirement in 1968.

Under the direction of Dr. Claus Globig, the center's mission was to improve existing grades and develop new papers, which included archival papers for libraries, xerographic copy papers and baryta-coated base papers for instant photography.

To improve understanding between Company researchers and manufacturers, Simpson's R&D decentralized in 1984, and established satellite laboratories for coated-paper research at Shasta and later at San Jacinto and Plainwell.

San Jacinto

About 25 percent of the U.S. pulp and paper industry's capacity changed hands between 1983 and 1988, although the prices for acquisitions had inflated.[2] Simpson was studying how to convert Tacoma Kraft into a white-paper mill when the opportunity came up in 1987 to purchase another Champion pulp and paper mill in Pasadena, Texas, near Houston.

Champion began operating the Pasadena mill in 1937, on a 162-acre site where General Santa Anna, the Mexican commander-in-chief, was captured in the Battle of San Jacinto, which was key to Texas gaining its independence from Mexico in 1836. A century later, the mill site was selected because it was near the East Texas "piney woods," an abundant source of pulpwood; the Houston Ship Channel and a network of railroads provided good transportation to major markets. It was the second mill in the United States to produce bleached sulfate pulp from southern pine, which could be used for making fine printing papers. (Previously, southern pine had been used only for making kraft and coarse papers.) In 1940, Champion added the first paper machine in Texas capable of producing coated paper grades. It eventually became the largest book-paper mill in the South, supplying *Life* magazine and other major "slick" publications.[3]

Simpson, then the major regional supplier of coated one-side papers to the western market, was looking for opportunities to expand its production of pulp and coated paper off the West Coast. "We were at the limit of our capacity at Shasta," Fannon recalled. "We had a large customer base that needed more coated products, and in order to maintain that base, we had to provide growth." The Company also wanted to expand its coated paper business in the Midwest and on the East Coast by buying another integrated mill with coated paper facilities. So the Company made a successful proposal to Champion to acquire the Pasadena mill – Simpson's biggest competitor in label paper – which became its largest paper acquisition.

Simpson's "SWAT" team descended upon the mill and liked what it saw. Champion had invested about $40 million to improve some of its basic components. The recovery boiler, the heart and most expensive part of a pulp mill, was in good shape. The mill was capable of making basically the same kinds of paper that Simpson made at Shasta, but because of the product mix, its average sales return was well below Shasta's.

The mill, which Simpson renamed "San Jacinto," expanded the Company's capacity for coated paper from 85,000 tons in January 1987 to 215,000, and extended distribution eastward. Simpson could then compete in coated paper against such major national players as Consolidated, Warren and Potlatch. Walt Duignan recalled, "before the Pasadena purchase, we determined that 60 percent of the merchants would probably support our national move, which would put us in good shape. In fact, 85 percent to 90 percent of the merchants supported us."

The San Jacinto Mill, located in Pasadena, Texas, was purchased from its builder, Champion International, in 1987. Champion had selected the site for its access to rail and marine transportation, available labor and proximity to the pine stands in East Texas.

Simpson's Plainwell Mill first produced paper in 1886. In 1954, it became part of the Hamilton Paper Company and was, for a time, a sister to the Valley Forge Mill.

The Centennial Mill, located in Gilman, Vermont, was purchased by Simpson in 1990 from Georgia-Pacific Corp.

Plainwell

Simpson's next expansion opportunity came in the form of the Plainwell Paper Company, just 30 miles north of Vicksburg on the banks of the Kalamazoo River.

Plainwell began life in 1886 as the Michigan Paper Company. Its 28-acre location was ideal for producing paper because of abundant water, proximity to Chicago, Detroit and the Great Lakes, and availability of raw materials. For most of its life, the mill had made fine white papers on a 76-inch Harper Fourdrinier machine. In 1954, the mill was sold to the Hamilton Paper Company and was, for a time, a sister to Simpson's Valley Forge Mill when it was also owned by Hamilton. Plainwell went through a series of ownership changes, from Weyerhaeuser to Philip Morris Incorporated to Chesapeake Corporation, before it was acquired by Simpson in December 1987. Together with Valley Forge and Harding-Jones, Plainwell became Simpson's third 100-year-old mill in seven years.

Plainwell brought to Simpson three paper machines – with an annual capacity of 85,000 tons, including 45,000 tons of coated paper – to produce premium coated and uncoated papers and technical specialty papers, such as supercalendered "release" paper – the backing for the sticky surfaces of name tags and countless other pressure-sensitive products – which complements Simpson's regular label papers.

With the acquisitions of San Jacinto and Plainwell, Simpson became a broad-based national supplier of virtually all varieties of high-quality paper – text and cover papers, coated paper, cotton fiber, commodity offset, technical and business papers.

Simpson was able to accomplish this by having the right strategy at the right time – and a lot of luck. With the pulp and paper industry consolidating at a rapid pace and the price of mills going up, Simpson "couldn't do today what we did when we acquired San Gabriel and Valley Forge," said Thurston Roach. "Most of our acquisitions have been discounted from the fixed-asset value. Today, the best we could do is book value."

Growth brings with it, of course, new challenges, including what Moseley called "the single biggest question: How do we stay nimble and quick? In this industry, there is almost an inverse relationship between size and financial performance. The bigger you get, the harder it is to continue to perform well."

Centennial

Not all purchases came about through careful courtships and methodical assessments. Around February 1, 1990, Furman Moseley received a phone call from Georgia-Pacific Corp. (G-P), asking if Simpson would be interested in purchasing G-P's Gilman, Vermont, paper mill.

Located on the banks of the Connecticut River in northeast Vermont, the mill made safety paper, a specialty treated paper for checks, securities certificates and other documents that need to be protected against forgery. It also produced diazo paper, which is used for engineering drawings and blueprints, and strippable wallpaper substrate grades of paper.

At the time of the call, G-P was in the midst of trying to acquire Great Northern Nekoosa Corp. Great Northern was arguing that G-P's presence in the safety paper business would give the merged company 80 percent of that business and open up potential antitrust allegations.

On February 12, Simpson and G-P signed a definitive agreement for Simpson to buy the Vermont mill, a converting plant in Burlington, Iowa, and two wet process machines and a precision sheeter from G-P's Warwick, New York, mill. The acquisition opened the door to new distributors for Simpson, which had, practically overnight, become a major supplier to a new, though small, market. The mill was named the Centennial Mill in recognition of the Company's 100th year.

A week later, Great Northern Nekoosa accepted G-P's bid, creating the nation's largest forest products company.

In August 1990, Simpson Paper Company signed a letter of intent to purchase the James River Corporation coated paper mill in West Linn, Oregon, about 12 miles south of Portland. (The acquisition was expected to be finalized after the publication of this book but before the end of 1990.)

By the time of Simpson's Centennial, Bill Reed's faith and persistent pursuit of the wood fiber business had been justified. The Company operated 10 pulp and/or paper mills, which annually produced nearly 2 million tons of wood fiber products and represented about 67 percent of Simpson's total business.

South of the Equator

Since the day Mark Reed first negotiated a contract with the Japanese for Simpson squared hemlock, the Company has looked to international markets for its products. Later, Hal McClary expanded Simpson International's interest in both export and import.

In the 1980s, Simpson became a net seller of pulp, thanks to strong export markets in Pacific Rim countries such as Japan, Korea, Taiwan and China. Some of the production out of the San Jacinto Mill went to Mexico and Venezuela; Humboldt and Tacoma pulp products were sold principally in Asia.

The future of the pulp business rests in producers' access to forest resources. Moseley told the American Paper Institute in November 1989, "Man-made forests, with nature's acceptance, represent the third wave in the evolution of fiber use by our industry: from rags to natural forest riches to engineered, plantation-grown cellulose."

Traditionally, wood chips for the Paper Company's pulp mills have come primarily from Timber Company timberlands and softwood lumber and plywood operations in Northern California and Washington. But near the end of the 1980s, the Timber Company, under the direction of Dr. John L. Walker, vice president, land and timber, looked beyond its existing supply for hardwood resources, which are easier to bleach and produce better-formed papers. Simpson planted a 10,000-acre drip-irrigated "paper farm" eucalyptus plantation near Corning, in California's Sacramento Valley, to supply high-quality wood fiber for Shasta's pulp mill. In 1989, Walker oversaw the planting of 568 acres of gmelina trees at a plantation in Guatemala, where wood fiber grew at a rate more than double that in North American forests. Simpson first became acquainted with gmelina in the 1950s, when industrialist Daniel Ludwig asked Tom Gleed for Simpson's help in assessing the paper-making potential of gmelina. Ludwig subsequently planted large gmelina plantations along the Amazon River in Brazil, where the trees grew at a rate in excess of 600 cubic feet annually. Gmelina mature to pulpwood size in five to seven years and represented a substantial wood fiber source for Simpson's San Jacinto Mill, 1,250 miles north by barge. The Company planned expansion of its plantations to more than 18,000 acres by 1995.

In the summer of 1988, the Company announced its active return to Chile, after an absence of two decades, with a plan to build a "greenfield" pulp mill that would have a daily capacity of 900 metric tons of bleached softwood kraft market pulp, intended primarily for export to Europe and Asia, following its start-up in 1991. The $600 million state-of-the-art mill was a 50/50 joint venture between Simpson Latin America, Ltd., and Compania Manufacturera de Papelas y Cartones S.A. (CMPC), the largest pulp and paper producer in Chile – and a company in which Simpson had held a significant minority ownership position since 1972. Thurston Roach was the president of Simpson Latin America, Ltd., and Pat Hassett, formerly Tacoma Kraft executive vice president, was vice president of the project. The mill, operated by a Chilean company, Celulosa del Pacifico S.A., was known as CelPac.

The mill, located in the small community of Mininco, about 400 miles south of Santiago, was designed to use radiata pine pulpwood from CMPC plantations. Radiata pine, which grown rapidly in Chile, yields high-quality, long-fibered raw material. The mill was also designed to manufacture hardwood pulp from the CMPC/Simpson joint-venture eucalyptus plantations, which were planted to yield more than 350 cubic feet of fiber per acre annually, compared to about 145 cubic feet from the average North American coastal Douglas fir site.

These fast-growing trees, produced in third-world countries by international forest products companies, represent a counterargument to the subject of tropical deforestation. By using up carbon dioxide and giving off oxygen, the trees help to counteract global warming, or the greenhouse effect.

The CelPac project was the result of an innovative financing package in which a group of international banks participated in a debt-to-equity conversion program. The banks and Simpson acquired U.S. dollar-denominated Chilean debt obligations and, through the Central Bank of Chile, converted the dollars to pesos, at a premium. These funds were invested in CelPac preferred stock. At the end of 10 years, investors have the right to repatriate their capital and accumulated dividends. This single transaction reduced Chile's total foreign debt by more than 2 percent.

In an interview 10 years before, Bill Reed had predicted that Simpson would one day make another stab at a major involvement in Chile. He never could have predicted that when the Company returned, it would be as a principal in one of the biggest private-capital industrial developments in the history of Chile.

Cogeneration

Simpson has generated electric power since 1926, when it co-owned and operated Shelton's Joint Power Operation Plant, which was fueled with scrap from the McCleary and Reed Mills.

The Crown Simpson Pulp Mill, which opened in 1964, became the Company's first cogeneration facility, which was defined by Simpson Director of Energy Wayne Meek as "any process that produces two forms of energy sequentially from one source of fuel." The Crown Simpson power plant used redwood scrap and bark – called "hog fuel" – from local mills to fuel its high pressure steam boiler, which turned a 20-megawatt turbine generator and supplied steam for use in the mill's pulping process. Before Crown Simpson was built, lumber mills had incinerated wood waste, which had filled the coastal air with smoke and ash.

With the success of the Crown Simpson power plant, the Company began planning additional self-generation facilities as a means of controlling its rising energy costs. In 1978, the Company's plans were accelerated with the passage of the federal Public Utility Regulatory Policies Act, which afforded private power producers an opportunity to sell electricity to local utilities and encouraged cogeneration. This reduced the need for building large, new public or private power facilities.

In 1983, Simpson built a cogeneration plant at its Shasta Mill. Its generator, which was turned with a natural gas-fueled 50,000-horsepower turbine jet engine, produced 36 megawatts of electricity, enough to furnish power for about 28,000 homes. Waste heat from the jet was used to convert water into steam for use in the mill. All of the plant's electricity was sold to Pacific Gas & Electric Company, which, in turn, resold it to Simpson and other PG&E customers.

The Shasta cogeneration plant was a technical and financial success, and in 1986, the Company built another cogeneration facility in Pomona at its San Gabriel Mill, which also produced 36 megawatts of electricity.

In 1988, the Company constructed a cogeneration plant at its Ripon Mill, which became the world's first full steam-injected power plant. Steam was injected into its General Electric LM 5000 turbojet engine, which improved the engine's efficiency and lowered the nitrous-oxide emissions. Ripon's generator had a capacity of 48 megawatts. Simpson joined three other San Joaquin County cogenerators and built a $19 million, 43-mile, high-voltage transmission line to the nearest Pacific Gas & Electric substation.

Including the San Jacinto Mill, which also produced electricity, the combined generating capacity of Simpson's power plants was 160 megawatts – enough to supply 125,000 homes.

Timber –
The Long-Term View

13

Timber –
The Long-Term View

Simpson Timber Company rode through a period of sporadic growth – partially propelled by inflation – from the mid 1960s through the end of the 1970s. National housing starts were running at over 2 million units a year, export markets were strong and the price of timberland was steadily rising. The consensus was that the boom would continue into the 1980s. Timber companies responded to the predicted demand for housing by feverishly bidding to buy stumpage on private, state and federal lands until the prices reached postwar peaks. From 1976 to 1980, the value of Douglas fir stumpage vaulted an incredible 145 percent, from $176 per thousand board feet to $432.[1]

Looking to utilize its second-growth timber, Simpson opened Sawmill Five in March, 1979. The $8.7 million mill could handle 11,000 pieces of wood a day, and convert logs, as small as four inches, and cores from the plywood mill into lumber. Hank Sandstrom, who was then vice president and general manager at Shelton, recalled, "We needed a facility to process the increasing volume of thinnings we were getting. Mill Five was a stud mill, and it put us into a major market segment in a big way."

The rosy predictions didn't pan out. By 1982, high interest rates and rampant inflation helped cut housing starts to almost 50 percent of recent highs, and Northwest wood products plunged into the greatest industry recession since the Great Depression. Stumpage prices shrank 25 percent from 1978 and 1979 highs. Commodity prices crumbled. With skyrocketing interest rates and a strong dollar, U.S. timber products were no longer competitive abroad, while rising operating costs made Northwest forest products less competitive at home. Many companies could not afford to harvest the timber they had purchased.[2]

"Buying timber at the top of the market in the late 1970s was a tough decision and a wrong decision," Gary Reed readily conceded. "Fortunately, unlike a lot of our small competitors, we never bought enough to jeopardize the Company."

In 1981 and 1982, Simpson ran at a loss and paid no dividend for the first time in more than 75 years. The Company took the lull in business to rethink its mission, which led to divesting itself of two subsidiary businesses. One was Simpson Building Supply Company, which distributed Simpson doors, plywood and lumber. The other was Simlog Leasing Company, a $125 million company that leased trucks and earth-moving equipment to Simpson Timber Company and other users.

In 1978, Simpson planted a Douglas fir orchard near Shelton, for producing genetically superior seed for nursery germination and replanting Company timberlands for future generations.

Gilbert L. Oswald

On January 1, 1983, after leading the Company for 13 years, Gil Oswald retired as president of Simpson Timber Company. Next to Mark Reed's 19 years, Oswald's tenure was the longest in the Company's history. He became its vice chairman until his retirement in 1984.

Oswald, a mechanical engineering graduate of Washington State University, concentrated on the productivity of Simpson's building products operations (which in 1978 represented about 73 percent of Company sales) and getting the right logs to the conversion facilities to maximize return. He served in a number of positions during his Simpson career, including vice president and general manager of Simpson Redwood, vice president of manufacturing, and vice president of the lumber and plywood group. He provided leadership in a number of industry trade associations, culminating as president and then chairman of the National Forest Products Association from 1977 to 1979. He was also active as a director of the World Forestry Center in Portland, Oregon.

Restructuring

In 1983, soon after Furman Moseley succeeded Oswald to become Simpson Timber Company's 10th president, record interest rates began to recede and housing starts began to rebound. But by this time, the Northwest wood products industry had fallen behind its southwestern U.S. and Canadian competition, which had increased its already major share of the U.S. softwood market.

Moseley decentralized management while continuing to close or sell off mills and properties that did not fit into the new corporate strategy. The Timber Company was restructured to become smaller and leaner, and its Northwest Operations concentrated on commodity lumber, its traditional strength.

In both Washington and California, Simpson was faced with an evolutionary change in its timber base – making the transition from the last of the large old-growth trees to second growth. The old sawmills had to be retrofitted with new equipment that could efficiently cut the smaller logs. Second-growth redwood's pronounced variation in color from old growth necessitated a completely different marketing strategy.

During the early 1980s, the entire industry lost one third of its mills in the pursuit of cost efficiency. Simpson reflected this trend by sharply reducing employment, through curtailments and an early retirement program. Laid-off workers were given as much as a year's notice, severance pay, and the assistance of comprehensive reemployment programs.

Simpson's second-growth stands were located on mostly flat terrain. Though flatland machinery did not replace fallers and chain saws, new equipment, such as this crawler-mounted, mandible-like hydraulic shear, proved to be both faster and safer for harvesting trees on level topography.

184

In 1985, Camp Grisdale, the last and the longest-running logging camp in the continental U.S., was closed. A ceremonial last logging train marked the finale of what writer Stewart Holbrook described in his book Far Corner as "one of the great sights daily at Camp Grisdale.... When the long train of great logs rolls past the town, pulled by a heavy mainline locomotive, bright with orange and green trimmings, her bell ringing, heading for the Shelton millpond..."

In 1970, Gilbert L. Oswald succeeded Hank Bacon as president of Simpson Timber Company. When he retired in January 1983, he had the second-longest presidential tenure in Company history. Only Mark E. Reed's 19-year presidency exceeded Oswald's time in office.

186

Simpson cut its overhead to a point where it could shut down during flat market periods and wait for business to improve and its trees to grow. The Company returned to profitability in 1983 and 1984, and the latter year's profits of $32.5 million on revenues of $823 million were third best in the Company's history.

Following the two-year improvement, timber prices collapsed in 1985. "Sawmills closed," wrote Dave James. "Small companies withered away into bankruptcy. Large corporations that had existed for decades, merged or sold out or scaled down to become shadows of what they had been. Hundreds of thousands of acres of Washington corporate timberland on the selling block went without buyers."[3]

Simpson's response to falling timber prices was to restructure its Shelton Working Circle operations and get out of logging high cost Forest Service timber.

The Timber Company closed its old-growth Sawmill Four and a planer mill in Shelton and trimmed its salaried and hourly payroll by 500 people. The Company also invested $24 million in mill modifications, it closed the McCleary Plywood Mill and consolidated its plywood production at the Olympic Plywood Mill, and it built a wood-fired power plant at Shelton.

By the end of the year, Simpson closed its two high country logging operations, Camp Govey and Camp Grisdale.

Camp Govey, in the Skokomish River drainage, was shut down after 30 years as a truck-operating and maintenance center – a "truck-fixin', saw-sharpenin', crew shufflin', log-shippin' workhorse," wrote Dave James. The Company transfer sites along the railroad – at Canyon River, Fir Creek, Vance Creek and Bingman Creek, where logs were loaded from trucks to railroad cars – were key links in the Grisdale-Govey system, "working places old loggers will remember as long as they recall yarders, loaders, and slack-line systems."[4]

Camp Grisdale, Simpson's CSYU logging headquarters in the south Olympic Mountains, was located on the same site for 40 years, the longest-standing, one-location woods operation in the continental United States. Its closure marked the end of community logging camps, which had been a way of life for many loggers in the U.S. since the 18th century.

The historical significance of Grisdale's closing was duly noted by the national media, which recorded in print and on videotape its final days, "the last loading of logs and poignant scenes of loggers' families moving from camp houses back to town," wrote James. "Today, the workers no longer go to camp. They live in neighborhoods or towns and ride to and from their daily jobs in cozy crew buses. They work in flatland country instead of in the steep mountains from which they retreated when Grisdale closed."[5]

It was fitting that the cleared site of Camp Grisdale was planted with seedlings to provide a new crop of timber for harvesting sometime in the 21st century.

The closing of Grisdale was the literal and symbolic gesture that personified the new reality of Simpson Timber Company. In 1980, Simpson Timber employed 4,225 workers, or 60 percent of Simpson Investment Company's total employment; by 1989, those figures had shrunk to 2,565 employees, or 32 percent.

"There is nothing left for us to do but tighten our chin straps and become more competitive," Moseley told a 1986 meeting of the Pacific Logging Congress. "If we have learned nothing else from these tough times we have relearned that the market is the master." Simpson's approach, he added, is to be "lean, flexible and alert to opportunities."[6]

At the same time, Simpson moved to the forefront of the industry in incentive bonus plans connected to improvements in productivity, quality and safety. By the end of 1989, these incentive plans covered the vast majority of employees.

In 1986, Moseley forecast "a future of better adventures and less adversity," in an article he wrote in *Pacific Northwest Executive* magazine. The Northwest's abundance of raw material and its capacity for growing high-quality softwood are advantages that "will become clear as we complete the shift from old-growth to young-growth trees that yield more chips per unit of lumber and generate better quality fiber products." And, he added, "because the harvestable trees are at lower elevations, the logging and hauling costs will be less, and reduced wood costs will once again become a Northwest strength."[7]

This outlook was confirmed over the next few years by increased demand for manufactured wood products and raw logs from both domestic and international markets, primarily the Pacific Rim. Export sales were also helped by the decline in value of the U.S. dollar.

A Growing Export Market

During the first half of the 1980s, Simpson did not aggressively pursue international markets because federal laws and the terms of the Shelton Cooperative Sustained Yield Unit "virtually restricted the Company from exporting even its own logs," recalled Gil Oswald.

The Company felt that the changing world and domestic markets for forest products necessitated an amendment to the 40-year-old CSYU agreement, which over the years had been altered by subsequent federal laws and regulations, and the government's changing objectives for the national forests.

The principal change sought by Simpson was the CSYU's so-called "80/20" rule. This regulation stipulated that a volume equal to 80 percent of the timber harvested in the unit had to be locally processed (within 10 miles of Shelton or McCleary), either by Simpson or another company. Simpson was allowed to dispense the other 20 percent of the logs in whatever way it saw fit, either through export or domestic sales.

Korbel Laboratory tissue culturist Dr. Kim Q. Doan.

Regenerating redwood tissue in a test-tube environment.

Once a standing redwood was selected as a superior tree, branch tip and root tissues were taken. The tissue cells went through a process of regeneration, first in test tubes, then petri dishes, then a nutrient-rich protected environment. When the clones of the parent tree matured into complete stem and root systems, they were moved from the laboratory environment to the nursery. Shown is tissue culture assistant Dorothy J. Bernardi.

By the mid 1970s, Simpson's redwood stands, though impressive in size, were few in number, and the Company began an intensive effort to develop superior trees for reforesting its cutover California timberlands.

(Next page) Redwood is stacked to air-dry in the coastal California breeze before it is manufactured into siding, fencing and decking lumber.

189

Since 1943, the Company has replanted more than 120 million seedlings and sown 60,000 pounds of seed on its California and Washington state timberlands. (A pound of Douglas fir seed contains about 45,000 potential trees, and redwood seed is even more prolific.)

Since 1973, a ban on export of logs from federal lands had been included annually in the Interior Appropriations bill. However, companies like Simpson that had purchased federal timber and exported their own timber from 1971 to 1973, were given an export quota based on historic practice. Ironically and unfortunately, Simpson's export markets had been weak during these three years, so the Company's assigned quota was only 8.5 million board feet (out of a cut of 220 million), or about 4 percent – rather than the 20 percent allowed by the CSYU agreement.

The Company was able to overcome the effects of this small quota in 1986, when it acquired, from Champion International, the Commencement Bay Mill in Tacoma, Washington. The transaction included Champion's export quota in the southern Puget Sound region of about 70 million board feet, which was combined with Simpson's Shelton quota of 8.5 million board feet.

This acquisition was the impetus for a dramatic, fundamental redirection. Log exports, primarily to Japan, were strong, and when the Company saw that it had an opportunity to export legally a larger volume (as long as it stayed within the 80/20 rule), recalled Timber Company President Tom Ingham, "we became more aggressive in buying private timber and/or logs in the southern Puget Sound region, so we would have enough total volume to still legally process domestically at least 80 percent of our fee harvest, and yet be able to export up to 78 million feet.

"That's what changed the ball game for us. We went from a net log seller to more of a net 'log merchandiser,' which includes selling logs in the best markets for the best value."

Ingham recalled that he didn't particularly want the Commencement Bay Mill. But, "once we agreed to the value, we asked, 'What do we have to do to make it work?' That was one of the healthiest things the management group went through. It forced us to become more creative. That laid the foundation from the 'Gee, ain't it awful' environment that we were coming from to 'Let's get on with it and figure out how to make it go.' We bought every log for that mill on the open market and learned how to compete with every other independent producer. Our first year was one of the best that mill ever had."

The use of historic log-export quotas was halted in August 1990, when President Bush signed the Customs and Trade Act of 1990. This legislation resulted primarily from reductions in U.S. Forest Service timber harvests in the Pacific Northwest, which Congress designated for non-timber uses, and the listing of the Northern Spotted owl as a "threatened" species – effective July 23, 1990. By 1995, under the new government policy Simpson's export of raw logs would drop to zero if it purchased federal timber, including that from the CSYU.

Maintaining Resources and the Environment

The evolution of the Pacific Northwest forest products industry prompted greater cooperation within the trade, as well as with other parties concerned with the region's greatest renewable natural resource. In 1985, Simpson and other companies joined with the Washington State Land Commissioner and the University of Washington's Center for International Trade in Forest Products to create the Evergreen

Partnership, a nonprofit corporation that was chartered to "identify policy needs, disseminate market information and serve as a forum for public discussion of forestry and forest products issues."

The following year, Simpson and other wood products companies united with environmentalists, government agencies and Indian tribes to devise the Timber/Fish/Wildlife Agreement, whose purpose was "to replace traditional legal confrontation and political pressuring for favorable regulatory clauses, with cooperative, collaborative management of the state's forest-related resources, with participation by all involved."[8]

The principal concerns of the pact were management of roads, riverbanks, upland areas, timber harvest and silviculture (production and maintenance of trees), as well as fish, wildlife, archaeological and cultural considerations. The agreement had jurisdiction over 17.7 million acres of commercial timberland in Washington, including lands controlled by the U.S. Forest Service, Department of Natural Resources, private individuals, the forest industry, Indian tribes and counties/cities. John Gorman, then Northwest resources manager, represented Simpson.[9]

Simpson had been observing many of these practices long before the Timber/Fish/Wildlife Agreement. In the early 1970s, the Company changed its method of road and landing construction within the CSYU. After soil was cut away, it was backhauled and stockpiled for reuse, instead of being shoved over the edge of fresh roadside banks. In both the Northwest and Redwood Operations, Simpson protected hillsides and streams that supported fish from damage caused by erosion.

Simpson had long believed that sound forestry began with fire prevention. The Company worked to protect the seedlings and maturing plantations that were its future timber supply. Back in 1941, with Simpson's encouragement, concerned citizens formed a "Keep Mason County Green" organization, which developed into a movement that spread statewide and nationwide. The Olympic Peninsula was also the birthplace of the Tree Farm program with Simpson among the earliest participants. By its centennial year, Simpson had reforested 241,937 acres in its California and Washington holdings, which had been planted with 120 million seedlings and sowed with 60,000 pounds of seed. The Company's long-term future wood supply outlook was bright because of forestry programs initiated 50 years ago.

Redwoods: The Park Land Settlement

Although efforts to "save the redwoods" date back to the Gold Rush days of the 1850s, Simpson and other redwood timberland owners faced intense pressure in the 1960s from preservationists and politicians to change their forestry practices and to curb cutting of old-growth redwood. Simpson argued that it had been a good citizen since it first entered the redwoods in 1948, when it began a policy of leaving timber along the banks of the Klamath River to preserve its scenic and recreational values. In 1968, Simpson made land available for California's Mad River Fish Hatchery and later for the building of a hatchery on Smith River in Del Norte County.

The Company's search for genetically superior redwood trees was directed by James Rydelius at the Korbel Research Nursery.

Simpson Timber Company's 1990 senior managers included (standing, from left) John L. Walker, vice president land and timber; Jess R. Drake, vice president and general manager – Northwest; James T. Brown, general manager – Arcata Redwood; and (seated, from left) Ronald R. Grant, vice president controller; Thomas R. Ingham, president; and David W. Kaney, general manager – Simpson Redwood.

During the 1980s, John Tylczak, in the spirit of Kinsey, traveled from camp to camp and mill to mill photographing men and women who made their living from the Pacific Northwest timberlands, including (on left) railroadmen Ross Gallagher, Frank Livingston and Bill Sylvester.

Tylczak's photographs included Sawmill Three filers (from left) David Whisnant, Lee Asche, Bob Oster, Vic Woodall and Bruce Maples.

196

That year, the United States Congress created the Redwood National Park, which included a legislative taking of approximately 6,000 acres of Simpson timberlands that had shared a 33-mile common border with the designated parkland. The agreement set a value of $4,933,850 on the Simpson land and timber, for which the Company received $783,850 in cash and 788 acres of government-owned land and timber in Del Norte County. Earlier, Simpson had acquired 809 acres of superlative old-growth redwoods adjacent to Jedediah Smith State Park, which it traded to the State of California for equivalent land and timber. [10]

Simpson's Vice President of Timberlands, Starr Reed, was chairman of the land committee representing the major California landholders. For his efforts, Reed was named the industry's outstanding leader on the park issue by the National Forest Products Association in Washington, D.C.

In 1978, despite hard-fought industry opposition, Congress enacted – and President Jimmy Carter signed – Public Law 95-250, which expanded Redwood National Park from 30,000 acres to about 76,000 acres. Again, by a legislative taking, the federal government acquired nearly 46,000 more acres of land (8,200 acres of Simpson, 10,700 acres of Arcata Redwood Company and 27,000 acres of Louisiana-Pacific Corp.) in Humboldt and Del Norte counties. Gil Oswald recalled, "The second taking took some awfully good second growth that was in an age group very important to Simpson. It affected the log-hauling route and we're not sure that we yet understand what the long-term impact will be." One result was to severely disrupt efforts of the industry to develop sustained yield redwood harvest plans. [11]

When the second taking was mandated, the price was to be set from the average of three cruises. However, the federal government did not agree with those results and arbitrarily set its own price. When the timber companies and the government could not agree on values, Simpson, Louisiana-Pacific and Arcata Redwood Company sued the government for additional compensation, a suit that would not be resolved for 10 years. (This was a pattern that also followed the creation of the original park in 1968.) Simpson ultimately received a cash payment of $49.8 million (before interest) on the second taking. The total cost to the taxpayers for the Redwood National Park expansion, which was originally estimated at $359 million in 1976 by the National Park Service, actually exceeded $1.5 billion. This made the park the most expensive of any of the nation's 49 national parks.

Forest Management

An important component of Simpson's sustained yield forest management program is reforestation, which encompasses the Company's efforts to improve and accelerate the natural tree-growing process.

From the early 1950s to the late 1960s, Simpson's redwood holdings (most of which were cutover lands that were purchased for their second-growth potential) became part of California's largest-ever private reforestation program, which protected and maintained those properties as a long-term source of timber. This was done in conjunction with the Company's transition into second-growth timber.

Simpson built near Korbel the largest private forestry laboratory in California for the study of forest soils and their influence on tree growth. Working closely with the University of California at Davis and the Humboldt County Agricultural Extension office, Simpson plunged into experimental projects for improving forestry methods and productivity of the land, including cell regeneration for cloning superior trees, the planting of superior tree seedlings, fertilization, proper tree spacing, and protection from fire, insects and disease. In the process, the Company more than doubled nature's own rate of wood growth.

Simpson's efforts at reforesting, until the middle of the 1970s, included sowing seeds by helicopter over thousands of acres. But this process was eventually abandoned because it was expensive and inefficient, produced inconsistent (either overly dense or overly sparse) stands, and didn't contribute to the genetic improvement of trees or control over the composition of species.

Instead, the Company concentrated on the annual hand-planting of millions of tree seedlings, which were grown in the controlled environment of a nursery that Simpson built in Korbel in 1975. In 10 months, the nursery's irrigated crop of baby trees grew from seed to six-inch seedlings and were ready for forest planting.

Using tissue culture processes developed at the University of California at Irvine, Company forester James Rydelius and his staff were able to put genetically superior redwood cell-sized tissue stock in test tubes filled with nutrient-dosed growing material, where each cell generated shoots, needles and roots. Although tissue culture was not in commercial use at Simpson by 1990, it offered much promise and the Company's research was continuing.

Near Anderson, California – a hot, dry area out of the natural range of redwood – the Company's 50-acre orchard produced families of superior "plus" redwoods that were duplicated by collecting the tips of branches for grafting to mature root stock.

In late 1978, Simpson established a Douglas fir tree seed orchard on a 55-acre site near Shelton. With genetically superior stock, trees were bred for improved height, volume, straightness, diameter and rate of growth. In 1989, the first improved seedlings to come out of the Shelton seed orchard were planted on Simpson lands.

"We used to manage for a 100-year rotation," said Dr. Joseph L. Weber, Simpson's geneticist-silviculturist at Shelton. "Now, it is 40 to 50 years. In 1987, we completed the first harvest in a Douglas fir timber stand that was planted just 30 years ago."

Thomas R. Ingham, Jr.

In December 1985, Moseley became president of Simpson Investment Company, a holding company for its timber, paper, plastic pipe and other units. He was succeeded as president of Simpson Timber Company by Thomas R. Ingham, Jr., a home-grown employee who had most recently been vice president and general manager – Northwest. Ingham, a native of Olympia, and an accounting/economics graduate of the University of Puget Sound, began with the Company as a management trainee in 1964, and rose through sales and manufacturing in Simpson's Northwest and Redwood Operations. Although his father was a first cousin of Bill Reed's and a partner in the Reed Ingham Olympia Oyster Company, Tom Ingham never used his middle name, Reed, in any Simpson documentation because, he said, "I felt it was better to earn my own spurs."

Ingham sat on the Timber Company board, along with Gary Reed, Moseley and Roach. Ingham's management included Jess Drake, vice president and general manager – Northwest; Ronald Grant, vice president controller; John L. Walker, vice president land and timber; David Kaney, general manager – Simpson Redwood; and James T. Brown, general manager – Arcata Redwood.

Timberlands

In 1990, many Washington and Oregon timber companies were faced with a dwindling supply of trees to log on private and public forestlands. Because most of the privately held old growth had been cut, timberland owners such as Simpson harvested mostly second-growth timber. Federal forests (which held most of the remaining stands of old growth) became less available because of increasing pressures to set aside more publicly owned forests for recreation and environmental protection for threatened or endangered species. In 1989, the northern spotted owl became a public symbol of the struggle among the various factions that debated about timber supply and the volume of trees to be harvested from public lands.

Simpson Timber Company, under Ingham, made several key moves to protect itself and to plan its long-range future in timber.

In 1988, Simpson Timber Company acquired 117,180 acres of immature second-growth western Oregon timberlands, on outstanding high-site ground, mostly in Tillamook and Lincoln counties, for approximately $50 million. This acquisition, from the Times Mirror Co., a Los Angeles-based media and information company, marked Simpson's reentry into the Oregon timberlands after a 20-year absence, and became the nucleus of a Simpson sustained yield forest that was planned for first production in about 2010.

Also in 1988, the Company acquired 78,000 acres, including additional stands of old-growth redwood contiguous with Simpson timberlands, with its purchase of the Arcata Redwood Company. Arcata Redwood came with fragmented and widely dispersed old-growth timberlands in the Klamath area and an old-growth sawmill at Orick, California. Arcata Redwood also operated a modern remanufacturing plant at Arcata, and had its own sales and marketing staff, which concentrated on old-growth umber sales. Old-growth redwood sold at a premium, but the size of the Company's harvest did not merit two old-growth sawmills. Furthermore, because Arcata Redwood's Orick sawmill and its Arcata remanufacturing plant were newer and more efficient, Simpson chose to shut down its old-growth mill at Klamath and its remanufacturing plant in Arcata and focus its attention on second-growth production at Korbel. This move signaled Simpson Redwood Company's exit from the old-growth business.

The Arcata acquisition "allowed us to broaden our whole land base, to be able to spread the operations out over time, get a larger total harvest," Ingham explained.

In 1988, the land base of the Shelton CSYU grew through acquisition more than in any other year since 1954. Simpson added 9,822 acres in Mason and Grays Harbor counties, bringing the total acreage in the CSYU to 361,273 – 111,240 acres belonging to the U.S. Forest Service and 250,033 to Simpson. The Company and the Washington Department of Natural Resources exchanged 47,459 acres in the CSYU and other areas of the state in order to consolidate both Simpson's and the state's holdings and to allow for more cost-efficient resource management. Simpson received 29,956 acres of immature timber in Mason, Grays Harbor and Thurston counties. Since the establishment of the CSYU in 1946, the only additions to its land base were made by Simpson; the U.S. Forest Service never added to the Shelton sustained yield land base.

The strict terms of the Shelton CSYU presented both advantages and disadvantages to Simpson. By pooling the CSYU old-growth and second-growth inventories into one management unit, the Company was able to make a smooth transition to a second-growth economy while waiting for those stands to mature to merchantable size. Although the CSYU had never really been profitable, it did provide cash flow, maintained business levels at Shelton and McCleary, and it represented stability to Simpson's lenders and work force.

"The bothersome thing is that nothing ever stays the same," said Ingham. "The conditions in the agreement have been altered over the years through either federal law changes or the regulatory climate, but the terms of the agreement haven't changed. That's where we have a very fundamental issue with our partner, the Forest Service. Any agreement needs to change with the times. The federal government is the one who is making up the new rules and we don't have much to say about that. People think that when we say we want to amend the agreement, that means we want to exit from the area. Nothing could be farther from the truth."

Simpson's total timberland holdings on the West Coast reached 780,000 acres – compared to the total of 30,000 largely cutover acres the Company held at the time of Mark Reed's death in 1933.

Family Trees

14

Family Trees

In 1984, William Garrard Reed, Sr., retired from the board of directors of Simpson Timber Company. Bill was named a director emeritus, giving him the privileges of directorship without the responsibility.

During his nearly half a century with the Company, Bill had grown from a too-wise Harvard Business School student who recommended that his father liquidate the Company to a canny, courageous entrepreneur/investor who overcame the deaths of his father and brothers to build Simpson far beyond their dreams. He delegated operational responsibilities to trusted managers. He diversified Simpson into pulp and paper, plywood, doors, chemicals and plastics and expanded its horizons to the redwoods, Canada and Chile. He recognized and encouraged Furman Moseley's talents just as Sol Simpson had Mark Reed's. And he groomed his son, Gary, to expand upon his vision, just as Bill's father had done for him. The line continued.

"He didn't have to do what he did," observed friend Charles M. Pigott, chairman of PACCAR Inc. "It would have been very easy for him to enjoy his considerable fortune and liquidate his companies, but that was not Bill Reed. He is proof that it isn't what your last name is, nor how you get to be head of a company, that counts; it is what you do when you get there."

Bill served on several boards of directors, including PACCAR, Seattle-First National Bank, The Boeing Company, Safeco Insurance Company of America and Northern Pacific Railroad. At board meetings, Bill always impressed Pigott with his "ability to see a side of a problem that would not necessarily occur to the rest of us."

Bill's personal business ethics were as much a part of his legacy as the next seedling planted by Simpson foresters. Gary Reed sheepishly recalled the time he raised the ire of his father by suggesting Simpson skirt an ethical line. This episode occurred in the early 1970s, when an East Coast grand jury was investigating charges of price fixing among pulp sellers. Simpson believed that it was innocent of any complicity (and was later proved so). Preparing for the initial inquiry, the Company came across an internal memo on the subject, written by a Simpson salesman, which could have been misinterpreted. "I told Dad that it would be so easy to remove the memo. Dad said, 'We do not destroy evidence!' I felt his heavy hand there and I have always been embarrassed that I even thought about it."

Tom Ingham observed that a strong sense of corporate ethics was a prerequisite for managing Simpson affairs. "We don't shut down operations willy-nilly. We agonize over proactive solutions, perhaps to a fault."

In the beginning, Sol Simpson was a contract logger who began the Company practice of retaining cutover land. By its centennial, Sol's company owned and managed 780,000 acres in Washington, Oregon and California.

Bill was a spiritual man, in a "reserved, traditional way," noted his daughter Susan Reed Moseley. A long-time senior warden at Seattle's Epiphany Parish, Bill possessed, in Susan's words, "a strong faith and a willingness to risk things, all based on an acceptance that life is good, that it was a gift and that he was a steward."

A special part of that stewardship were the employees of Simpson who lived and worked in Shelton, where Bill always kept his voting address. Irene S. Reed High School, Sol G. Simpson Library and the William G. Reed Library (dedicated in 1989) typified the family's generosity in Shelton, which Gary Reed described as "Simpson's roots."

After his retirement, Bill devoted some of his energy to the Matlock Foundation, a charitable fund that traditionally provided grant money for institutions and organizations in communities where Simpson has operations. The family members continued to be actively involved in their community and to contribute time and money to a variety of nonprofit organizations that ran the gamut from environmental to health care to arts and education.

Certainly, men and women in Bill Reed's position were expected to donate their share to worthy causes, but Reed literally and metaphorically gave more than his share. He had always been troubled that the fates had taken away his siblings and that he, the survivor, inherited everything. "I have had a special motivation to give money away for philanthropic purposes," he once noted. "I felt I deserved only one third of the family estate."

Bill ultimately fulfilled his objective "to give away property equal in value to what I had inherited from Frank, with the proviso that I wouldn't give away Simpson stock because I wanted to keep the family control of Simpson for my children's generation."

Regrettably, Bill contracted Alzheimer's disease in the early 1980s and died at 81 on October 20, 1989. His illness prevented him from fully appreciating the rewards of his vision and the accomplishments of the Company and its employees under the leadership of Gary Reed and Furman Moseley.

Family Ownership

Although the Reeds long maintained the controlling interest in Simpson, they never owned quite all of its stock. Over the course of time, shares of the heirs of the Alfred H. Anderson estate had been dispersed through marriage, divorce settlements, gifts and sales to investors; some of those owners disposed of shares in an ever-increasing outside market for Simpson stock.

The CelPac complex, scheduled to begin production in the fall of 1991, was built at Mininco, about 400 miles south of Santiago, Chile. It included a 900-metric-ton pulp mill, employee housing, a school, mercantile and a hospital.

Simpson entered the pulp and paper business in 1926, when Mark Reed invested in the Rainier Pulp & Paper Company in Shelton. By 1990, Simpson produced pulp at 4 locations, including the Humboldt Pulp Mill, Tacoma Kraft Mill, San Jacinto Mill, and the Shasta Mill. In its centennial year the Company's pulp mills produced 335,000 air-dried metric tons of pulp beyond that required to source its paper mills.

The Celulosa del Pacifico S.A. (CelPac) 1990 management group included (from left) Project Controls Manager Fernando Ramirez; Mill Manager Ricardo Wainer; Project Vice President Patrick Hassett; General Manager Antonio Larrain; Finance Manager Pedro Iriberry; Technical Manager Eugenio Grohnert; and, Procurement Manager Carlos Torretti.

203

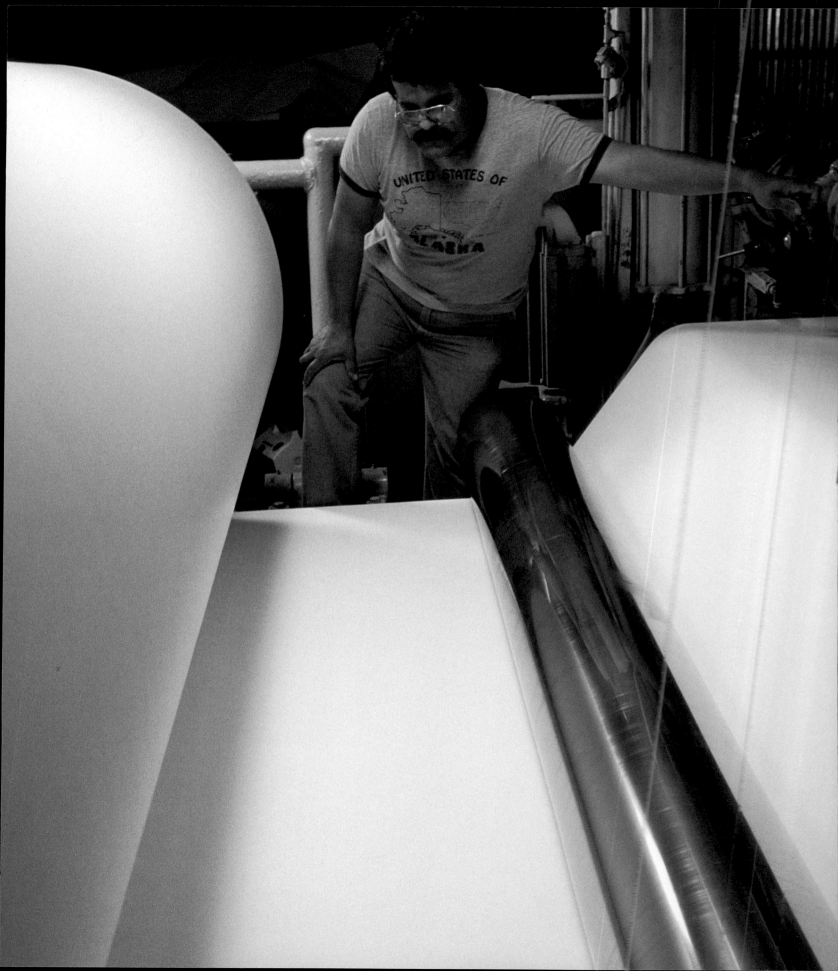

For many years, Bill tried to buy out all non-family shareholders. At the end of 1969, 85 percent of the outstanding shares of Simpson stock were controlled by Simpson Reed & Company or its partners, namely the five members of the William G. Reed family. The balance of the Company's stock was held by outside stockholders. Simpson, which was essentially a private company, felt that having to make financial disclosures to a few outside shareholders was an unfair burden that potentially could provide crucial information to its competitors.

In a March 13, 1970, letter, Reed informed "Certain Stockholders of the Simpson Timber Company" that Simpson would not be increasing its dividends and that the majority shareholders "believe that it is more important to maintain Simpson's competitive size and strength while keeping the corporate debt within safe limits." As to whether the Company would ever be merged, sold or liquidated and whether the shares would be listed on a stock exchange, Reed wrote, "All of these events are unlikely, for the Company believes that its independent growth will bring benefits to stockholders, customers, suppliers, employees, governments, and other members of the communities of which it is a part."[1]

By 1974, the number of shareholders of the Timber Company who were not heirs of the founders or Company executives had dwindled to 25. That year, Simpson devised a reverse, 1-for-10 stock split, which reduced the 50,000 authorized shares to 5,000. (Those who held fractional shares were not allowed votes.) The reason for the reverse split, the Company announced, was that it no longer needed to maintain the 50,000 shares, and that the Reed family had established a series of trusts designed to maintain and increase family ownership of the Company for at least the next several generations.

Bill Reed hoped that move would prompt the sale of the remaining shares by the minority shareholders, whom he believed were only speculators. In fact, some of them were on record as believing that a death in the family would force the Reeds to take Simpson public in order to pay taxes.[2]

These shareholders did not know that Bill Reed, acutely aware of the tax implications, had dispersed stock within the family so that his death would not become a tax burden. In addition, the family planned to transfer the shares owned by the family and the trusts to a family holding company. In a 1974 letter to stockholders Reed wrote, "The family has no need, desire or intent for the Company to become publicly held. The family has sufficient liquid assets to avoid selling Company stock to the public to pay estate and inheritance taxes."[3]

Minority stockholders were offered $807 per share until June 30, 1974. After that date, the price of stock would be subject to a performance formula that, computed at the time, would have priced shares at $777 each.

Not surprisingly, that action got the shareholders' attention. One shareholder had written to Reed for his reaction to her broker's opinion that Simpson stock was "substantially undervalued." He wrote back that "many people have different notions of value," but he felt that Simpson was of comparable value

It took a crew of four to run the Ripon Mill paper machine. Shown is Fourth Hand Joe Loya, who assisted the third hand at the winder and inspected paper for any imperfection.

to competitors that were already publicly traded, such as Pope & Talbot, Southwest Forest Industries and Bohemia, Incorporated. In response to his correspondent's "interesting question" on why the stock would be a good investment for the Reed family and a poor one for outsiders, Reed wrote,

> *I can say that my attachment to the Company, and I believe that of the members of my family, goes far beyond ordinary business considerations. Perhaps some people would call it emotional. Simpson was founded by my grandfather, developed by my father, managed for 40 years by my brother and myself, and is now headed by my son. I was born and reared within sight of its operations and have spent all my life in it. I think it is truly a family company...* [4]

For those reasons, Bill confessed his difficulty in answering the question of value because "you may be thinking only in economic terms, whereas I am thinking also in family and personal terms. Perhaps it is a little like saying that I am more interested in my own children than I am in the children of strangers."

Ten years went by and the Reed family had secured control of 98.3 percent of the 3,792 outstanding shares. According to Washington state law, if fewer than five percent of the shares are in public hands, a company can retire them at fair market value. On July 11, 1984, Simpson's Senior Vice President, Finance, Robert Hutchinson wrote to outside shareholders and offered them $75,000 a share. Some agreed, but the owners of the remaining shares held out for a better offer.

Finally, on July 11, 1988, after a month-long trial, Simpson agreed to pay $7.4 million, or $197,500 per share – $97,500 for "fair value" and $100,000 in interest and legal fees. For the first time, the descendants of Sol Simpson completely owned the Company.

During this period, the corporate name of Simpson Timber Company was changed to Simpson Investment Company (which it had been called in Sol Simpson's lifetime) and it became the holding company for the timber, paper, plastics and other operations. The Investment Company's board of directors included Gary Reed, Furman Moseley, Bob Hutchinson and Gil Oswald. The fifth board member was Eleanor Reed, who was described by her son, Gary, as someone with "a wonderful sense about people and very good insight into how they operate."

The Family Business

The family business, wrote *The New York Times*, "is being rediscovered as the embodiment of the management practices and business values needed to help the nation's industries regain their competitive edge." The article, and others in a 1986 series on the subject, cited family companies' commitments to product quality, fair treatment of employees and the long term – a set of values that some felt Japan had

Simpson's primary means of reforesting its California Timberlands consisted of planting 440 seedling trees to the acre. Shown is Simpson Redwood Timberlands Manager Lou Blaser inspecting sprouts from freshly cut stumps, a secondary and natural means of redwood reforestation.

(Next page) By 1990, Simpson had become one of the most sophisticated tree-growing companies in the industry, cultivating sustained yield production of more than 780,000 acres in Washington, Oregon and California.

The 1990 Simpson Investment Company board included (from left) President (retired) Gilbert L. Oswald; Chairman Wm. G. Reed, Jr.; Eleanor Henry Reed; President Furman Moseley; and Senior Vice President, Finance (retired) Robert B. Hutchinson.

Simpson Investment Company's 1990 senior managers included (from left) Vice President and Chief Financial Officer J. Thurston Roach; Vice President and Treasurer Robert J. Day; Vice President, Human Resources Cynthia P. Sonstelie; Vice President, Investments Allen E. Symington; Vice President and General Counsel Joseph R. Breed; and Vice President, Public Affairs Joseph L. Leitzinger.

210

cultivated and that many American firms had ignored or neglected. The series also pointed out that "America's infatuation with the entrepreneur has turned family business…into respectable places to work."[5]

Moseley believed that family ownership has "never been bad, it's only recently become fashionable. We can get wonderful management people because we can compensate them in ways that you can't do in a publicly-owned company. We pay for success and we're happy to do it."

With the exception of Arcata Redwood's old growth, none of Simpson's most recent transactions were made for immediate payback. Simpson, unlike some publicly traded timber companies, calculated its return in terms of decades rather than immediate profits. "This is why publicly owned companies are willing to sell things to us," said Gary. "We are able to look at a very long-range future and not worry at all about the impact on next quarter's or next year's earnings. We know that these will be excellent investments."

Simpson didn't have to grow merely for the sake of adding sales dollars. Acquisitions were motivated by opportunities that the management of the Paper, Timber and Plastics Companies identified as important from a competitive point of view – such as supporting a product. "I am not dreaming of acquisitions and great things to do," Gary admitted. "I am very much involved as a final decision maker, but I am not trying to do anything more than challenge Mo's view of the future and make sure that it is sound."

Family-owned businesses are vulnerable to inbred and homogeneous thinking. "You need to have the discipline that comes from outside directors poking holes in your ideas," said Moseley.

Simpson Paper Company's 1990 board consisted of Gary Reed, Furman Moseley, John Fannon, Bob Seidl and three outside directors – Whitney MacMillan, chairman of Cargill, Inc., a grain storage, marketing and shipping company, which in 1990 was the largest privately held firm in the U.S.; Jorge Ross, a Chilean businessman, who joined the board in 1976; and H. G. (Pat) Pattillo of Pattillo Construction Co., Inc., Decatur, Georgia. MacMillan offered the board a broad perspective on global resource movement and offshore investment. Ross contributed insights into Chile and Simpson's business in South America. Pattillo, the Company's newest outside director, brought to the board a well-schooled understanding of business and risk management associated with expansion.

Family Responsibility

As Bill relinquished the reins of the Company, Gary assumed greater responsibility over family affairs. Susan Moseley observed that, although "Gary hasn't had to deal with the tragedy that my father has had in his life, Gary has assumed the responsibility that comes with this position with grace and enthusiasm. He and my father are much more alike than different. They are both anchors for the family."

Gary was the only male descendant of Sol Simpson because his young cousins, the children of Frank and Georgine Reed, had all perished in that tragic fire in 1942. Throughout his early life, Gary was keenly sensitive to that twist of fate. He once confided to his father that he carried a sense of guilt because all of the potential contenders for his job had died. Bill eased his son's conscience when he explained that he had arranged, before the accident, to acquire Frank's interest in Simpson Logging Company.

Moseley shared that same sense of family – particularly as it related to the action of the Company. "I can think of a couple of instances where, if I had been running a paper company that was publicly held and only my job was at risk, I would have made a different decision – as opposed to risking the wealth of my children and that of their cousins, aunts, uncles and grandparents."

Many privately owned companies are forced to pay out more for dividends as the number of family members grows, and they eventually sell when those dividends are no longer sufficient. Gary speculated that "eventually Simpson could go public because of the geometric way that families grow, and the possibility that we won't be employing all the family members. We can expand only by internally generated funds and borrowings. As families get older, they want to manage down the debt, so that limits the opportunity."

Management succession, a consideration for all companies, can be a particularly thorny one for family-owned firms. According to *The New York Times,* "only 30 percent of family businesses survive their founders and make it into the second generation" and only 50 percent of those survivors will continue as family businesses into the third or fourth generations. Simpson must constantly evaluate whether its present structure makes "good sense or whether we're making sacrifices disproportionate to the rewards," said Gary. [6]

The quest for fulfillment, more than money for money's sake, has long been a goal of the descendants and successors of Sol Simpson, Mark Reed and Bill Reed. At the root of their interests was a unified desire to do well while doing good, by providing jobs, manufacturing needed products, enriching lives and taking care of the land for the generations to come.

Jorge Ross, who has observed Simpson from the inside and outside since 1962, aptly summarized this remarkable transgenerational centennial saga: "People sometimes wonder if you can be successful in business without being greedy, without being cocksure of yourself and without stepping on other people's toes. The answer is that you can. The proof is the story of Simpson."

Simpson Investment Company Chairman Gary Reed (left) and President Furman Moseley.

Appendices

Officers and Directors

Simpson Investment Company

Chairman:
Wm. G. Reed, Jr.
1985 - present

President:
F. C. Moseley
1985 - present

Directors:
R. B. Hutchinson
1985 - present
G. L. Oswald
1985 - present
F. C. Moseley
1985 - present

Eleanor H. Reed
1985 - present
Wm. G. Reed, Jr.
1985 - present
W. G. Reed (Emeritus)
1985 - 1989

Simpson Timber Company

Chairman:
W. G. Reed
1946 - 1971
Wm. G. Reed, Jr.
1971 - present

President:
Sol G. Simpson
1890 - 1906
Alfred H. Anderson
1906 - 1913
Mark E. Reed
1914 - 1932
Frank C. Reed
1933 - 1942
W. G. Reed
1943 - 1945
C. H. Kreienbaum
1946 - 1948
W. G. Reed
1949 - 1950

Thomas F. Gleed
1951 - 1961
C. Henry Bacon, Jr.
1962 - 1970
G. L. Oswald
1970 - 1982
F. C. Moseley
1983 - 1985
T. R. Ingham, Jr.
1986 - present

Directors:
Sol G. Simpson
1895 - 1906
Alfred H. Anderson
1895 - 1913
James Campbell
1895 - 1904
J. A. Campbell
1900 - 1904
C. E. Holmes
1900 - 1904

Mark E. Reed
1905 - 1933
A. B. Govey
1914 - 1942
Frank C. Reed
1930 - 1942
Katheryn Wilson
1933 - 1960
A. E. Hillier
1933 - 1949
W. G. Reed
1933 - 1977
1980 - 1984
(Emeritus)
1985 - 1989
C. H. Kreienbaum
1941 - 1962
Thomas F. Gleed
1943 - 1970
Helen Bunn
1947 - 1950

Chapin Henry
1947 - 1948
1959 - 1972
Eleanor H. Reed
1949 - 1985
J. A. Priest
1951
C. Henry Bacon, Jr.
1962 - 1979
Wm. G. Reed, Jr.
1962 - present
F. C. Moseley
1970 - present
G. L. Oswald
1970 - 1985
R. B. Hutchinson
1978 - 1985
T. R. Ingham, Jr.
1986 - present
J. L. Roach
1986 - present

Simpson Lee Paper Company/Simpson Paper Company

Chairman:
W. G. Reed
1959 - 1967
F. C. Moseley
1969 - present

President:
Thomas F. Gleed
1959
Maxwell D. Bardeen
1959 - 1967
Malcolm McVickar
1968 - 1970
F. C. Moseley
1971 - 1973
R. J. Seidl
1974 - 1979

J. J. Fannon
1980 - present

Directors:
W. G. Reed
1959 - 1984
(Emeritus)
1985 - 1989
Thomas F. Gleed
1959 - 1966
C. Henry Bacon, Jr.
1959 - 1979
C. H. Kreienbaum
1960 - 1962
Maxwell D. Bardeen
1960 - 1968

Norman Bardeen
1960 - 1965
Merrill W. Taylor
1960 - 1963
John C. Howard
1960 - 1972
Wm. G. Reed, Jr.
1963 - present
Albert A. Christian
1964 - 1965
Elliot L. Ludvigsen
1966 - 1978
George V. Powell
1966 - 1980
Fred C. Lake
1967

Malcolm McVickar
1968 - 1970
F. C. Moseley
1969 - present
R. J. Seidl
1975 - present
Jorge Ross O.
1976 - present
J. J. Fannon
1980 - present
Whitney MacMillan
1980 - present
H. G. Pattillo
1988 - present

Pacific Western Extruded Plastics Company

Chairman:
Wm. G. Reed, Jr.
1972 - present

President:
G. L. Oswald
1972 - 1981

J. K. Rash
1982 - present

Directors:
Wm. G. Reed, Jr.
1972 - present
G. L. Oswald
1972 - 1982

R. B. Hutchinson
1972 - 1984
F. C. Moseley
1983 - present
J. K. Rash
1983 - present
J. T. Roach
1985 - present

Calendar of Significant Events

1890 – Sol. G. Simpson formed S. G. Simpson & Company, Matlock, Washington.

1895 – Simpson Logging Company was incorporated, along with, Peninsular Railway Company, the Satsop Railroad Company and Puget Sound and Grays Harbor Railroad Company.

1925 – Reed Mill opened.

1927 – Reed Shingle Mill opened.

1941 – Simpson Logging Company acquired Henry McCleary Timber Company.

1943 – Simpson Logging Company acquired Olympic Plywood Company, Shelton.

1945 – Simpson Logging Company entered the redwoods with the purchase of Requa Timber Company, Del Norte County, California.

1946 – Simpson Logging Company and U. S. Forest Service signed the 100-year Shelton Cooperative Sustained Yield Unit (CSYU) agreement.

1947 – Simpson Insulating Board Plant opened.

1948 – Simpson acquired Coast Redwood Company, Klamath, California.

1951 – Simpson acquired the Everett (Washington) Pulp & Paper Company.

1954 – Simpson Redwood Company founded.

1955 – Simpson Logging Company acquired Schafer Brothers Logging Company, Aberdeen, Washington.

1956 – Simpson Redwood Company acquired the Sage Land and Lumber Company, Klamath, California.

1956 – Simpson Redwood Company acquired Northern Redwood Lumber Company, Korbel, California, which included the Arcata and Mad River Railroad and Korbel operations.

1956 – Simpson Redwood Company acquired M&M Woodworking Company, Portland, Oregon.

1956 – Simpson Timber Company formed as parent of Simpson Logging Company, Simpson Redwood Company and Simpson Paper Company.

1959 – Simpson Paper Company was merged with Lee Paper Company, Vicksburg, Michigan, to form Simpson Lee Paper Company.

1960 – Simpson Logging Company and Simpson Redwood Company were merged into Simpson Timber Company.

1961 – Simpson Paper Company opened the Ripon (Calif.) Mill.

1961 – Simpson Research Center opened.

1965 – Simpson Timber Co. (Saskatchewan) Ltd. was founded.

1966 – Simpson Timber Company and Crown Zellerbach Corporation opened their joint venture Crown Simpson Pulp Company at Fairhaven, California.

1967 – Simpson Timber Company acquired Gil-Wel Manufacturing Company, Eugene, Oregon, which was later renamed Simpson Extruded Plastics Company.

1972 – Simpson Lee Paper Company acquired the Kimberly-Clark Corporation Pulp and Paper mill at Anderson, California, and renamed it the Shasta Mill.

1973 – Simpson Timber Co. (Alberta) Ltd. was founded.

1977 – Simpson acquired all of the outstanding stock in the Paper Company and changed its name to Simpson Paper Company.

1977 – Simpson Extruded Plastics Company acquired the Robintech, Inc. plant, Sunnyside, Washington.

1979 – Simpson Paper Company acquired a Pomona, California paper mill from Potlatch Forests, Inc. It was renamed the San Gabriel Mill.

1980 – Simpson Paper Company acquired a paper mill in Miquon, Pennsylvania from Weyerhaeuser Company. It was renamed the Valley Forge Mill.

1982 – Simpson Paper Company acquired the Crown Zellerbach interest in the Crown Simpson Pulp Mill, and changed its name to the Humboldt Pulp Mill.

1982 – Simpson Extruded Plastics Company purchased a Visalia, California plastics plant from Gifford-Hill Company, Inc.

1983 – Simpson Paper Company acquired the Harding-Jones Mill in Middletown, Ohio.

1985 – Simpson Extruded Plastics Company acquired three Western Plastics Company plants—in Tacoma, Washington and Union City and Downey, California.

1985 – Simpson Extruded Plastics Company's name was changed to Pacific Western Extruded Plastics Company (PWPipe).

1985 – Simpson Tacoma Kraft Company, a newly-formed subsidiary of Simpson Paper Company, acquired a Tacoma, Washington, pulp and paper facility from Champion International.

1985 – The corporate name of Simpson Timber Company was changed to Simpson Investment Company and became the holding company for Simpson Timber, Simpson Paper, and Pacific Western Extruded Plastics companies.

1986 – Simpson Tacoma Kraft Company acquired the Tacoma, Washington, Commencement Bay Stud Mill from Champion International.

1987 – Simpson Pasadena Paper Company, a subsidiary of Simpson Paper Company, acquired a pulp and paper mill in Pasadena, Texas from Champion International Corporation. It was renamed the San Jacinto Pulp and Paper Mill.

1987 – Simpson Paper Company acquired the Plainwell Paper Company, with its paper mill in Plainwell, Michigan, from Chesapeake Corporation.

1987 – Pacific Western Extruded Plastics Company acquired Certainteed Company's electrical and waterworks pipe plant in Cameron Park, California.

1988 – Simpson Timber Company acquired the Arcata Redwood Company near Arcata, California, from Arcata Corporation.

1988 – Simpson Timber Company acquired 117,000 acres of northwestern Oregon timberland from the Times Mirror Land and Timber Company.

1989 – Pacific Western Extruded Plastics Company acquired Certainteed Company's electrical and waterworks pipe plant at Perris, California.

1990 – Simpson Paper Company acquired Georgia-Pacific Corporation's safety paper mill in Gilman, Vermont, and converting plant in Burlington, Iowa.

1990 – Pacific Western Extruded Plastics Company acquired two Air Products and Chemicals, Inc., polyvinyl chloride resin plants: one at Calvert City, Kentucky, and another at Pace, Florida.

Footnotes

Preface:

1. *Time, Tide and Timber,* p. 153

2. *The Mill on the Boot,* p. 52

3. *Green Commonwealth,* p. 33

4. Ibid. p. 35

Chapter One:

1. *Green Commonwealth,* p. 34-35

2. *Lumber and Politics,* p. 14

3. *Green Commonwealth,* p. 52

4. *Lumber and Politics,* p. 14

5. *Green Commonwealth,* p. 64

6. *Simpson Lookout,* November 1955

7. *Green Commonwealth,* p. 64

8. Ibid. p. 62

9. *Green Commonwealth,* p. 101, 107; *Simpson Lookout,* November 1950 and June 1955

10. *The Last Wilderness,* p. 191-2

11. These and other quotes from William G. Reed were taken from his memoirs, *Four Generations of Management,* and *Family Trees,* unless otherwise identified.

12. *Simpson Lookout,* May 1951

13. Simpson letter to John A. Campbell and James Campbell, June 14, 1902; Simpson Logging Co. letter to Port Blakely Mill Co., September 16, 1899; Arthur B. Govey letter to Port Blakely Mill Co., April 29, 1901; Simpson letter to Port Blakely Mill Co., April 28, 1902; Port Blakely Mill Co. papers

Chapter Two:

1. Mark E. Reed letter to James H. Davis, April 18, 1922, Simpson Logging Co. papers; *Lumber and Politics,* p. 9

2. Newspaper clipping, Mark E. Reed folders, Washington State Biography File, Northwest Collection, University of Washington Library; *Lumber and Politics,* p. 9

3. *Green Commonwealth,* p. 55-56; *Lumber and Politics,* p. 11

4. *Green Commonwealth,* p. 56-57

5. *They Tried to Cut It All,* p 77-78

6. *Grisdale: Last of the Logging Camps,* p. 31

7. Ibid.

8. *Lumber and Politics,* p. 12

9. Simpson letter to Reed, September 2, 1901, Simpson Timber Company papers; *Lumber and Politics,* p. 18-19

10. *Mason County Journal,* May 5, 1906

11. Simpson Timber Company papers, February 12, 1904; February 17, 1905; *Lumber and Politics,* p. 19

12. *The History of the Northern Pacific Land Grant, 1900-1952* (Ph.D. diss., University of Idaho, 1966, p. 257-260); *The Forested Land,* p. 95

13. *Green Commonwealth,* p. 63

14. *Lumber and Politics,* p. 23

Chapter Three:

1. *Lumber and Politics,* p. 22

2. *Mason County Journal,* August 7, 1914

3. Ibid. July 22, 1927

4. *The Forested Land,* p. 148-149; *West Coast Logger,* Vol. XXXIII, March 1, 1918, p. 19; *Lumber and Politics,* p. 38-40

5. *The Seattle Times,* February 18, 1923

6. *Seattle Post-Intelligencer,* November 20, 1923

7. Ibid.

8. *Argus,* May 21, 1932

9. *Green Commonwealth,* p. 135-136

10. *Lumber and Politics,* p. 63

11. *Simpson Lookout,* July 1950

12. *Lumber and Politics,* p. 67-75

13. *Mason County Journal,* February 4, 1921

14. *Green Commonwealth,* p. 94

15. *Green Commonwealth,* p. 140-141; *Mason County Journal,* April 25, 1924

16. *Mason County Journal,* July 7, 1924

17. *Green Commonwealth,* p. 141

18. *Lumber and Politics,* p 72-73; 142-143

19. *Four Generations of Management,* p. 27; *The Forested Land,* p. 175; letter from Donworth, Todd and Holman to Simpson Logging Company, December 10, 1926

20. *Mason County Journal,* January 24, 1929

21. *Ibid.* April 24, 1924

22. *Mason County Journal,* May 14, 1926; *Lumber and Politics,* p. 135, *Four Generations of Management,* p. 63

23. *Lumber and Politics,* p. 140-141; *Mason County Journal,* December 22, 1927

24. *Mason County Journal,* December 13, 1928

25. *Lumber and Politics,* p. 74

Chapter Four:

1. *Lumber and Politics,* p. 22

2. Letter from Alex Polson to James Tyson, Charles Nelson Co., S.F., January 26, 1927

3. *Green Commonwealth,* p. 141-142

4. *Lumber and Politics,* p. 183

5. *A Forester's Log,* p. 136

6. *The Forested Land,* p. 193

7. These and other quotes from George L. Drake were taken from his memoirs *A Forester's Log* unless otherwise identified

8. *Lumber and Politics,* p. 206-207

9. *Washington, A Centennial History,* p. 114-115

Chapter Five:

1. *The Development of a Sustained-Yield Industry: The Simpson-Reed Interests in the Pacific Northwest, 1920s to 1960s,* p. 77, letter to C.H. Watzek, 8/7/34

2. *The Development of a Sustained-Yield Industry: The Simpson-Reed Lumber Interests in the Pacific Northwest, 1920s to 1960s,* p. 55, p. 118

3. William G. Reed letter to T.R. Ingham, June 1936

4. These and other quotes from Chrysogonus H. Kreienbaum were taken from his memoirs *The Development of a Sustained-Yield Industry: The Simpson-Reed Lumber Interests in the Pacific Northwest, 1920s to 1960s.*

5. *This Forested Land: A History of Lumber in Western Washington,* p. 226

6. *Green Commonwealth,* p. 156-157

Chapter Six:

1. *Journal of Forest History,* October, 1987, p. 192

2. W. G. Greeley letter to Roderic Olzendam, May 7, 1946; *Journal of Forest History,* October, 1987, p.195

3. *Simpson Lookout,* January 1952

4. *Simpson Diamond,* June 1972

5. *Simpson Lookout,* July 1947

6. *Grisdale: Last of the Logging Camps,* p. 62

7. *Redwood Cone,* December 1958

Chapter Seven:

1. *Four Generations of Management.* p. 155

2. *Fortune* Magazine, December 1976

3. W. G. Reed-Hartley interview, p. 24-25

4. *Redwood Cone,* March 1956, December 1958

5. *Redwood Cone,* March 1960

6. Ibid.

Chapter Eight:

1. *Simpson Lookout,* March 1960

2. W. G. Reed letter to Kreienbaum, January 28, 1960

3. Bacon-Hartley interview, p. 9

4. *Simpson Diamond,* August 1963

5. *Simpson Diamond,* July 1965

6. Bacon-Hartley interview, p. 11

7. Bacon-Hartley interview, p. 12

8. Seidl-Erickson interview, p. 6

9. *Simpson Diamond,* January 1966

10. *Simpson Diamond,* September/October 1967

11. *Simpson Diamond,* November 1968

Chapter Nine:

1. *Commercial Express,* September 28, 1980, p. 32, Section III

2. Ibid.

3. Ibid.

4. Ibid., p. 33

5. *Humboldt Standard,* July 20, 1967

6. Ibid.

7. Bacon-Hartley interview, p. 13

Chapter Ten:

1. Bacon-Hartley interview, p. 13-14

Chapter Eleven:

1. *Simpson Paper Company: A Review of 1969 to 1979*

2. *Ibid*

3. *Welcome to Shasta,* Dedication brochure, Shasta division, Kimberly-Clark Corporation, June 7, 1965.

4. *Simpson Diamond,* July/August 1971

5. *Simpson Diamond,* June 1971

6. *Simpson Paper Company History, A Review of 1969 to 1979*

Chapter Twelve:

1. *Simpson Shasta Newsletter,* April-May, 1986.

2. *Reuters,* April 3, 1988

3. Champion International press releases, January 17, 1952 and September 8, 1960.

Chapter Thirteen:

1. *The Northwest Wood Products Industry: A Specialized Lending Approach,* by Robert M. Ingram III, Rainier National Bank

2. Ibid.

3. *Grisdale: Last of the Logging Camps,* p. 7

4. Ibid., p. 103

5. Ibid., p. 7

6. *American Forests,* May/June 1987

7. *Pacific Northwest Executive,* October 1986

8. Ibid.

9. Ibid.

10. *Simpson Diamond,* January/February 1967

11. *Simpson Magazine,* April 1978

Chapter Fourteen:

1. W. G. Reed letter to Simpson Timber Company stockholders, March 13, 1970

2. *Seattle Weekly,* October 5, 1988, citing depositions, Simpson Timber Company vs. Dr. John Taylor Ellis II and Marian Coldwell. et al

3. W. G. Reed letter to Simpson Timber Company stockholders, March 1, 1974.

4. W. G. Reed letter to unnamed Simpson Timber Company stockholder, March 6, 1974.

5. *The New York Times,* June 11, 1986.

6. Ibid.

Bibliography

Books and Monographs

Andrews, Ralph W., *This Was Logging: Selected Photographs of Darius Kinsey.* Seattle: Superior Publishing Company, 1954.

Angle, Grant C. and William D. Welsh, *A Brief History of Shelton. Washington.* Shelton: 1941.

Borden, Stanley T., *Arcata and Mad River: 100 Years of Railroading in the Redwood Empire.* San Mateo: The Western Railroader, 1954.

Bureau, William H., *What the Printer Should Know about Paper.* Pittsburgh: Graphic Arts Technical Foundation, 1982.

Clark, Norman H., *Washington: A Bicentennial History.* New York: W. W. Norton & Company, Inc., 1976.

Coman, Edwin T., Jr., and Helen M. Gibbs, *Time, Tide and Timber. A Century of Pope & Talbot.* Stanford: Stanford University Press, 1949.

Drake, George L. with Elwood R. Maunder, *A Forester's Log: Fifty Years in the Pacific Northwest.* Santa Cruz: Forest History Society, 1975.

Ficken, Robert E., *The Forested Land: A History of Lumbering in Western Washington.* Seattle: University of Washington Press, 1988.

Ficken, Robert E., *Lumber and Politics: The Career of Mark E. Reed.* Seattle: University of Washington Press, 1988.

Ficken, Robert E., *Washington, A Centennial History.* Seattle: University of Washington Press, 1988.

Hamilton, W. C. & Sons, *Along the Pathway from Fibre to Paper.* [Self-published company history; undated]

Hidy, Ralph W., Frank Ernest Hill and Allan Nevins, *Timber and Men: The Weyerhaeuser Story.* New York: The Macmillan Company, 1963.

Holbrook, Stewart, *Green Commonwealth.* Shelton, Washington: Simpson Logging Company, 1945.

Holbrook, Stewart, *Half Century in the Timber: A Narrative of Schafer Bros. Logging Company.* Aberdeen, Washington, 1945.

Holbrook, Stewart, *Loggers Profiles.* San Francisco: Bethlehem Pacific Coast Steel Corporation, 1948.

James, David A., *Grisdale: Last of the Logging Camps.* Belfair, Washington: Mason County Historical Society, 1986.

Kreienbaum, C. H., with Elwood R. Maunder, *The Development of a Sustained Yield Industry: The Simpson-Reed Lumber Interests in the Pacific Northwest, 1920s to 1960s.* Santa Cruz: Forest History Society, 1972.

Lavender, David, *California: Land of New Beginnings.* Lincoln, Nebraska: University of Nebraska Press, 1972.

Lavigne, John R., *Pulp & Paper Dictionary.* San Francisco: Miller Freeman Publications for the Pulp and Paper Industry, 1986.

Markham, John H., *Seventy Years in the Northwest Forests.* Chehalis, Washington: Loggers World Publications, 1977.

Molineaux, Grace and others, *Water over the Dam: Vicksburg Then and Now.* Vicksburg, Michigan: Vicksburg Historical Society, Inc., 1972.

Morgan, Murray, *The Last Wilderness.* New York: The Viking Press, 1955.

Morgan, Murray, *The Mill on the Boot: The Story of the St. Paul & Tacoma Lumber Company.* Seattle: University of Washington Press, 1982.

Paper Trade Jounral staff, *250 Years of Papermaking in America.* Chicago: Lockwood Trade Journal Co., Inc., 1940.

Perry, Thomas D., *Modern Plywood,* New York, Chicago: Pitman Publishing Corporation, 1942.

Price, Andrew, Jr., *The Port Blakely Mill Company,* Seattle: 1990.

Randall, Roger, *Labor Relations in the Pulp and Paper Industry of the Pacific Northwest.* Portland, Oregon: Northwest Regional Council in cooperation with The Bonneville Power Administration and The Pacific Northwest Regional Planning Commission, 1942.

Reed, William G., *Family Trees.* Seattle: unpublished, 1981.

Reed, William G., with Elwood R. Maunder and Charles Buchwalter, *Four Generations of Management: The Simpson-Reed Story.* Santa Cruz: Forest History Society, 1977.

Reed, William G., *The Katheryn Wilson Memoirs.* Seattle: Simpson Timber Company, 1979.

Ross, John R., *Maverick: The Story of Georgia-Pacific.* Georgia-Pacific: 1980.

Sindall, R. W., *The Manufacture of Paper.* New York: D. Van Nostrand Co., 1919.

Smith, David C., *History of Papermaking in the United States {1691-1969}.* New York: Lockwood Publishing Co., 1970.

Stevens, James, *Green Power: The Story of Public Law 273.* Seattle: Superior Publishing Company, 1958.

Teagle, Ernest C., *Out of the Woods: The Story of McCleary.* McCleary: Simpson Logging Company, 1956.

Twining, Charles E., *Phil Weyerhaeuser, Lumberman.* Seattle: University of Washington Press, 1985.

Van Syckle, Edwin, *They Tried to Cut It All.* Seattle: Pacific Search Press, 1980.

Weidenmuller, Ralf, *Papermaking.* Translated from the German by John Kalish. San Diego: Thorfinn International Marketing Consultants Inc.

Whitney, Roy P., *The Story of Paper.* Atlanta: Technical Association of the Pulp and Paper Industry, 1980.

Williams, Guy, *Logger Talk: Some Notes on the Jargon of the Pacific Northwest Woods.* Seattle: University of Washington Chapbooks, 1930.

Articles

de Biasi, Victor, "Continuous Cogeneration Weds IM5000 to US Industry," *Gas Turbine World,* July 1982.

Blackman, Ted, "Computers Help Aged Sawmill to Cut Second-Growth Timber," *Forest Industries,* March 1982.

Huckendubler, Roger, "Simpson Cogeneration Plant Features Innovative Technology," *American Papermaker,* November 1987.

"Logging at Grisdale," *The Timberman,* Vol. 49, No. 11.

Lowe, Kenneth E., "Simpson Lee Modernizes, Expands Anderson, Calif., Fine Paper Mill," *Pulp & Paper,* September 1976.

Mason, David T., and Karl D. Henze, "The Shelton Cooperative Sustained Yield Unit," *Journal of Forestry,* Vol. 57, No. 3, March 1959.

Palais, Hyman and Earl Roberts, "The History of the Lumber Industry in Humboldt County," *The Pacific Historical Review,* Vol. XIX, No. 1, February 1950.

Robbins, William G., "Lumber Production and Community Stability: A View from the Pacific Northwest," *Journal of Forest History,* October 1987.

Scates, Shelby, "Sol Simpson and Mark Reed Laid Foundation for Simpson Empire," *Argus,* December 11, 1964.

Seidl, Robert J., "Plantation Grown Douglas Fir – A Perspective," *Pilchuck Tree Farm Notes,* 1987.

Trade Periodicals, Business Publications and Newspapers

Albany Democrat-Herald (Oregon)

American Forests

American Papermaker

Blue Lake Museum Society Newsletter

Bremerton Sun

Business Week

California Forest Facts, California Forest Communications Council

California Redwood: Nation's Lumber Masterpiece

The Commercial-Express, Vicksburg, Michigan

Daily Journal of Commerce

Forestry Digest

Forest Industries

Fortune

The Herald (Everett)

The Humboldt Historian

The Humboldt Times

Mason County Journal

Modesto Bee

The New York Times

Northcoast View

Pacific Northwest Executive

Pacific Papermill News

"People, Land and Trees: Shelton Cooperative Sustained Yield Unit Progress Reports

PG and E Week

Plywood & Panel

Pomona Business Guide

The Pomona Progress Bulletin

Puget Sound Business Journal

Pulp & Paper

The Recorder

Redding (Calif.) Record Searchlight

Report to the Communities: The Fifteenth Anniversary of the Shelton Cooperative Sustained Yield Agreement

Reuters

Ripon Record

Seattle Post-Intelligencer

Seattle Star

The Seattle Times

Seattle Weekly

The Shasta Profile

Simpson Diamond

Simpson Lee News

Simpson Lookout

Simpson Magazine

Simpson Paper Company: Shasta Mill

Simpson Redwood Cone

Simpson Redwood Serviceline

Simpson Timberlines

Stockton Record

The Tacoma News Tribune

Timber/Fish/Wildlife: A Report from the Northwest Renewable Resources Center, Volume I, Number One, Summer 1987.

USA Today

The Valley Post

The Vicksburg Commercial

The Wall Street Journal

Western Printer & Lithographer

Private Papers and Correspondence

Port Blakely Mill Company

Rayonier Pulp and Paper Company

Irene Simpson Reed

Mark E. Reed

William G. Reed

Simpson Investment Company

Simpson Paper Company

Simpson Timber Company

Outside Company Notes (related to Simpson plants and operations) and Publications

American Cyanamid Company, Paper Dyelines, August 1970

American Paper Institute

American Plywood Association

Arcata Redwood Company

Champion Paper and Fibre Company, Houston Division

Dolbeer & Carson Lumber Co.

Fernstrom Paper Mills

Harding-Jones Paper Company

Kimberly-Clark Corporation, Shasta Division

Lee Paper Co.

Northern Redwood Lumber Co.

Pacific Papermill

Potlatch Forests, Inc.

Rainier Bancorporation, Rainier Economic Perspective, June 1984, March 1986

Rayonier Pulp and Paper Company

Redwood Sales Co.

St. Regis, Kraft Division, Tacoma: "How Paper Is Made"

Weyerhaeuser Company

Reports and Dissertations

Bingham, C. W., "Forest Products Exports: The 1980s in Perspective," Forest Products Trade Symposium, March 22, 1983

"Decision Time for California National Forests," Western Timber Association, 1979

Guy, Daniel E., "Korbel and Korbel Brothers," Eureka, California, 1956

Ingram, Robert M., III, "The Northwest Wood Products Industry: A Specialized Lending Approach," March 1986

Simpson Lee Paper Company Annual Report: 1974

"Simpson Paper Company: A Review of 1969 to 1979"

"The Story of the Redwood Forest," 1986

"The Story of the Redwood Lumber Industry," 1984

Oral Interviews (102)

Al Adams
Wayne Alberda
Betty Anderson
John Anderson
Henri J. Appy
C. Henry Bacon, Jr.
Maxwell Bardeen
Philip Bayley
Ross E. Bell
Louis A. Blaser
Harold Boyce
Herbert F. Brehmeyer
David Carstairs
Ralph W. Casselman
Paul Craig
George Crout
Norman Cruver
Gordon Daniels
David J. De Young
Charles Dickens
Kim Q. Doan
Walt A. Duignan
John Eisenman
D. B. "Barney" Elking
Judy Ellstrom

Elmer Evans
John J. Fannon
Robert A. Ficken
Tim Foley
Kenneth Fredson
Charles Gardner
Dr. F. Claus Globig
John F. Gorman
Fritz Graff
Hugh B. Hanson
Otis Harper
George Hempler
William Hill
Ralph L. Hirt
Helge Holm
Robert B. Hutchinson
Thomas R. Ingham
David A. James
Hank V. Jones
Ina Jones
David W. Kaney
Don Klein
Edward Kolodge
Bart Kouba
E. Guy Lalouche

Joseph L. Leitzinger
Peter W. Lowe
Whitney MacMillan
Eliot Marple
LeRoy McCormick
Wayne L. Meek
Byron "Barney" Miller
Roy Miller
Wade Miller
Frank Moore
Philip Morrison
Furman C. Moseley
Susan Reed Moseley
Clem Mulholland
Vern Myers
Dub Nelson
Delmar E. Orren
Gilbert L. Oswald
James Pauley
Bud Pennegar
James R. Perry
Charles M. Pigott
Calvin Rantz
James K. Rash
Eleanor H. Reed

Starr W. Reed
William G. Reed, Jr.
Teodoro E. Reinhardt
Everett Reichman
Peter Replinger
Emma Richert
J. Thurston Roach
John L. Robins
Jorge Ross
James A. Rydelius
Henry F. Sandstrom
Max Schmidt, Jr.
William A. Schul
Bryce Seidl
Robert J. Seidl
Leroy Shelton
Fred Snelgrove
Gary L. Snider
Cynthia P. Sonstelie
Alan Symington
Henry K. Trobitz
Emil Warnez
Dr. Joe Weber
William West

Other Interviews

Bacon, C. Henry, by James A. Hartley, "Managing Three Decades of Growth by Simpson Timber Company: The Recollections of C. Henry Bacon, Jr.," May 1-3, 1979

Reed, William G., by James A. Hartley, "Memories of Mark E. Reed and the Growth of Simpson Timber Company," June 29, 1979

Seidl, R. J., by Karen Erickson, August 26, 1980

Index